CHAPTER APPROVED

GAMING IN THE 41ST MILLENNIUM

CONTENTS

PRODUCED BY GAMES WORKSHOP IN NOTTINGHAM

With thanks to the Mournival and the Infinity Circuit for their additional playtesting services

Chapter Approved: 2018 Edition © Copyright Games Workshop Limited 2018. Chapter Approved: 2018 Edition, GW, Games Workshop, Space Marine, 40K, Warhammer, Warhammer 40,000, the 'Aquila' Double-headed Eagle logo, and all associated logos, illustrations, images, names, creatures, races, vehicles, locations, weapons, characters, and the distinctive likenesses thereof, are either ® or TM, and/or © Games Workshop Limited, variably registered around the world. All Rights Reserved.

No part of this publication may be reproduced, stored in a retrieval system, or transmitted in any form or by any means, electronic, mechanical, photocopying, recording or otherwise, without the prior permission of the publishers.

This is a work of fiction. All the characters and events portrayed in this book are fictional, and any resemblance to real people or incidents is purely coincidental. British Cataloguing-in-Publication Data. A catalogue record for this book is available from the British Library. Pictures used for illustrative purposes only.

Certain Citadel products may be dangerous if used incorrectly and Games Workshop does not recommend them for use by children under the age of 16 without adult supervision. Whatever your age, be careful when using glues, bladed equipment and sprays and make sure that you read and follow the instructions on the packaging.

Games Workshop Ltd, Willow Rd, Lenton, Nottingham, NG7 2WS
games-workshop.com

INTRODUCTION

Welcome to *Chapter Approved: 2018 Edition*, a compendium of material for use in your games of Warhammer 40,000. Inside you'll find pages more packed with offerings than a Black Ship bringing sacrifices to the Emperor, including new and updated rules, datasheets, missions and much more.

In the grim darkness of the far future, there is only war. Marked by glory and lurid scars, veteran squads win renown through their deeds upon the field of battle. Great champions and leaders arise, living legends who inspire their followers and strike fear into the hearts of their enemies. Armies clash amidst the urban confines of continent-spanning cities, while skirmish forces engage in brief and bloody conflicts, the outcome of their battles affecting the balance of power in the larger theatre of war. This is a galaxy filled with uncountable factions, each ever ready for war. Ork hordes swell their planet-crushing numbers with salvaged vehicles, and the greatest living heroes of the Farsight Enclaves enter the fray to turn the tide. Meanwhile, the Orders Militant of the Adepta Sororitas seek to purify the million worlds of the Imperium with bolt and flame.

Chapter Approved provides a Mek's toolbox of new rules and missions that you can use in your games of Warhammer 40,000, all of which are separated into the following sections:

OPEN PLAY: Open play is Warhammer 40,000 without limits. Included here are rules for Ork players to add looted vehicles to their armies, as well as rules for all players to use in creating their own bespoke special characters with unique abilities.

NARRATIVE PLAY: This style of gaming aims to make the 41st Millennium truly come alive on the tabletop. Players will find a Battle Honours system to add a new level of progression to their campaigns, as well as an expansion, Cities of Death, which is designed to recreate the unremittingly harsh urban conflicts of the far future.

MATCHED PLAY: This section is packed with new Eternal War and Maelstrom of War missions, available for use in your matched play games.

APPENDIX: Here we have collected updated rules for battlefield terrain, updated datasheets and updated points values. You will also find a beta codex for the Adepta Sororitas, an index containing datasheets and Detachment abilities for Renegade Knights, and rules for fielding the legendary warriors of the Farsight Enclaves known as the Eight in your games of Warhammer 40,000.

To make full use of the contents in this book you will need a copy of the Warhammer 40,000 *rulebook. To find out more about* Warhammer 40,000, *visit* warhammer40000.com.

WAYS TO PLAY WARHAMMER 40,000

Warhammer 40,000 offers three distinct styles of game for players to choose from, depending upon their preferences, the collections they have available, and what they want to get out of the game. These styles are open play, narrative play and matched play, and each has its own strengths.

OPEN PLAY

For those who simply want to gather part or all of their miniatures collection, get it onto the tabletop and start rolling dice, open play is the perfect way to game. As its name would suggest, open play has few restrictions. Force sizes are not limited, and do not need to be in any way balanced against the army they are facing. Players are free to invent whatever storyline or framework for the battle they wish, whether that involves using the Only War mission provided in the core rules, or simply inventing their own scenario based upon the sort of game they feel like playing.

In this section of *Chapter Approved*, we present ways in which you can make your games of open play even more exciting. Starting with Looted Wagons (pg 8-13), Ork players will find rules allowing them to use kustomised vehicles in their armies. From transports to battle tanks and even super-heavy vehicles, open play gives you the flexibility to try units such as these in games of all sizes.

Also included in this section is a set of guidelines for creating your own unique champions and leaders (pg 14-17). These provide you with the opportunity to field completely new characters – such as the Chapter Master of a Space Marine Chapter of your own devising – or to recreate famous figures from the 41st Millennium, such as Black Library favourites Ibram Gaunt and Uriel Ventris, and even the infamous Doomrider.

These are just some examples of the kind of things you can do when playing open play games. The only limits to open play gaming are the models in your collection, the gaming space you have available, and your imagination.

NARRATIVE PLAY

Games inspired, driven and regulated by a particular pre-generated storyline are usually known as narrative play battles. *Chapter Approved* provides a range of new content for use with this sort of gaming.

First up is Battle Honours (pg 20-25). The Battle Honours rules can be applied to any campaign system, and they enable players to accrue experience points for their units when they perform certain deeds in battle. After each battle these units can gain new ranks, and with them, new abilities. These rules also accommodate using Battle Honours in one-off battles.

The section that follows, Cities of Death (pg 26-43), contains missions and rules that allow players to fight exciting close-quarters battles in the depths of ruined Imperial hives.

MATCHED PLAY

Utilising points values and Battle-forged armies, matched play adds an element of competitive balance to games of Warhammer 40,000. In this section of *Chapter Approved*, you will find the latest matched play rules alongside new missions to play – choose from Eternal War missions (pg 48-53), in which both players compete to achieve the same objective, and Maelstrom of War missions (pg 54-59), in which random Tactical Objectives can change the face of the game in a heartbeat. Both types of game are popular with players attending organised events such as tournaments, or playing 'pick-up games' against new opponents.

AND MORE!

To make your games even more varied and exciting, you can use the rules provided in the rest of the book. They work with any style of gaming: open, narrative and matched.

The terrain rules on pages 62-67 can be used to represent all manner of otherworldly landscapes, from deadly alien jungles and city-sized manufactorums to the ruins of urban hive worlds.

This edition of *Chapter Approved* includes a beta codex for the Adepta Sororitas (pg 68-99), an elite sisterhood of warriors. This includes background, datasheets and army-wide rules such as Acts of Faith, Warlord Traits, Stratagems and a set of Order Convictions that allow you to represent these iconic forces on the tabletop.

This is a beta codex that we are inviting you, the player, to try out and give us feedback on as we start development of a full Adepta Sororitas codex, which will coincide with the release of a suite of new Sisters of Battle Citadel Miniatures.

Following the Adepta Sororitas codex is *Index: Renegade Knights* (pg 100-106). The datasheets and Detachment rules in this section allow you to field the corrupted walkers of those Nobles turned traitor in all their dark majesty, and include a unique Warlord Trait, Relic and Stratagems.

On pages 108-119 of the appendix you will find background for the Eight, the greatest living legends of the Farsight Enclaves, along with rules on how to field these mighty, battlesuit-clad champions on the battlefields of the 41st Millennium.

Lastly, we have included updated datasheets for several units, and updated points values that can be used in your points-based games, including some from the Forge World range (pg 124-139).

OPEN PLAY

'Without let up, without fail, the
greenskinned ones attack, assail,
and invade. There has been no
peace with this alien race, nor will
there ever be, for they understand
but one thing: war! They are
savage in victory, unrepentant in
defeat. Look to your weapons, for
they are your only hope.'

- *Commander Farsight*

LOOTED WAGONS

Enemy armoured vehicles that have been captured and repurposed by Orks are known as Looted Wagons. They provide greenskins of all clans with a wider range of mechanised support, and besides, Orks think there is something inherently funny about blowing foes up with their own weapons.

Orks have a knack for salvaging, and nothing is more valuable to them than weaponry. Scrap teams haul off damaged or abandoned enemy vehicles, often not even waiting until a battle is over. Ork Mekboyz pay many mouthfuls of teef for the recovered wrecks, and they delight in patching up and kustomising them to improve upon their speed, dakka, and general design.

Most often the base of a Looted Wagon is Imperial in nature. This is, in part, because the Imperium is the single largest empire in the galaxy, but is also a testament to the sturdiness of Imperial vehicles, which allows them to survive the ensuing 'tinkering' of a Mekaniak. A few anti-grav xenos skiffs withstand the brutal modification process, but most are quickly destroyed by Meks who regularly fix complex mechanisms by applying heavy blows from blunt instruments.

While Looted Wagon is a catch-all term, and can cover any number of modified vehicles, there are three basic categories. Karts are Mek-tinkered transport vehicles. Most often these are made using a chassis from an Astra Militarum Chimera, Goliath Truck or Space Marine Rhino. They are ideal for getting Ork Boyz to the front lines of combat as quickly as possible.

The second category of looted vehicles, Wagons, sacrifices transport capacity in favour of a larger weapon and thicker armour. Leman Russ Battle Tanks are the most common core for Wagons, but Orks will try out almost anything. The largest pilfered vehicles are Battle Fortresses, mobile strongholds that bristle with weaponry, gun turrets, and additional armour plates. They are frequently based on Imperial super-heavy tanks such as the Baneblade or Shadowsword.

CONVERTING MODELS FOR OPEN PLAY GAMES

Many hobbyists enjoy the creative challenge of converting some or all of the models in their collection by customising them with parts taken from other Citadel Miniatures kits. You can convert models to tie them to a story you have read, or simply to make them stand out even more on the tabletop. Looted Wagons present a wealth of opportunities for this sort of thing, being converted from almost any other Citadel kit you like. On the following pages you will find a guide on how to build and convert a Looted Wagon from a Leman Russ Battle Tank, but the same idea can be applied to almost any kit from the Citadel range, from the humble Rhino to the massive Baneblade! We also include some example datasheets you can use in your open play games for three broad categories of Looted Wagons; Karts, Wagons and Battle Fortresses. Because these datasheets don't have a points value, they can't be used in matched play games, but they are ideal for open play games in which you can field any unit you like.

KART

DAMAGE
Some of this model's characteristics change as it suffers damage, as shown below:

REMAINING W	M	BS	A
6-10+	12"	5+	3
3-5	6"	6+	D3
1-2	3"	6+	1

NAME	M	WS	BS	S	T	W	A	Ld	Sv
Kart	*	5+	*	6	7	10	*	6	3+

A Kart is a single model equipped with a big shoota.

WEAPON	RANGE	TYPE	S	AP	D	ABILITIES
Big shoota	36"	Assault 3	5	0	1	-
Shoota	18"	Assault 2	4	0	1	-
Skorcha	8"	Assault D6	5	-1	1	This weapon automatically hits its target.
Stikkbomb launcha	12"	Assault 2D6	3	0	1	This weapon can be fired once per battle.

WARGEAR OPTIONS
- This model may take up to two additional weapons from the following list: big shoota, skorcha.
- This model may take up to six shootas.
- This model may take a stikkbomb launcha.

ABILITIES

Explodes: If this model is reduced to 0 wounds, roll a D6 before removing it from the battlefield and before any embarked models disembark. On a 6 it explodes, and each unit within 6" suffers D3 mortal wounds.

Dakka! Dakka! Dakka!: Each time you roll an unmodified hit roll of 6 for an attack with a ranged weapon made by a model in this unit, that hit roll succeeds regardless of any modifiers. In addition, immediately make an additional hit roll against the same target using the same weapon. These additional hit rolls cannot themselves generate any further hit rolls. When firing a weapon with randomly determined characteristics (e.g. a bubblechukka), any additional hit rolls use the same characteristics as the hit roll that generated the additional hit roll. This ability does not affect weapons that automatically hit their target.

Big Red Button: Once per battle, at the start of the Shooting phase, the driver of the Kart can hit the inviting and mysterious red button mounted on his dashboard. When he does, roll a D3 on the table below to see what happens.

D3	Result
1	**Boosta:** Immediately move this model 6" as if it were your Movement phase (models cannot disembark from the vehicle before doing so).
2	**More Dakka:** Add 1 to the Strength characteristic of this model's ranged weapons until the end of the phase.
3	**Auto-welder:** This model regains D3 lost wounds.

TRANSPORT
This model can transport 10 **Flash Gitz** or **<Clan> Infantry** models. Each **Mega Armour** or **Jump Pack** model takes the space of two other models.

FACTION KEYWORDS
Ork, <Clan>

KEYWORDS
Vehicle, Transport, Looted Wagon, Kart

OPEN PLAY

WAGON

A Wagon is a single model equipped with a big shoota.

NAME	M	WS	BS	S	T	W	A	Ld	Sv
Wagon	*	5+	*	7	8	12	*	6	3+

DAMAGE

Some of this model's characteristics change as it suffers damage, as shown below:

REMAINING W	M	BS	A
7-12+	10"	5+	3
4-6	7"	6+	D3
1-3	4"	6+	1

WEAPON	RANGE	TYPE	S	AP	D	ABILITIES
Big shoota	36"	Assault 3	5	0	1	-
Killkannon	24"	Heavy D6	8	-2	D3	-
Lobba	48"	Heavy D6	5	0	1	This weapon can target units that are not visible to the bearer.
Rokkit launcha	24"	Assault 1	8	-2	3	-
Skorcha	8"	Assault D6	5	-1	1	This weapon automatically hits its target.
Stikkbomb launcha	12"	Assault 2D6	3	0	1	This weapon can be fired once per battle.
Zzap gun	36"	Heavy 1	2D6	-3	3	Before firing this weapon, roll to determine the Strength of the shot. If the result is 11+, do not make a wound roll – instead, if the attack hits it causes 3 mortal wounds. The bearer then suffers 1 mortal wound.

WARGEAR OPTIONS

- This model may take a killkannon, lobba or zzap gun.
- This model may replace its big shoota with a skorcha or zzap gun.
- This model may take up to two additional weapons from the following list: big shoota, skorcha, rokkit launcha.
- This model may take a stikkbomb launcha.

ABILITIES

Explodes: If this model is reduced to 0 wounds, roll a D6 before removing it from the battlefield. On a 6 it explodes, and each unit within 6" suffers D3 mortal wounds.

Dakka! Dakka! Dakka!: Each time you roll an unmodified hit roll of 6 for an attack with a ranged weapon made by a model in this unit, that hit roll succeeds regardless of any modifiers. In addition, immediately make an additional hit roll against the same target using the same weapon. These additional hit rolls cannot themselves generate any further hit rolls. When firing a weapon with randomly determined characteristics (e.g. a bubblechukka), any additional hit rolls use the same characteristics as the hit roll that generated the additional hit roll. This ability does not affect weapons that automatically hit their target.

Mobile Fortress: This model ignores the penalty for moving and firing Heavy weapons.

Shoot 'Em Again!: If this model remains stationary or moves under half speed in its Movement phase (i.e. it moves a distance in inches less than half of its current Move characteristic) it can shoot twice in the following Shooting phase with its killkannon or lobba (the weapon must target the same unit both times).

Big Red Button: Once per battle, at the start of the Shooting phase, the driver of the Wagon can hit the inviting and mysterious red button mounted on his dashboard. When he does, roll a D3 on the table below to see what happens.

D3	Result
1	**Boosta:** Immediately move this model 6" as if it were your Movement phase. This model cannot use the Shoot 'Em Again! ability this turn.
2	**More Dakka:** Add 1 to the Strength characteristic of this model's ranged weapons until the end of the phase. This modifier counts towards the result when rolling for a zzap gun's Strength.
3	**Auto-welder:** This model regains D3 lost wounds.

FACTION KEYWORDS	ORK, <CLAN>
KEYWORDS	VEHICLE, LOOTED WAGON, WAGON

OPEN PLAY

BATTLE FORTRESS

DAMAGE

Some of this model's characteristics change as it suffers damage, as shown below:

REMAINING W	M	BS	A
14-26+	10"	5+	9
7-13	7"	6+	6
1-6	4"	6+	3

NAME	M	WS	BS	S	T	W	A	Ld	Sv
Battle Fortress	*	5+	*	9	8	26	*	8	3+

A Battle Fortress is a single model equipped with a deffkannon, killkannon, big shoota, twin big shoota and krushin' tracks.

WEAPON	RANGE	TYPE	S	AP	D	ABILITIES
Big shoota	36"	Assault 3	5	0	1	-
Deffkannon	72"	Heavy 3D6	10	-4	D6	-
Killkannon	24"	Heavy D6	8	-2	2	-
Lobba	48"	Heavy D6	5	0	1	This weapon can target units that are not visible to the bearer.
Mega-gatler	48"	Heavy 4D6	7	-2	1	-
Rokkit launcha	24"	Assault 1	8	-2	3	-
Skorcha	8"	Assault D6	5	-1	1	This weapon automatically hits its target.
Stikkbomb launcha	12"	Assault 2D6	3	0	1	This weapon can be fired once per battle.
Twin big shoota	36"	Assault 6	5	0	1	-
Twin skorcha	8"	Assault 2D6	5	-1	1	This weapon automatically hits its target.
Zzap gun	36"	Heavy 1	2D6	-3	3	Before firing this weapon, roll to determine the Strength of the shot. If the result is 11+, do not make a wound roll – instead, if the attack hits it causes 3 mortal wounds. The bearer then suffers 1 mortal wound.
Krushin' tracks	Melee	Melee	User	-2	D3	-

WARGEAR OPTIONS	• This model may replace its deffkannon with a mega-gatler. • This model may replace its killkannon with a twin big shoota, zzap gun or lobba. • This model may take up to two additional weapons from the following list: big shoota, skorcha, rokkit launcha. • This model may take either two sponsons, or four sponsons; each sponson is equipped with either a zzap gun or a rokkit launcha, and either a twin big shoota or twin skorcha (e.g. rokkit launcha and twin skorcha). • This model may take up to two stikkbomb launchas.

ABILITIES	**Battle Fortress:** This model can Fall Back in the Movement phase and still shoot and/or charge in the same turn. In addition, this model ignores the penalty for moving and firing Heavy weapons, and can – except when firing Overwatch – still fire its weapons if enemy units are within 1" of it (but only its twin big shootas or twin skorchas can target units that are within 1" of it – other guns must target other units). Finally, this model only gains a bonus to its saving throws for being in cover if at least half of the model is obscured from the firer. **Dakka! Dakka! Dakka!:** Each time you roll an unmodified hit roll of 6 for an attack with a ranged weapon made by a model in this unit, that hit roll succeeds regardless of any modifiers. In addition, immediately make an additional hit roll against the same target using the same weapon. These additional hit rolls cannot themselves generate any further hit rolls. When firing a weapon with randomly determined characteristics (e.g. a bubblechukka), any additional hit rolls use the same characteristics as the hit roll that generated the additional hit roll. This ability does not affect weapons that automatically hit their target.	**Big Red Button:** Once per battle, at the start of the Shooting phase, the driver of the Battle Fortress can hit the inviting and mysterious red button mounted on his dashboard. When he does, roll a D3 on the table below to see what happens. **D3 Result** **1 Boosta:** Immediately move this model 6" as if it were your Movement phase (models cannot disembark from the vehicle before doing so). **2 More Dakka:** Add 1 to the Strength characteristic of this model's ranged weapons until the end of the phase. This modifier counts towards the result when rolling for a zzap gun's Strength. **3 Auto-welder:** This model regains D3 lost wounds. **Explodes:** If this model is reduced to 0 wounds, roll a D6 before removing it from the battlefield and before any embarked models disembark. On a 6 it explodes, and each unit within 2D6" suffers D6 mortal wounds.

TRANSPORT	If this model is equipped with a mega-gatler, it gains the TRANSPORT keyword and can transport 30 FLASH GITZ or <CLAN> INFANTRY models. Each MEGA ARMOUR or JUMP PACK model takes the space of two other models.

FACTION KEYWORDS	ORK, <CLAN>

KEYWORDS	VEHICLE, TITANIC, LOOTED WAGON, BATTLE FORTRESS

OPEN PLAY

KONVERSION GUIDE

For those who want to channel their inner Mekboy, the following is a guide detailing how to create a Looted Wagon using a Leman Russ Battle Tank and parts from the Ork Battlewagon kit. Follow the advice step by step or use the principles as inspiration for your own mad mechanisations.

To make a Looted Wagon, Ork Mekboyz start by getting their grubby hands on a vehicle and then they 'kustomise' it by adding their own improvements (i.e. Orky details). That is exactly the process that the Games Workshop Design Studio has followed here. This Wagon began its life as a Leman Russ Battle Tank, and was modified with parts from the Ork Battlewagon kit.

It is worth noting that Mekboyz are notorious for their fast and loose building style – after all, why measure to see if something will fit properly when you can simply hammer it into shape later or weld something even bigger over it! Emulating Mek design ethos is all well and good, but humans are more prone to injury, so please practise safe precautions when using sharp instruments.

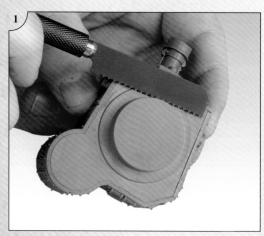

1

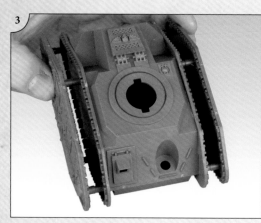

Carefully cut the cylindrical 'lug' off the bottom of the Battlewagon turret with a Citadel Saw.

2

Centre that offcut circle over the Leman Russ turret ring, and draw around it with a pencil.

3

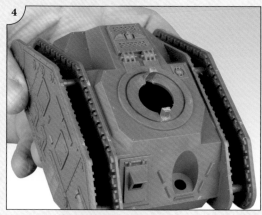

This photo shows the pencil line drawn around the Leman Russ turret ring, which indicates where the Battlewagon turret will fit.

4

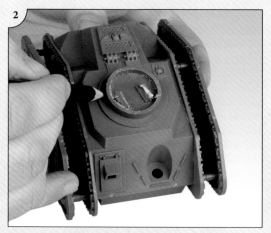

Small offcuts of plastic frame were glued onto the turret ring to hold the Battlewagon turret in place.

5

Add the Battlewagon turret. Note that the raised pieces of sprue offcut will allow the Battlewagon turret to be rotated freely, so do not use glue during this stage if you wish to keep the turret mobile.

6

Using a Citadel Saw, cut the Leman Russ heavy bolters off the sponson mounts.

7

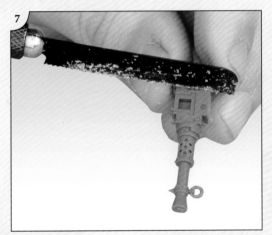

The big shootas were cut with a Citadel Saw to produce a squared-off edge that would fit against the Leman Russ sponson mounts.

8

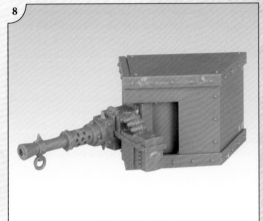

Glue the big shoota to the Leman Russ sponson. Making 'dakka dakka dakka!' sounds at this stage is purely optional, but highly recommended.

The photos above show two different angles of the completed Looted Wagon. As you can see, Ork crew, glyph plates and other greenskin decorations have been added. The model is now ready for painting!

'Done, boss? Course it ain't, they always need more 'ammerin'… but it's done enough for killin'!'

- Orkimedes, Big Mek

CUSTOM CHARACTERS

This section allows you to create datasheets for bespoke named characters, either those of your own devising or any of the storied heroes detailed in the Warhammer 40,000 universe who do not already have a datasheet of their own.

The rules presented here allow you to create unique characters for use in your open play games. Whether designed for a one-off scenario or an epic campaign, these characters add a personal dimension to your battles. Using this system to create datasheets, either for heroes from your favourite Warhammer 40,000 story or characters of your own devising, is great fun, and can lead to a host of new modelling and painting opportunities that ultimately result in inspiring new miniatures to add to your collection.

When it comes to creating models and rules for these characters, there are broadly two different approaches. The first is to start by modelling and converting an awe-inspiring miniature, and then select the attributes and upgrades you feel are most fitting for its appearance and personality. The second is to create the rules for your character, research (or in the case of your own narrative creations, devise) its backstory, and then convert and paint a miniature to best represent them.

Creating your Characters

To create a datasheet for a named character, pick a **CHARACTER** datasheet from your army (other than a named character) and decide if you want to create a Hero, Mighty Hero or Legendary Hero. For each of these types of character, you can make a number of selections from the tables on the following pages. You can make up to 4 selections for a Hero, up to 6 selections for a Mighty Hero, and up to 8 selections for a Legendary Hero.

To make a selection, simply choose one of the following tables and either pick the result most suited to your character or, alternatively, roll the dice indicated on that table to randomly determine your selection and let destiny shape your champion! The following restrictions apply:

- No selection can be made more than once.

- You cannot select an ability that has the same effect as one your character already has, either through one of their own innate abilities or an ability gained through a Warlord Trait or relic.

- Weapon improvements cannot be applied to relics.

- Psychic enhancements are only available to **PSYKERS**.

If you are randomly generating your selections, and you roll a result that breaks any of the above restrictions or simply cannot be applied (for example, an upgrade to a ranged weapon for a character without ranged weapons), simply roll again.

<Sub-faction> Keywords

Some of the results on the Additional Abilities table contain the <**SUB-FACTION**> keyword. Whenever you see this, you should substitute it for the appropriate term for the sub-faction your **CHARACTER** is taken from.

For example, if you pick a Space Marine Captain, the <**SUB-FACTION**> keyword should be substituted for <**CHAPTER**>. If your character does not have any Sub-factions, as is the case with Genestealer Cults characters, substitute the <**SUB-FACTION**> keyword for the least general Faction Keyword it has (in this example, it would be **GENESTEALER CULTS** and not **TYRANIDS**).

'It is not easy to teach Orks anything, but I think we have, at last, taught them not to enter hab-block 77…'

Sergeant Zarr, Donian 188th, the Foestalkers

ADDITIONAL ABILITIES

D66	ABILITY
11	**Inspirational Fighter:** Re-roll hit rolls of 1 in the Fight phase for friendly <Sub-faction> units within 6" of this model.
12	**Beast Hunter:** You can re-roll failed wound rolls for attacks made by this model in the Fight phase if the target is a **Monster** unit.
13	**Heroic:** This model can perform a Heroic Intervention if, after the enemy has completed all of their charge moves, it is within 6" of any enemy units, and can move up to 6" when doing so.
14	**Duellist:** Add 1 to this model's Strength and Attacks characteristics while it is within 1" of any enemy **Character** units.
15	**Zealot:** You can re-roll failed hit rolls for this model in the Fight phase if it made a charge move, performed a Heroic Intervention, or was charged this turn.
16	**Deadly Charge:** Add 1 to the Attacks characteristic of this model in the Fight phase if it made a charge move this turn.
21	**Targeting Augury:** Enemy units do not gain the benefit of cover to their saving throws against attacks made by friendly <Sub-faction> units within 6" of this model when the attack is made.
22	**Directed Fire:** Re-roll hit rolls of 1 in the Shooting phase for friendly <Sub-faction> units within 6" of this model.
23	**Deadly Marksman:** Add 1 to the Damage characteristic of ranged weapons used by this model.
24	**Sundering Shots:** Each wound roll of 6+ made for this model's ranged attacks inflicts 1 mortal wound on the target in addition to any normal damage.
25	**Keen Eye:** This model can target enemy **Character** units in the Shooting phase even if they are not the closest enemy model.
26	**Defensive Fighter:** When this model fires Overwatch, it successfully hits on rolls of 5 or 6, instead of only 6.
31	**Grudge:** You can re-roll any hit, wound and damage rolls made for this model's attacks that target the enemy Warlord.
32	**Resilient:** Each time this model loses a wound, roll a dice; on a 5+ it does not lose that wound.
33	**Camouflage:** Add 2 instead of 1 to saving throws made for this model when it is receiving the benefit of cover.
34	**Stealth Assault:** Enemy units cannot fire Overwatch at this model.
35	**Indomitable:** All damage suffered by this model is halved (rounding up).
36	**Impervious:** This model regains 1 lost wound at the start of your turn.
41	**Infiltrator:** During deployment, you can set up this model in ambush, instead of placing it on the battlefield. At the end of any of your Movement phases it can reveal its location – set it up anywhere on the battlefield that is more than 9" from any enemy models.
42	**Stealthy:** Subtract 1 from hit rolls for attacks made with ranged weapons that target this model.
43	**Hard to Kill:** Wound rolls of 1, 2 or 3 made for attacks that target this model always fail, even if the attack has a Strength characteristic higher than this model's Toughness characteristic.
44	**Strategic Feint:** At the start of the first battle round but before the first turn begins, you can pick a friendly <Sub-faction> unit within 6" of this model and set it up again, anywhere wholly within your deployment zone. If your opponent has any units with similar abilities, roll off; starting with the winner of the roll-off, take it in turns to resolve these abilities.
45	**Swift Strike:** You can always choose this model to fight first in the Fight phase even if it did not charge. If the enemy has units that have charged, or that have a similar ability, alternate choosing units to fight with, starting with the player whose turn is taking place.
46	**Foresight:** Once per battle, if this model is on the battlefield, you can re-roll one hit roll, wound roll, damage roll or saving throw.
51	**Inspirational Leader:** Friendly <Sub-faction> units can use this model's Leadership instead of their own while they are within 6" of it.
52	**Rallying Cry:** You can re-roll failed Morale tests for friendly <Sub-faction> units while they are within 6" of this model.
53	**Icon of Retribution:** Roll a dice each time a friendly <Sub-faction> model within 6" of this model is slain in the Fight phase. On a 6, the unit that made the attack that slew the model suffers 1 mortal wound after it has finished making its attacks.
54	**Impetuous:** You can re-roll failed charge rolls for this model.
55	**Terrifying:** Subtract 1 from the Leadership characteristic of enemy units while they are within 3" of this model.
56	**Savage Riposte:** Each time you roll an unmodified saving throw of 6 for this model in the Fight phase, the enemy unit that made the attack suffers 1 mortal wound after it has resolved all of its attacks.
61	**Air Strike:** Once per battle, in your Shooting phase, you can pick an enemy unit, other than a **Character** unit, that is visible to this model and roll a D6. On a 1-4 nothing happens. On a 5+ the target unit suffers D3 mortal wounds.
62	**Swift Advance:** When this model Advances, add 6" to its Move characteristic for that Movement phase instead of rolling a D6.
63	**Reactive Tactics:** This model, and friendly <Sub-faction> units within 6" of them, can charge even if they Fell Back that turn.
64	**Strike and Fade:** After this model has fought in the Fight phase, it can immediately pile in D3+3" in any direction, not just towards the closest enemy model.
65	**Final Strike:** If this model is slain, you can select an enemy unit within 3" of it and roll a D6; on a 2+ that unit suffers D3 mortal wounds.
66	**Direct Fire:** Each time you make a wound roll of 6+ in the Shooting phase for a friendly <Sub-faction> unit within 6" of this model, the AP characteristic of that attack is improved by 1 (e.g. AP -1 becomes AP -2).

WEAPON IMPROVEMENTS

2D6	RESULT
2	**Auto-loader:** Pick one of this model's ranged weapons. Increase the number of shots this weapon makes by 1 (e.g. a Pistol 1 weapon becomes a Pistol 2 weapon).
3	**Penetrator Rounds:** Pick one of this model's ranged weapons. Improve that weapon's AP characteristic by 1 (e.g. AP -1 becomes AP -2).
4	**High Calibre:** Pick one of this model's ranged weapons. Add 1 to that weapon's Strength characteristic.
5	**Improved Sights:** Pick one of this model's ranged weapons. Add 6" to that weapon's Range characteristic.
6	**Inferno Round:** Pick one of this model's ranged weapons. Add the following ability to that weapon: 'Units do not receive the benefit of cover to their saving throws against attacks made with this weapon.'
7	**Artificer Weapon:** Pick one of this model's weapons. Add 1 to that weapon's Damage characteristic.
8	**Finely Balanced:** Pick one of this model's melee weapons. Add the following ability to that weapon: 'Each time the bearer fights, it can make 1 additional attack with this weapon.'
9	**Shredder:** Pick one of this model's melee weapons. Add the following ability to that weapon: 'You can re-roll failed wound rolls for attacks made with this weapon.'
10	**Brutal:** Pick one of this model's melee weapons. Improve that weapon's Strength characteristic by 1 (e.g. User becomes +1, +1 becomes +2).
11	**Razor-edged:** Pick one of this model's melee weapons. Improve that weapon's AP characteristic by 1 (e.g. AP -1 becomes AP -2).
12	**Heirloom:** Pick one of this model's melee weapons. Add the following ability to that weapon: 'Each unmodified hit roll of 6 made for attacks with this weapon scores 2 hits instead of 1'.

> **Designer's Note:** *If a weapon has more than one profile, the weapon improvement applies to each of that weapon's profiles.*

PSYCHIC ENHANCEMENTS

D3	RESULT
1	**Psychic Might:** Add 1 to the number of psychic powers this character can attempt to manifest in your Psychic phase.
2	**Adamantium Will:** Add 1 to the number of psychic powers this character can attempt to deny in your opponent's Psychic phase.
3	**Master of Lore:** Add 1 to the number of psychic powers this model knows from one of the psychic disciplines available to them.

CHARACTERISTIC MODIFIERS

2D6	RESULT
2	**Old War Wound:** Select a result from this table, or roll 2D6 to randomly select a result (re-roll if you get this result again). Subtract or worsen this model's characteristic by the amount described in the result you picked instead of adding or improving it (e.g. if the Ferocious Combatant result was selected, an Attacks characteristic of 3 would become 2, while if the Dead-eyed result was selected, a BS of 3+ would become 4+).
3	**Courageous:** Add 1 to this model's Leadership characteristic.
4	**Ferocious Combatant:** Add 1 to this model's Attacks characteristic.
5	**Mighty:** Add 1 to this model's Strength characteristic.
6	**Dead-eyed:** Improve this model's Ballistic Skill characteristic by 1 (e.g. BS 3+ will become BS 2+), to a maximum of 2+.
7	**Fleet:** Add 2" to this model's Move characteristic.
8	**Blademaster:** Improve this model's Weapon Skill characteristic by 1 (e.g. WS 3+ will become WS 2+), to a maximum of 2+.
9	**Enhanced Physiology:** Add 1 to this model's Toughness characteristic.
10	**Toughened Armour:** Improve this model's Save characteristic by 1 (e.g. Sv 5+ will become Sv 4+), to a maximum of 2+.
11	**Divine Protection:** Improve this model's invulnerable save by 1 (e.g. an invulnerable save of 5+ will become an invulnerable save of 4+), to a maximum of 3+. If this model does not have an invulnerable save, it instead gains a 6+ invulnerable save.
12	**Heroic Constitution:** Add 1 to this model's Wounds characteristic.

CAPTAIN ARGENTUS

Captain Argentus is a Space Marine Captain of the Silver Skulls Chapter, represented by a Primaris Captain miniature with a subtle head-swap kitbash. This example explains how we created a custom named-character datasheet appropriate for this famed champion of Humanity.

As the starting point we used the Primaris Captain datasheet from *Codex: Space Marines*, arming Argentus with a power sword and a master-crafted stalker bolt rifle, as well as a bolt pistol and frag and krak grenades. To have achieved his rank, Argentus must be a greatly skilled warrior and a veteran of many campaigns – to reflect this we made him a Mighty Hero, allowing six selections to be generated from the tables on the previous pages. We decided to pick the selections, rather than rolling them randomly, to ensure they fit with his equipment, personality, style of leadership and tactics.

The first thing we chose to improve is Argentus' equipment. Having fought in many battles against the T'au Empire, Argentus uses his bolt rifle, Silverstrike, to pierce the armour of their battlesuits and slay the pilot within. To represent this, we selected the Penetrator Rounds and Artificer Weapon results from the Weapon Improvements table to improve the Armour Penetration and Damage characteristics of his master-crafted stalker bolt rifle to match this storied weapon.

Next, we wanted to show how Argentus commands his company in battle. Argentus directs the firepower of his warriors with consummate skill. As such, we chose the Targeting Augury and Direct Fire abilities from the Additional Abilities table.

As the Silver Skulls are known for their use of prognosticators to divine the future, we also selected the Foresight ability to represent the visions of the future presented to Argentus by his advisors.

Finally, we chose the Ferocious Combatant result from the Characteristic Modifiers table to increase Argentus' Attacks characteristic, representing the Silver Skulls' practice of slaying powerful enemies in close combat.

NARRATIVE PLAY

'The propaganda of the T'au claims their ways are more enlightened than ours, but the xenos made a mistake when they entered our hive city. In that claustrophobic hell every advance cost them more blood than any so-called civilised race would dare pay.'

- Sergeant Nikita Petrov, 731st Vostroyan Firstborn Regiment

BATTLE HONOURS

Many famous units exist in Warhammer 40,000, whether it is the Catachan veterans known as Harker's Hellraisers, the many storied squads of the Ultramarines 2nd Company, or Boss Snikrot's Red Skull Kommandos. Battle Honours can be used to represent such superlative groups in your games of Warhammer 40,000.

Even amongst the most elite forces in the galaxy there are formations who stand above their peers. These are the units whose names and deeds are spoken in awed tones by their comrades, and with fear by their foes. Chosen for the most dangerous of missions, emerging bloody but victorious against impossible odds time and time again, these warriors anchor the centre of the battle line in the face of the enemy's depthless hatred. When others turn to retreat, it is these squads who stand fast. When all hope is lost, it is these legendary figures who rise up to turn the tide.

The rules presented in this section enable you to create such peerless units and use them in your Warhammer 40,000 campaigns. Incorporating these rules will greatly enhance the narrative of your games, allowing units to gain experience as they fight in battles and gain additional abilities, called Battle Honours, as they are promoted in rank in between your games.

There are hosts of different abilities available to units each time they are promoted, and how you choose to upgrade your units and forge their reputation is ultimately up to you. You could choose Battle Honours that best suit the backstory and personality you have invented for the unit, or you could select the abilities that echo the very deeds the unit performed in previous battles. Alternatively, you could choose those upgrades you feel will give your promoted unit the greatest tactical advantage in the remainder of your campaign. Will you make the unit better at what they already do well, such as adding extra firepower to your shootiest unit? Or will you shore up their weaknesses, perhaps by adding mobility to a slower formation? Whatever you do will set the unit apart from its peers in the rest of your army.

So what are you waiting for? Your troops have distinguished themselves in the heat of battle – glory and honour await...

'We kill everyfing 'cept those we let escape so they can tell their mates 'bout how we'z da stabbiest.'

- Boss Snikrot
Red Skull Kommandos

Using Battle Honours

Battle Honours is an expansion for Warhammer 40,000 that allows players to represent experienced and especially skilled units in their campaigns. The rules presented in this section supplement the Warhammer 40,000 core rules and can be used as part of any campaign system, whether it is one from the *Warhammer 40,000* rulebook, or one of your own creation.

When playing a campaign, all units, other than **Characters**, **Swarms**, **Drones** and **Buildings***, will gain experience points for fighting in a battle, and for performing certain deeds during that battle. At the start of the campaign, every unit begins with 0 experience points. If new units are added to your army roster during the campaign, they also begin with 0 experience points.

The table on page 22 details all the different ways a unit can earn experience points and how many experience points are awarded for each deed performed during a battle. Keep a tally of how many experience points each unit earns during each battle, and, at the end, make a note on your army roster of each unit's experience points total.

***Designer's Note:** *Swarms, drones and buildings are not known for their ability to learn new skills, and characters are already experienced veterans, who typically have access to a variety of wargear and a suite of rules such as relics and Warlord Traits to further personalise them and boost their combat potential. If you and your opponent want to create even more bespoke characters for use in your campaigns, consider using the Custom Characters open play rules presented on pages 14-17.*

Gaining Battle Honours

At the end of each battle, you should check to see if any of your units have accumulated enough experience points to be promoted a rank by consulting the table on page 22. If a unit gains any ranks, it will also gain new Battle Honours, which you should write down on your army roster.

The type of Battle Honour you can select for it depends on what kind of unit it is. If it is a **Vehicle**, you must select from the Vehicle Battle Honours (pg 25). If it is a **Monster**, you must select from the Monster Battle Honours (pg 24). For all other units, select from the Warrior Battle Honours (pg 23). In any case, you cannot select a Battle Honour that is for a higher rank than the unit is.

The Power Rating of a unit also increases by 1 for each Battle Honour it has. For example, the Power Rating of a unit with 3 Battle Honours is increased by 3.

Recover and Resupply

If a unit that has any Battle Honours is destroyed during a battle, the controlling player must roll a D6 for it at the end of the battle. On a 1, that unit must recover and resupply – it will not be available in the next game in your campaign. This represents the unit returning to friendly lines to recover from its injuries, repair battle damage, train fresh recruits, etc.

Vehicle Squadrons and Monstrous Broods

In the case of units containing models that are split into separate units during deployment, each of those models is treated as a separate unit for the purposes of Battle Honours i.e. the deeds they perform, and the experience, ranks and Battle Honours they subsequently gain, are their own, The only exception to this is that for each Battle Honour held by these models, the parent unit's Power Rating is increased by 1, rather than the model's.

Battle Honours in One-off Games

Battle Honours can be used in one-off narrative games as well, if both you and your opponent agree. If you wish to do so, at the start of deployment, before any units are set up on the battlefield, each player gains a number of experience points equal to their army's Power Level that they can distribute to units in their army as they wish, exactly as if they had earned those experience points in a campaign. If this would increase their rank, they gain an appropriate Battle Honour as well (note, however, that if their Power Rating increases as a result, you do not gain an additional experience point).

Representing Battle Honours

If you wish, you can customise the miniatures belonging to those units that have accrued Battle Honours so as to better represent their veteran status. Adding a customised elite unit to your Warhammer 40,000 army increases the character of your collection and gives you a chance to tool up your army on the tabletop.

Those who are keen on painting can use Battle Honours as inspiration for extra details. You might decide that a campaign marking, medal or barbaric tattoo upon a banner, pauldron or bare head is befitting of the unit's elevated status, or perhaps adding some simple kill stripes or tallies to their armour, wargear or hulls is the way to go. It may be that you wish to denote Battle Honours by applying extra decal transfers to your models.

Others may select Battle Honours that can become modelling projects. Displaying the severed heads of your foes is a gruesome way to represent the Assassins Battle Honour, and nothing will spark a rivalry like a favoured gaming opponent spotting a captured banner painted up in their army's colours.

BATTLE DEED	EXPERIENCE POINTS
Unit took part in the battle	+1
Unit was controlling an objective marker at the end of the battle	+2
Unit destroyed enemy units during the battle (excluding **Vehicle**, **Monster** or **Titanic** units)	+1 per unit
Unit destroyed enemy **Vehicle** units during the battle (excluding **Titanic** units)	+2 per **Vehicle** unit
Unit destroyed enemy **Monster** units during the battle (excluding **Titanic** units)	+2 per **Monster** unit
Unit destroyed enemy **Titanic** units during the battle	+3 per **Titanic** unit
Unit destroyed the enemy Warlord during the battle	+D3
Unit of the match (at the end of the battle, each player selects one of their units to have performed this deed)	+D3
Unit was destroyed during the battle.	-D3 (a unit cannot lose more experience points for being destroyed than it gained during a battle)

EXPERIENCE POINTS	RANK	BATTLE HONOUR
0-4	Green	None.
5-9	Blooded	Pick a Rank 1 Battle Honour for the unit.
10-24	Experienced	Pick a Rank 2 Battle Honour for the unit. Alternatively, you can pick a different Rank 1 Battle Honour for the unit.
25-39	Veteran	Pick a Rank 3 Battle Honour for the unit. Alternatively, you can pick a different Rank 1 or Rank 2 Battle Honour for the unit.
40-59	Elite	Pick a Rank 4 Battle Honour for the unit. Alternatively, you can pick a different Rank 1, Rank 2 or Rank 3 Battle Honour for the unit.
60+	Legendary	Pick a Rank 5 Battle Honour for the unit. Alternatively, you can pick a different Rank 1, Rank 2, Rank 3 or Rank 4 Battle Honour for the unit.

WARRIOR BATTLE HONOURS

SHARPSHOOTERS

Rank 1 Warrior Battle Honour

When deadly accurate fire is called for, this squad has proved itself more than up to the task.

Re-roll hit rolls of 1 for this unit in the Shooting phase.

AGILE

Rank 1 Warrior Battle Honour

These fighters cross the battlefield with uncanny agility.

You can re-roll Advance and Charge rolls for this unit.

DEADEYE SHOTS

Rank 1 Warrior Battle Honour

These masters of the kill know precisely where to place their shots for maximum damage.

Each time you roll an unmodified wound roll of 6 for an attack with one of this unit's ranged weapons, increase the Damage characteristic of that attack by 1.

GRIZZLED

Rank 1 Warrior Battle Honour

These warriors have seen the greatest horrors the galaxy has to offer, and have developed an unshakeable nerve in the process.

This unit ignores penalties to their Leadership characteristic.

LUCKY

Rank 2 Warrior Battle Honour

Despite having fought in the bloodiest of battles, these warriors remain intact.

Roll a D6 each time a model from this unit loses a wound; on a 6 the model does not lose that wound.

COMBAT SPECIALISTS

Rank 2 Warrior Battle Honour

These fighters have honed their close-combat skills, and destroy their enemy in a storm of well-placed blows.

Re-roll hit rolls of 1 for this unit in the Fight phase.

ASSASSINS

Rank 2 Warrior Battle Honour

Knowing well the value of disrupting the enemy's command structure, these fighters set out to slay the foe's leaders.

Add 1 to wound rolls for attacks made by models in this unit that target an enemy **Character** unit.

BREACHERS

Rank 3 Warrior Battle Honour

Veteran besiegers all, these warriors are adept at picking the enemy out of fortified positions.

Add 1 to wound rolls for attacks made by models in this unit if the target of those attacks is receiving the benefit of cover.

TROPHY TAKERS

Rank 3 Warrior Battle Honour

These ferocious combatants adorn their equipment with pieces of the enemies they have slain – only their most experienced foes can look upon this display of might and hold their nerve.

Subtract 1 from the Leadership characteristic of enemy units while they are within 6" of this unit.

DISCIPLINED

Rank 4 Warrior Battle Honour

Even when face to face with their enemy, these redoubtable warriors remain calm.

This unit can shoot or charge during a turn in which it Fell Back.

BRUTAL

Rank 5 Warrior Battle Honour

These fighters attack in a particularly aggressive fashion, clubbing their enemies to the ground.

Add 1 to the Strength and Attacks characteristic of models in this unit during any turn in which they made a successful charge move.

MONSTER BATTLE HONOURS

UNSTOPPABLE BEAST
Rank 1 Monster Battle Honour
This creature crashes into its enemies with great force, crushing them beneath its bulk and shattering their battle lines.

After this model completes a charge move, roll a D6 for each enemy unit within 1" of it. On a 4+ that unit suffers 1 mortal wound.

MONSTROUS REGENERATION
Rank 1 Monster Battle Honour
Healing at horrifying speed, the wounds inflicted on this towering monstrosity are sealed over in moments.

This model regains 1 lost wound at the start of each of your turns.

TERRIFYING
Rank 2 Monster Battle Honour
Some monsters are so huge and horrifying that even seasoned warriors will flee rather than stand against them.

Subtract 1 from the Leadership characteristic of enemy units while they are within 6" of this model.

LASHING LIMBS
Rank 2 Monster Battle Honour
Blows landed upon this monster are instantly responded to with ferocious violence.

Each time you roll an unmodified saving throw of 6 for this model in the Fight phase, the enemy unit that made that attack suffers 1 mortal wound after it has resolved all of its attacks.

INHUMAN RESILIENCE
Rank 3 Monster Battle Honour
This beast shrugs off even the most devastating attacks, its battle-toughened hide proof against the blows of the enemy.

Roll a D6 each time a model in this unit loses a wound; on a 5+ the model does not lose that wound.

SWEEPING BLOWS
Rank 3 Monster Battle Honour
This creature reaps all before it with great scything blows, felling entire formations with each swing.

Each unmodified hit roll of 6 made for this model's attacks in the Fight phase score 2 hits instead of 1.

VIOLENT DEATH THROES
Rank 4 Monster Battle Honour
Some Tyranid beasts are at their most dangerous in their final moments.

If this model is destroyed, its controlling player can choose for it to automatically trigger death throes (see *Codex: Tyranids*) – no dice roll is required.

JUGGERNAUT
Rank 4 Monster Battle Honour
When this monster fights, it lets nothing and no one stand between it and its favoured target.

You can re-roll charge rolls for this model.

JUST MAKING IT ANGRY
Rank 5 Monster Battle Honour
The fury of this abomination in battle remains undiminished through even the most grievous of wounds.

If this model has a damage table, double the number of wounds it has remaining for the purposes of determining what its Strength and Attacks characteristics are.

EAGER
Rank 5 Monster Battle Honour
This creature surges ahead of its comrades, drawn to the foe by an insatiable battle-lust.

At the start of the first battle round but before the first turn begins, you can move this model up to 5". It cannot end this move within 9" of any enemy models. If both players have units that can do this, the player who is taking the first turn moves their units first.

VEHICLE BATTLE HONOURS

FAMED COMMANDER
Rank 1 Vehicle Battle Honour
This tank is commanded by a celebrated and honoured officer, who inspires his crew to fight on despite serious damage.

Roll a D6 each time a model in this unit loses a wound; on a 6 the model does not lose that wound.

SKILLED DRIVER
Rank 1 Vehicle Battle Honour
This vehicle's driver can pick their way through battlefield debris swiftly, guiding his steed with practised ease.

You can re-roll Advance rolls for this unit.

EXPERIMENTAL AMMUNITION
Rank 2 Vehicle Battle Honour
The experienced crew of this vehicle have been granted access to powerful cutting-edge munitions.

Select one of the ranged weapons used by one or more models in this unit. Add 1 to the Damage characteristic of that weapon for attacks made by that unit.

ADVANCED TARGETING
Rank 2 Vehicle Battle Honour
This vehicle's sensors enable its crew to lock onto a target at great range, even through the thickest fighting.

Add 6" to the maximum range of this unit's Heavy and Rapid Fire weapons that have an unmodified maximum range of 24" or longer.

ABLATIVE ARMOUR
Rank 3 Vehicle Battle Honour
The hull of this vehicle has been covered in additional armour plating, offering substantial protection against all but the most penetrative of weapons fire.

Attacks against this unit that have an AP characteristic of -1 are treated as having an AP characteristic of 0 instead.

STORIED VEHICLE
Rank 3 Vehicle Battle Honour
This vehicle has a long and colourful history, and those chosen to crew it feel an immense pride in their assignment.

You can re-roll one hit roll or wound roll for this unit in each of your Shooting phases.

BLESSED DRIVE
Rank 4 Vehicle Battle Honour
The crew of this engine ensures it is in top working order at all times, knowing that mobility is often the key to survival.

If this model has a damage table, double the number of wounds it has remaining for the purposes of determining what its Move characteristic is.

LAST RETORT
Rank 4 Vehicle Battle Honour
This vehicle's hardened crew have resolved to deliver one final destructive message to their enemies should they meet their end upon the battlefield.

If a model in this unit is destroyed, the controlling player can choose for it to automatically explode – no dice roll is required.

PROMINENT TROPHY
Rank 5 Vehicle Battle Honour
Whether the bones of a great enemy, or a captured relic, this vehicle displays an item that inspires its allies and demoralises the foe.

Add 1 to the Leadership characteristic of friendly units while they are within 6" of this unit. Subtract 1 from the Leadership characteristic of enemy units while they are within 6" of this unit.

BLESSED WEAPONS
Rank 5 Vehicle Battle Honour
This crew have vowed to maintain the full fury of their guns until their dying breath.

If this model has a damage table, double the number of wounds it has remaining for the purposes of determining what its Ballistic Skill characteristic is.

CITIES OF DEATH

In the nightmare of the far future, armies battle one another to annihilation amid the shattered ruins of vast corpse-strewn cities. The Cities of Death expansion allows both players to recreate the brutal, close-confines nature of urban warfare.

In a galaxy of war, cities make for the bloodiest of battlefields. Bombed from orbit, the blasted city ruins are overrun by hordes of slavering aliens or crushed to rubble beneath the footfalls of titanic war machines. Warriors engage in bitter close-quarters battles whilst mighty battle tanks smash through crumbling buildings, grinding bricks and bodies both beneath their steel treads. Victory will only be won by an army ruthless and determined enough to drive its enemy from every collapsed building, root out and eradicate every firebase, and level entire strongholds to deny their foes a vantage point. Every building, staircase and hallway becomes a battleground fought over by dozens of warriors, no quarter given until the floor is carpeted with the bodies of the dead and the walls are blasted rubble. In these cramped confines, warriors fight on long after their ammunition is spent. With the butts of rifles and scavenged weapons, they bludgeon, stab and hack their foes to death.

Battle lines are drawn from one street corner to another and soldiers dart across shell-pocked roads. No man's land is watched over by merciless snipers waiting for the next fool to stray into their sights. Forward units employ stealth to close the distance to such threats – launching pinpoint strikes under cover of darkness – or stage daring raids from labyrinthine sewer networks in an attempt to ambush the ambushers. In such battles, combatants are at their most base and low, and no tactic is too desperate, no rule unbreakable if it might increase the chance of victory. City fighting takes all the horrors of war and magnifies them. Territory is more important, lives are cheaper, and survival is all but impossible.

PLAYING CITIES OF DEATH

Cities of Death is an expansion that incorporates brutal urban warfare missions into Warhammer 40,000. In these missions, one player takes the role of the Attacker, and their opponent the Defender. As a result, the missions presented in this expansion are designed primarily for narrative play, telling the story of bitter inner-city warfare. As with any game that puts players in different roles, we recommend replaying these missions, but switching the Attacker and Defender around to give both players a chance to test out a different set of tactics.

This expansion supplements the core rules with additional abilities, Warlord Traits (below), Stratagems (pg 32-35) and Battlezones (pg 36-37) that reflect the tactics deployed when playing a Cities of Death mission.

CITIES OF DEATH MISSIONS

This expansion includes six Cities of Death missions designed for narrative play games. If you wish to play a Cities of Death battle, you should first select a mission from the table below, or roll to randomly select which mission you will play.

D6	MISSION
1	The Gauntlet (pg 38)
2	Total Devastation (pg 39)
3	Relief Force (pg 40)
4	Grand Assault (pg 41)
5	Thunder Run (pg 42)
6	Decapitation (pg 43)

CITIES OF DEATH ARMIES

The Armies section of each Cities of Death mission provide instructions on how to determine which of the players will be the Attacker and which the Defender, and may include guidelines on the models which make up the armies.

Regardless of which mission you use, we recommend that you include several smaller units of infantry, instead of fewer, larger units. Large units are tricky to manoeuvre in Cities of Death battlefields whilst smaller units are better able to take full advantage of the cover available and the obscured rules introduced later in this section. Also bear in mind that large models such as vehicles will not be able to traverse all parts of the battlefield. Whilst they remain powerful, they will require support from other units in Cities of Death.

CITIES OF DEATH BATTLEFIELDS

In a Cities of Death mission, the battlefields are characterised by the increased density of the terrain. As such, unless the mission you are playing instructs you otherwise, we recommend having at least 3-4 terrain features in each 2' by 2' area, at least half of which (rounding up) should be ruins or Sector Mechanicus structures. Irrespective of the size of your battlefield, you must include at least 6 ruins or Sector Mechanicus structures (otherwise you will not have enough terrain features on which to place objective markers for many of the missions in this expansion). The streets and areas between the ruins and Sector Mechanicus structures should be liberally littered with obstacles, barricades, wreckage and other detritus so that troops have some shelter as they dash from one building to another.

On pages 62-67 you will find expanded battlefield terrain rules, some of which update those found in the *Warhammer 40,000* rulebook. In Cities of Death, you must use the expanded rules for battlefield terrain.

Objective Markers

Many missions use objective markers – these represent sites of strategic import that both sides are attempting to secure. These can be represented by any appropriate markers or models you have available. A player controls an objective marker if they have more models within 3" of it than their opponent does. When measuring distances involving objective markers, always measure to and from the centre of the marker.

CITIES OF DEATH WARLORDS

If you are playing a Cities of Death mission, you can use the following Warlord Traits when choosing your army:

D3	WARLORD TRAIT
1	**Cityfight Specialist:** If your army is Battle-forged, you receive 3 additional Command Points. These can only be spent to use Cities of Death Stratagems (pg 32-35).
2	**Conqueror of Worlds:** If this Warlord is within range of an objective marker (see above) it controls that objective marker even if there are more enemy models within range of the same objective marker. If an enemy unit within range of the same objective marker has a similar ability, then the objective marker is controlled by the player who has the most models within range of it as normal.
3	**Urban Warrior:** This Warlord treats all soft cover it is entirely on or within, or that it is receiving the benefit of cover from, as hard cover (pg 30). In addition, enemy units do not receive the benefit to their saving throws for being in cover against attacks made by this Warlord.

CITIES OF DEATH ABILITIES

Cities of Death missions use the following additional rules:

Obscured Targets

In urban environments, troops can make use of the dense terrain as they advance into position to obscure them from the enemy's sights.

After you have chosen a unit to shoot with and you have chosen the target unit, or units, for the attacks, you must determine if any of the targets are obscured.

A target unit is obscured if every model in it is obscured from the point of view of the firing model. An individual model is obscured unless all parts of it that are facing the firing model are visible from the point of view of the firing model (a **VEHICLE** or **MONSTER** is instead obscured unless 50% or more of the model facing the firing model is visible from the point of view of the firing model). If unsure, stoop down and get a look from behind the shooting model to see if any part of it is obscured. For the purposes of determining whether or not a model is obscured, a model can see through other models in its own unit and other models in the target unit. Models with the Flyer Battlefield Role are never obscured, even if less than 50% of the model is visible to the firing model.

Subtract 1 from hit rolls for attacks with ranged weapons if the target is obscured.

Note that it is possible for a target unit to be obscured from the point of view of some models in a firing unit and not from others. In such cases, only the models to whom the target unit is obscured suffer the penalty to their hit rolls.

Designer's Note: *When checking to see if a model is obscured, consider the main body of the firing model and its target – do not include the models' bases or parts that are 'sticking out' like aerials, banners, weapons or particularly impressive hairstyles, but do include all limbs.*

We recommend that players agree about what constitutes the main body of a model before the battle begins. We have also found that it pays to be gracious when judging if a target is obscured or not – in other words, if there is any doubt at all as to whether a target is obscured or not, then count it as obscured. If both players take this approach the game will flow more smoothly and will be much more satisfying.

From this angle, this unit of Aggressors is obscured – every model in the unit is at least partially obscured by the ruin they are occupying.

When these Guardian Defenders choose their targets, the Flash Gitz are not obscured to any of them – every model in the Guardian unit can see at least one of the Flash Gitz without any obstruction.

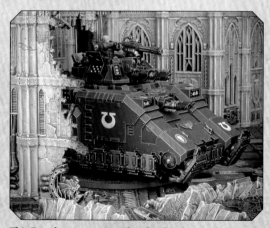

This Repulsor is not considered to be obscured, as it is a vehicle and more than 50% of the model is visible to the firing unit from this angle.

Lucky Hit

Sometimes, despite making best use of available cover and all efforts to conceal your position, a stray shot or ricochet will nonetheless find its mark.

A hit roll of 6 always hits the target, irrespective of any modifiers that may apply.

Streets and Roads

Forces can move quickly across streets and roads, but doing so often leaves them exposed to enemy fire.

After you have created the battlefield, the players should agree what areas count as streets and roads. If a model spends its entire Movement phase on a street or road, its Move characteristic is increased by 3" until the end of the phase. This has no effect on units that can **FLY**.

Dangerous Terrain

Many war-torn city ruins are verging on total collapse and are extremely perilous to those that shelter within, who may be crushed by loose masonry or fall through unstable floors.

Some terrain is classed as dangerous terrain. Each time a model Advances or charges through dangerous terrain, roll a D6; on a 1, that model's unit suffers 1 mortal wound.

Height Advantage

In urban warfare, every soldier in a tall building is a sniper, raking fire onto those below. Combating foes with such a height advantage is a dangerous proposition indeed.

A model gains a height advantage whilst it is occupying the upper levels of a ruin or a Sector Mechanicus structure and it shoots at a unit that is either at street level or within a lower level of a ruin or Sector Mechanicus structure. To gain a height advantage, every model in the target unit must be on levels that are 3" or more below that of the firing model.

If a model makes an attack with a ranged weapon against an enemy unit over which it has a height advantage, the Armour Penetration characteristic of that weapon is improved by 1 (e.g. AP0 becomes AP-1, AP-1 becomes AP-2, and so on).

Soft Cover and Hard Cover

In the close confines of building-to-building warfare, cover is the key to survival – but not all cover offers the same degree of protection.

In a Cities of Death mission, terrain features are classed as either soft cover or hard cover. After you have created the battlefield, players should agree what terrain features fall into which class (see the guidelines below). Then, instead of using the rules for cover as described in the core rules, use the following rules:

If a unit is entirely on or within any terrain feature, or it is receiving the benefit of cover from a terrain feature, add 1 to its models' saving throws against shooting attacks if the terrain feature is classed as soft cover, or add 2 if the terrain feature is classed as hard cover. Invulnerable saves are unaffected. Units gain no benefit from cover in the Fight phase.

Improving the Benefits of Cover

Some models have abilities that improve the bonus a model receives to its saving throw when it is receiving the benefit of cover, e.g. 'add 2 to saving throws made for models in this unit when they receive the benefit of cover instead of 1.' If a model has an ability like this, you only add the bonus to its saving throw when it receives the benefit of soft cover. If such a model is receiving the benefit of hard cover, you instead add an additional +1 bonus to its saving throws, regardless of the actual number listed in its ability. In the example above, this would mean you add 3 to the saving throws made for the unit when it benefits from hard cover.

Ignoring the Benefits of Cover

Some weapons and models have abilities that ignore the benefit a target might otherwise receive to its saving throws from being in cover, e.g. 'units attacked by this weapon do not gain any bonus to their saving throws for being in cover' or 'enemy units do not receive the benefit to their saving throws for being in cover against attacks made by this model.' If a model has an ability like this, or is shooting a weapon that has an ability like this, it makes no difference whether the target is receiving the benefit of soft or hard cover – it gains no bonus to its saving throws. Note, however, that such abilities only ignore the bonus a target might otherwise have gained to its saving throws; it does not ignore any penalty incurred to the firer's hit rolls as a result of the target being obscured (pg 28).

Agreeing on Cover

The following table provides guidance as to whether a terrain feature is soft cover or hard cover. If a terrain feature does not appear on the table below, players should agree after creating their battlefield whether it is classed as soft or hard cover.

SOFT COVER	HARD COVER
• Death World Forest (including Eldritch Ruins, Grapple Weeds, Shardwrack Spines and Barbed Venomgorse)	• Sector Mechanicus structures (including Haemotrope Reactors, Galvanic Servohaulers, Thermic Plasma Regulators* and Thermic Plasma Conduits*)
• Woods	• Ruins
• Battlescape	• Fuel Pipes*
• Craters	• Barricades
• Imperial Statuary	• Fortifications
• Obstacles	

Fuel Pipes, Thermic Plasma Regulators and Thermic Plasma Conduits have a chance of inflicting a mortal wound on a unit that uses them as cover. To see if this happens in games of Cities of Death, roll a D6 each time you make an unmodified saving throw of 6 for such units, instead of a modified saving throw of 7+. On a 1, the model's unit suffers 1 mortal wound.

Narrative Play
Mission Special Rules

Most narrative play missions use one or more additional special rules to better represent the different tactics and strategies used by Attackers and Defenders. Some of the more in-depth mission special rules are collected below and referenced by the missions that appear later.

Concealed Deployment

In some battles, commanders have had time to conceal the positions of their forces from their enemy.

If a mission uses Concealed Deployment, the Defender will need a set-up marker for each unit in their army that they intend to start the battle deployed on the battlefield. You do not need any markers for units that will start the battle embarked on a **Transport**, only a marker for the transport itself. Each marker needs to be distinct (for example, by having a different number) so it can correspond to a specific unit. The Defender must write down which unit each marker represents and keep this information secret from their opponent.

When the Defender deploys their army, they set up the markers instead of their models. Once the Defender has set up all their markers, the Attacker deploys all their forces. Once this has been done, the Defender then reveals which marker corresponds to which unit, setting up the appropriate models as they do so. The first model in each unit must be placed exactly where the unit's set-up marker was placed, and the entire unit must be set up wholly within the player's own deployment zone.

Dawn Raid

Cunning commanders may attack under cover of darkness to better conceal their advance from the foe.

If your mission uses Dawn Raid, both players must subtract 1 from all hit rolls made in the Shooting phase during the first battle round of the game.

Preliminary Bombardment

In a major offensive, the attacker will often launch a heavy bombardment prior to the main attack.

If your mission uses Preliminary Bombardment, then at the start of the first battle round, but before the first turn begins, the Attacker should roll a dice for each enemy unit that is on the battlefield (do not roll for units that are embarked inside **Transports**). On a roll of 6, that unit has been hit by a Preliminary Bombardment; that unit suffers D6 mortal wounds. **Infantry** units that are hit by a Preliminary Bombardment can choose to go to ground before the damage is determined – if they do, they only suffer D3 mortal wounds, but cannot take any actions during their first turn.

Random Battle Length

War is rarely predictable, and the time available to achieve your objectives is never certain.

If your mission uses Random Battle Length, at the end of battle round 5, the player who had the first turn must roll a D6. On a roll of 3+, the game continues, otherwise the game is over. At the end of battle round 6, the player who had the second turn must roll a D6. This time the game continues on a roll of 4+, otherwise the game is over. The battle automatically ends at the end of battle round 7, or when one army has slain all of its foes.

Reserves

Reserves are forces which are not directly present at the start of battle, but are available as reinforcements.

If a mission uses Reserves, it will detail which units in your army start the game in Reserve – these units are not deployed with the rest of your army.

The mission will usually state when the units placed in Reserve arrive on the battlefield – this is typically at the end of a particular Movement phase. If the mission does not specify when units arrive, roll for each unit at the end of your second Movement phase (and at the end of each of your Movement phases thereafter) – this is called a Reserve roll. On a 3+, the unit being rolled for arrives from Reserve. Note that if a unit placed into Reserve is embarked within a **Transport**, they will arrive when their transport does, not separately (if rolling, make a single roll for the transport and the units embarked in it).

The mission will explain how and where to set up units when they arrive from Reserve.

Sustained Assault

Occasionally, an army will possess overwhelming superiority in numbers.

If your mission uses Sustained Assault, any of the Attacker's units that are destroyed can be brought back into play later in the battle, to represent their almost limitless supply of reinforcements. At the end of each of the Attacker's Movement phases, roll a dice for each of their destroyed units, adding 2 to the result if that unit has the Troops Battlefield Role. On a 4+, immediately set up that unit within 6" of a battlefield edge – the mission will specify which.

The Attacker can also, at the end of any of their turns, remove any of their units from the battlefield that have a quarter or less of their starting number of models (or, in the case of single-model units, a quarter or less of its starting number of wounds). This unit then counts as having been destroyed for all purposes, and so can be brought back into play later as described above.

STRATAGEMS

If you are playing a Cities of Death mission, you can spend Command Points (CPs) to use the following Stratagems.

1CP — BREACHING GEAR
Cities of Death Stratagem
Assault troops use breaching gear to improve access and manoeuvrability when storming enemy-held structures.

Use this Stratagem if an **INFANTRY** unit in your army declares a charge against only one enemy unit in your Charge phase, and that unit is entirely on or within a ruin or Sector Mechanicus structure, but before making the charge roll. After making the charge roll, you can change one of the two dice results to a 6.

1CP — REINFORCED POSITION
Cities of Death Stratagem
Upgrading a position's defensibility can take many forms, such as affixing armoured plating to improve density, or hanging flak-mesh to ward off shrapnel.

Use this Stratagem after both sides have deployed, but before the first battle round begins. Pick a terrain feature that is classed as soft cover and is wholly within your deployment zone. For the remainder of the battle that terrain feature is classed as hard cover instead.

2CP — HUNKER DOWN
Cities of Death Stratagem
For troops experienced in city fighting, it becomes second nature to dart behind rubble and take cover in sight-obscured spaces at the crack of a rifle shot.

Use this Stratagem at the start of your opponent's Shooting phase. Choose a unit from your army that is entirely on or within a ruin or Sector Mechanicus structure. Until the end of the turn, add an additional 1 to saving throws for models in this unit that are receiving the benefit of cover.

1CP — SIEGE SHELL
Cities of Death Stratagem
These are massive shells that can blast the foe out of cover and render the ruins they hide in unstable.

Use this Stratagem in your Shooting phase before making attacks with a **MONSTER** or **VEHICLE** from your army. Select one of that model's ranged weapons that makes a random number of attacks (e.g. Heavy D6, Heavy 2D6). That weapon can target a single ruin or Sector Mechanicus structure as if it were an enemy unit. To do so, make a single hit roll using the model's Ballistic Skill (ignore modifiers). If the hit roll is successful, roll a D6 and add the weapon's Damage characteristic to the result. If the total is 8 or more, the terrain feature is classed as dangerous terrain for the rest of the battle and you immediately roll a D6 for each model that is entirely on or within that terrain feature – on a 1, that model's unit suffers 1 mortal wound.

1CP — WRECKER
Cities of Death Stratagem
Wrecker balls, seismic drills, sophisticated lascutters, or similarly destructive devices can bring an extra level of devastation to city fighting, shattering both ruins and the squads hidden within.

Use this Stratagem at the end of your Fight phase if a **MONSTER** or **VEHICLE** model from your army is within 1" of a ruin or Sector Mechanicus structure. Select one of that model's melee weapons and make a single hit roll using the model's Weapon Skill (ignore modifiers). If you hit, roll a D6 and add the weapon's Damage characteristic to the result. If the total is 8 or more, the terrain feature is classed as dangerous terrain for the rest of the battle and you immediately roll a D6 for each model that is entirely on or within that terrain feature – on a 1, that model's unit suffers 1 mortal wound.

PLASMA FEED

1CP

Cities of Death Stratagem

With a suitable energy source nearby, a plasma weapon can be supercharged to fire devastatingly potent blasts.

Select an **INFANTRY** unit from your army that is within 1" of any Thermic Plasma Regulators or Conduits before it shoots in the Shooting phase, or before it fires Overwatch. Until the end of this phase, add 1 to the Strength and Damage characteristics of all plasma weapons the unit is equipped with. For the purposes of this Stratagem, a plasma weapon is any weapon whose name includes the word 'plasma' (e.g. plasma pistol, plasma gun, plasma rifle, plasma incinerator).

EXPERT GRENADIER

1CP

Cities of Death Stratagem

Those who survive in the close-quarters hell of urban combat learn to use their grenades to optimal effect.

Use this Stratagem when a model from your army throws a Grenade at an enemy unit that is entirely on or within a ruin or Sector Mechanicus structure. You can re-roll failed wound rolls when resolving that Grenade's attacks. Furthermore, if that Grenade makes a random number of attacks, it always makes the maximum number of attacks instead (e.g. a Grenade D6 profile would instead be treated as a Grenade 6 profile when thrown at a unit that is entirely on or within a ruin or Sector Mechanicus structure).

OPERATE SERVOHAULER

1CP

Cities of Death Stratagem

Through desperation, technical know-how or intuition, some warriors have a knack for being able to operate any equipment to their advantage.

Use this Stratagem at the end of your Movement phase if an **INFANTRY** unit from your army is within 1" of a Galvanic Servohauler and there are no enemy units within 1" of the same Galvanic Servohauler. You can move that Galvanic Servohauler in any direction, as if it were a **VEHICLE** unit in your army with a Move characteristic of 6" (it cannot Advance as part of this move, and cannot move within 1" of any enemy model). If the Galvanic Servohauler is towing a crane, both the Servohauler and the crane are moved.

SIPHON PROMETHIUM

1CP

Cities of Death Stratagem

A quick and risky transfusion of refined promethium makes flamer weapons all the more lethal.

Select an **INFANTRY** unit from your army that is within 1" of any Fuel Pipes before it shoots in the Shooting phase, or before it fires Overwatch. Until the end of this phase, double the range of all flame weapons the squad is equipped with and add 1 to any wound rolls made for these weapons. For the purposes of this Stratagem, a flame weapon is an Ork burna, skorcha or any weapon whose name includes the word 'flame' (e.g. flamer, heavy flamer, flamestorm gauntlet).

PLUNGING FIRE

1CP

Cities of Death Stratagem

When targeting quarry from above, a shooter can pinpoint the weakest part of enemy armour.

Use this Stratagem before a unit from your army makes its attacks in the Shooting phase. Until the end of the phase, attacks made by models in that unit which have a height advantage over their target are resolved with an additional improvement of 1 to their Armour Penetration characteristic (e.g. an AP of '-1' becomes '-2', '-2' becomes '-3', and so on).

LONG BOMB

1CP

Cities of Death Stratagem

Munitions hurled from on high rain down with fury.

Use this Stratagem before a unit from your army shoots in the Shooting phase. If a model in that unit has a height advantage, you can double the range of any Grenade weapons it uses this phase.

SIEGE ARMOUR

1CP

Cities of Death Stratagem

Experienced crews seek to protect their vehicles from plunging fire by adding armour to the tops of their engines of war.

Use this Stratagem before the battle. Choose a **VEHICLE** model from your army: during the battle, enemy attacks do not gain any bonus to their Armour Penetration characteristic for having a height advantage when targeting that vehicle.

OVERLOAD POWER CORE

1CP

Cities of Death Stratagem

Crudely desecrated, this volatile device makes a potent bomb.

Use this Stratagem before an **Infantry** model from your army that is within 1" of a Plasma Conduit shoots a ranged weapon at a unit within 6". Instead of firing that weapon, that model hurls a power core at the unit. Make a single hit roll; if you hit the target, it suffers D3 mortal wounds.

GRAPPLING HOOKS

1CP

Cities of Death Stratagem

An effective means of claiming the high ground.

Use this Stratagem at the start of your Movement phase. Select one of your **Infantry** units. For the duration of your turn, models in that unit can ascend or descend ruins or Sector Mechanicus structures when they move, even without a ladder, wall or girder. Furthermore, for the duration of your turn, do not count any vertical distance that unit moves against the total they can move that turn (i.e. moving vertically is free for those models).

DEMOLITIONS

1CP

Cities of Death Stratagem

Combat engineers can degrade assets, denying their utility to the foe. Many such acts of sabotage are best resolved through the use of high explosives.

Use this Stratagem at the end of your Movement phase. Choose an objective marker you control and roll a D6: on a 4+ the objective marker is removed from the battlefield and the ruin or Sector Mechanicus structure in which the objective marker is located is now classed as dangerous terrain. You can only use this Stratagem once per battle.

BLOOD IN THE STREETS

1CP

Cities of Death Stratagem

Cover is the key to survival in urban combat, and those that move out in the open sign their own death warrant.

Use this Stratagem before a unit from your army makes its attacks in the Shooting phase. Until the end of the phase, you can re-roll failed wound rolls for attacks made by models in that unit, provided that the target is entirely at street level and is neither obscured nor receiving the benefit of cover.

MASTER SNIPERS

1CP

Cities of Death Stratagem

The most skilled marksmen can thread nigh-impossible shots through the densest of terrain to take out enemy officers.

Use this Stratagem before a unit from your army makes its attacks in the Shooting phase. Until the end of the phase, enemy units do not receive the benefit to their saving throws for being in cover against attacks made by weapons in your unit that have an ability that says 'A model firing this weapon can target an enemy **Character** even if they are not the closest enemy unit.' In addition, models firing such weapons ignore all negative modifiers to their hit rolls until the end of the phase so long as they remained stationary during their previous Movement phase.

RUBBLE AND RUIN

1CP

Cities of Death Stratagem

Years of sustained bombardment have reduced many a sturdy structure to a rubble-strewn deathtrap.

Use this Stratagem at the start of the first battle round, but before the first turn begins. Select a ruin or Sector Mechanicus structure on the battlefield – you cannot select one that is currently occupied by any models. That terrain feature is dangerous terrain for the rest of the battle.

POINT-BLANK OVERWATCH

2CP

Cities of Death Stratagem

It takes a cool hand to hold fire until the optimal moment against an oncoming foe, but sometimes waiting until the target is as close as possible is the defenders' only hope for survival.

Use this Stratagem when an enemy unit declares a charge against a unit from your army. Instead of firing Overwatch as soon as the enemy unit declares its charge, the enemy unit makes its charge roll as normal. If this is insufficient to end a move within 1" of the target, no Overwatch is fired at the charging unit. Otherwise, all models in the charging unit are considered to be within line of sight of all models in the unit being charged, and within half range of all of its ranged weapons, when resolving the Overwatch.

SEWER RATS

2CP

Cities of Death Stratagem

By squeezing through pipes and wading through filth, these infiltrators have navigated underground sewer systems, using them to attack the foe from an unexpected quarter.

Use this Stratagem just before you set up a **SWARM** or **INFANTRY** unit during deployment. Instead of setting up that unit on the battlefield, you can place them to one side and say that they are infiltrating a sewer network. At the end of any of your Movement phases, you can set the unit up anywhere on the battlefield at street level that is more than 9" from any enemy models and is not within a ruin or a Sector Mechanicus structure.

RIGGED TO BLOW

2CP

Cities of Death Stratagem

Placing explosive traps where the enemy is sure to set them off is a classic city-fighting tactic.

Use this Stratagem at the end of your turn. Secretly pick an objective marker that is not currently controlled by your opponent, and write this down. The first time a unit in your opponent's army ends a move within 3" of that objective marker, roll a D6: on a 1 nothing happens, on a 2-5 the unit suffers D3 mortal wounds, and on a 6 it suffers D6 mortal wounds. In addition, roll a D6 if the objective marker was on or within a ruin or Sector Mechanicus structure: on a 4+ that terrain feature is now classed as dangerous terrain.

BOOBY TRAPS

2CP

Cities of Death Stratagem

Urban combat is a dirty business. The cluttered terrain and close quarters are perfect conditions for troops to rig deadly devices in the enemy's path.

This Stratagem is used after both sides have deployed, but before the first battle round begins. Secretly pick a single ruin or Sector Mechanicus structure that is not currently occupied by any models, and write it down. The first time any model moves within 1" of that terrain feature, they trigger booby traps and their unit suffers D3 mortal wounds (D6 if they Advanced this turn). In addition, roll a D6: on a 4+ that terrain feature is now classed as dangerous terrain.

PROXIMITY MINES

2CP

Cities of Death Stratagem

Plasma mines rigged to a sensor are set off by nearby movement, heat or any number of different triggers: a nasty surprise for an unsuspecting foe.

Use this Stratagem when an enemy unit is set up as reinforcements during the battle. Roll a D6 for each model in the unit: for each 6, that unit suffers 1 mortal wound.

URBAN BATTLEZONES

So long as you and your opponent agree, any Cities of Death battle can use one or more of the three Urban Battlezone rules sets on these pages. These rules allow you to recreate battles that are fought in cityscapes that are even more hostile and hazardous to the combatants than usual. These can be used in addition to, or instead of, any other Battlezone rules.

Battlezone: Industrial Worlds

Some rules presented in Battlezone: Industrial Worlds (printed first in *Chapter Approved: 2017 Edition*) also feature as part of the rules found in this book (for example, the rules for Height Advantage on page 29). As a result, if you are using Battlezone: Industrial Worlds in conjunction with Cities of Death, the rules published in this book take precedence.

URBAN BATTLEZONE: INFESTATION

Unbeknownst to either army, the shattered ruins of this city district have become infested with foul creatures. Warriors must contend not only with enemy forces, but bestial hunters that lurk in the shadows of buildings, or that can burst from sewers to claw and savage their prey.

Infested City: Before the battle, the players jointly must gather at least four infestation units. These can be any units that have a Power Rating of 10 or less, but we recommend that players select units that do not share Faction keywords with any units from their own armies.

In matched play games, infestation units can be any of the following units: BEAST units, SWARM units, GENESTEALER units, LICTORS, SPORE MINES or POXWALKERS. In open play and narrative play games, infestation units can be any unit, and players are encouraged to choose forces that best suit their own story, irrespective of their Power Rating. Perhaps a pack of Helbrutes is rampaging through the city slaying all in their path, or an Officio Assassinorum Execution Force lurks in the ruins ready to strike. Your choice is limited only by your miniatures collection.

Lurking in the Shadows: Before either side deploys, you must first infest the city. To do so, you will need six objective markers: if there are fewer than six objective markers on the battlefield, the players must alternate setting up extra objective markers on different ruins or Sector Mechanicus structures until there are six (these extra objective markers have no effect on any victory conditions). The players then randomly select three different objective markers, setting up a randomly selected infestation unit on each (all models in an infestation unit must be set up within 6" of their objective marker).

Infested Sewers: Each time a player sets up a unit using the Sewer Rats Stratagem (pg 35), roll a D6 for each model in that unit: for each roll of 1, one model, chosen by the controlling player, was slain by the creatures infesting the sewers. In addition, at the end of each battle round, both players roll a D6. If the combined score is less than 6, a new infestation unit is set up on the battlefield. The players roll off and the winner sets up a new, randomly selected infestation unit anywhere on the battlefield at street level that is more than 9" from any other unit and is not within a ruin or a Sector Mechanicus structure.

Infestation Units: Infestation units are treated as enemy units by both players. In the Fight phase, infestation units fight after all other units unless they have charged in their turn (see below). When resolving attacks or making saving throws, etc. for infestation units, we recommend your opponent rolls the dice. The Command Re-roll Stratagem cannot be used to re-roll dice rolls made for infestation units.

The Infestation Turn: At the end of each battle round, the infestation units have a 'turn'. In their Movement phase, each infestation unit will move as far as possible towards the closest objective marker (unless they are already within 3" of one), but they will not Fall Back or Advance. If they are a PSYKER, they will attempt to manifest *Smite* in their Psychic phase (they will never attempt to Deny the Witch). In their Shooting phase, each model will shoot at the closest visible unit. If they are within 12" of any unit in their Charge phase they will attempt to charge the closest unit. In their Fight phase, each model will target the closest unit with all of its attacks.

In all cases, infestation units will never target other infestation units, and if two units are equally close, randomly select which they will charge or target with their attacks. If any sequencing issues arise, the players roll off and the winner decides the order in which the rules in question are resolved.

URBAN BATTLEZONE: CONFLAGRATION

An inferno is sweeping across the city, flames leaping from building to building, transforming them into blazing deathtraps. Troops must battle not only with the enemy, but the fires consuming the city, fighting through flame and smoke to reach their objectives. Only the insane and the foolish can withstand the heat in such a war zone for long.

Set Ablaze: After both sides have deployed, and at the end of each battle round thereafter, the players roll off. The winner then rolls a D6 for each ruin and Sector Mechanicus structure on the battlefield that is not ablaze. Add 1 if there are any other terrain features that are ablaze within 6" of the terrain feature being rolled for. On a 6+, the terrain feature being rolled for catches ablaze and is treated as dangerous terrain for the remainder of the battle.

Flames Intensify: When a terrain feature is set ablaze for the first time, place a 'blaze dice' on it, with the dice showing 1. At the start of each battle round, the number on each blaze dice on the battlefield increases by 1 (to a maximum of 6).

Pillars of Smoke: Models cannot see through or over terrain features that are ablaze. This means that a unit is not visible, and so cannot be targeted, if a terrain feature that is ablaze is in between it and the firing model. Units that are on or within a terrain feature that is ablaze can be seen and targeted normally.

Consumed by Fire: At the end of the battle round, after rolling to see if any terrain features are set ablaze, each player must roll a dice for each of their models that is entirely on or within a terrain feature that is ablaze. Add the result of that terrain feature's blaze dice to the score. For each roll of 7+ that model's unit suffers 1 mortal wound.

STRATAGEMS

In this Battlezone, you and your opponent can both use Command Points (CPs) to use the following Stratagems:

1CP

FIREFIGHTERS
Conflagration Stratagem

Use this Stratagem at the start of your Shooting phase. Select an **INFANTRY** unit that is on or within a terrain feature that is ablaze. That unit cannot make any attacks this phase, but immediately decrease the blaze dice of the terrain feature it is on or within by 1 (to a minimum of 1).

1CP

ARSONISTS
Conflagration Stratagem

Use this Stratagem at the start of your Shooting phase. Select a ruin or Sector Mechanicus structure that is within 6" of a unit from your army. That unit cannot make any attacks this phase. If the terrain feature is ablaze, immediately increase the blaze dice of the terrain feature by 1 (to a maximum of 6). If the terrain feature is not ablaze, it is instead set ablaze.

URBAN BATTLEZONE: POLLUTION

A dense layer of poisonous smog covers the city, shrouding everything in thick clouds of toxic dust. Acid rain pours onto the streets below, exposed flesh sizzling and burning in the deluge. Centuries of such pollutants have compromised the integrity of the buildings themselves, their crumbling walls and weakened floors liable to collapse at any moment.

Acid Rain: Subtract 1 from the Toughness characteristic of models unless their unit is entirely on or within a ruin or Sector Mechanicus structure, or they are a **MONSTER**, or they are a **VEHICLE** with a Toughness characteristic of 7 or more that does not have the Open-topped ability.

Shrouding Smog: Targets are obscured even if they are completely visible to the firing model or they have the Flyer Battlefield Role. In addition, the maximum range of Rapid Fire, Assault and Heavy weapons is halved in this Battlezone.

Crumbling City: All ruins and Sector Mechanicus structures are dangerous terrain (pg 29). In addition, terrain features that would provide hard cover instead only provide soft cover, unless the Reinforced Position Stratagem (pg 32) is used.

STRATAGEMS

In this Battlezone, you and your opponent can both use Command Points (CPs) to use the following Stratagem:

1CP

BLIND FIRING
Pollution Stratagem

Use this Stratagem before a unit from your army makes its attacks in the Shooting phase. Rapid Fire, Assault and Heavy weapons fired by this unit this phase can shoot up to their full range, but will only hit targets over half their maximum range on hit rolls of 6, irrespective of any modifiers that may apply.

CITIES OF DEATH NARRATIVE PLAY
THE GAUNTLET

The defender's forces have been cut off and surrounded. Rather than stay and fight, they decide to break out in the dead of night before the attacker can tighten the noose. The opposing side must try to prevent them slipping away under the cover of darkness.

THE ARMIES

The players must first decide who will be the Attacker and who will be the Defender. Both players then select a Battle-forged army. Neither army can include any Fortifications. This mission works especially well when both forces have a roughly equal Power Level, or when the Attacker's Power Level is slightly higher than the Defender's. This mission works best with ground-based armies that contain few, if any, units that can **FLY**.

THE BATTLEFIELD

Create a battlefield using the deployment map below and then set up terrain as described on page 27.

DEPLOYMENT

After terrain has been set up, the Attacker sets up their army and then the Defender sets up their army. A player's models must be set up wholly within their deployment zone, and the Attacker must set up as equal a number of units as possible in each of their two deployment zones.

CUT OFF AND SURROUNDED

The Defender cannot use any abilities or Stratagems that allow their units to be set up off the battlefield and arrive as reinforcements later.

FIRST TURN

After both sides have deployed, the Defender rolls a D6: on a 6 the Defender has the first turn, otherwise the Attacker has the first turn.

DAWN RAID

This mission uses the Dawn Raid rules (pg 31).

ESCAPE ROUTE

Any Defender unit can move off the battlefield edge labelled 'Escape Route' so long as all of its models can move off the board in the same phase. Any units that do so have escaped the ambush – they are removed from the battlefield and take no further part in the battle.

BATTLE LENGTH

The players should use the Random Battle Length rules (pg 31) to determine how long the battle lasts.

VICTORY CONDITIONS

At the end of the battle, add up the Power Ratings of all the Defender's escaped units (see Escape Route, above) and compare this to the Power Level of their army (count the entire unit's Power Rating, even if only a single model escaped). If the combined Power Rating of the escaped units is one third or more of the army's Power Level, the Defender wins a major victory. Any other result is a major victory for the Attacker.

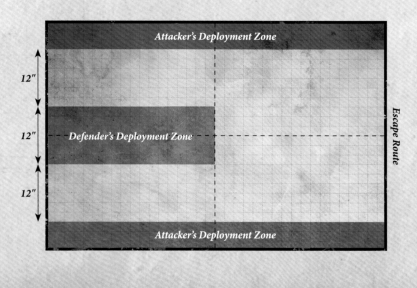

CITIES OF DEATH NARRATIVE PLAY
TOTAL DEVASTATION

A single city ruin is being used as a safe house and strongpoint for the defender's senior leaders. The attacker is under orders to locate and destroy this haven, and is fully prepared to flatten the entire block to accomplish their mission.

THE ARMIES

The players must first decide who will be the Attacker and who will be the Defender. Both players then select a Battle-forged army. The Defender's army can include up to one Fortification and the Attacker's army cannot include any Fortifications. This mission works especially well when both forces have a roughly equal Power Level, or when the Attacker's Power Level is slightly higher than the Defender's.

THE BATTLEFIELD

Create a battlefield using the deployment map below and then set up terrain as described on page 27. After terrain has been set up, the Defender must set up 6 objective markers. Each must be set up on or within a different ruin or Sector Mechanicus structure.

DEPLOYMENT

After terrain has been set up, the Defender sets up their army using the Concealed Deployment rules (pg 31) and then the Attacker sets up their army. A player's models must be set up wholly within their deployment zone.

PRELIMINARY BOMBARDMENT

Once both sides have been set up, the Attacker launches a Preliminary Bombardment (pg 31).

FIRST TURN

The players roll off and the winner chooses who has the first turn.

STRONGPOINT

The Defender has 6 additional Command Points in this mission, which must all be used on the Reinforced Position Stratagem (pg 32). After reinforcing their positions, the Defender must secretly pick one objective marker to denote their strongpoint.

RAZE AND RUIN

The Attacker can use the Demolitions Stratagem (pg 34) for free (i.e. it costs 0 CPs) and can do so any number of times during the battle.

BATTLE LENGTH

The players should use the Random Battle Length rules (pg 31) to determine how long the battle lasts.

VICTORY CONDITIONS

If, at the end of the battle, the Demolitions Stratagem has been used on the Defender's strongpoint, or the terrain feature containing the strongpoint has become dangerous terrain (as the result of, for example, the Wrecker or Siege Shell Stratagem) the Attacker wins a major victory. Any other result is a major victory for the Defender.

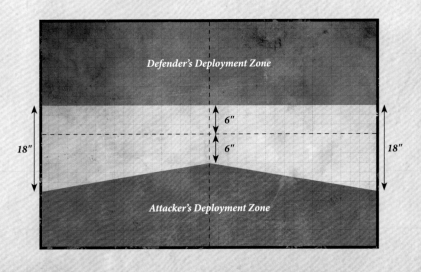

Defender's Deployment Zone

6"

18"   6"   18"

Attacker's Deployment Zone

CITIES OF DEATH NARRATIVE PLAY
RELIEF FORCE

A unit occupying a vital building has been cut off and isolated. They have held out for days against several waves of attackers, but now the odds stacked against them seem insurmountable. A relief force has been sent to secure the building and save the garrison before the enemy overwhelms their position.

THE ARMIES

The players must first decide who will be the Attacker and who will be the Defender. Both players then select a Battle-forged army. The Defender's army can include up to one Fortification (but not a **Building**) and the Attacker's army cannot include any Fortifications. This mission works especially well when both forces have a roughly equal Power Level, or when the Attacker's Power Level is slightly higher than the Defender's.

THE BATTLEFIELD

Create a battlefield using the deployment map below and then set up terrain as described on page 27. Ensure that there is at least one ruins or Sector Mechanicus structure wholly within 12" of the centre of the battlefield to be the Vital Building. The streets and roads around this building should contain plenty of barricades and obstacles to represent this building's outer defences. After terrain has been set up, the Defender sets up 1 objective marker on or within the Vital Building.

DEPLOYMENT

After terrain has been set up, the Defender sets up one or two **Infantry** units from their army entirely on or in the Vital Building. If the Defender's army includes a Fortification, they set this up within 6" of the Vital Building. The remainder of the Defender's army starts in Reserves (pg 31). The Attacker then sets up their army wholly within their deployment zone.

FIRST TURN

The Attacker has the first turn.

RELIEF FORCES

When the Defender's units arrive from Reserves, they are set up wholly within 6" of the Defender's battlefield edge (units may still use any abilities they may have that allow them to arrive elsewhere, such as 'Teleport Strike').

VITAL BUILDING

The Defender has 1 additional Command Point in this mission. Neither player can use the Demolitions Stratagem (pg 34) on the Vital Building objective marker.

BATTLE LENGTH

The players should use the Random Battle Length rules (pg 31) to determine how long the battle lasts.

VICTORY CONDITIONS

At the end of the battle, the Attacker wins a major victory if they control the Vital Building objective marker. Any other result is a major victory for the Defender.

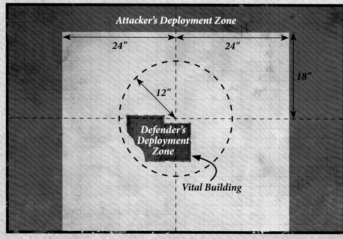

Defender's Battlefield Edge

CITIES OF DEATH NARRATIVE PLAY
GRAND ASSAULT

After weeks, months or even years of brutal urban conflict, the opportunity has arisen for one army to strike a decisive blow, either to push the invaders out of their city or alternatively to crush the last vestiges of resistance.

THE ARMIES

The players must first decide who will be the Attacker and who will be the Defender. Both players then select a Battle-forged army. The Defender's army can include up to one Fortification and the Attacker's army cannot include any Fortifications. This mission works especially well when both forces have a roughly equal Power Level, or when the Attacker's Power Level is slightly higher than the Defender's.

THE BATTLEFIELD

Create a battlefield using the deployment map below and then set up terrain as described on page 27. After terrain has been set up, the Defender must set up 6 objective markers in their deployment zone. Each must be set up on or within a different ruin or Sector Mechanicus structure.

DEPLOYMENT

After terrain has been set up, the Defender sets up their entire army, and then the Attacker sets up their entire army. A player's models must be set up wholly within their deployment zone.

PRELIMINARY BOMBARDMENT

Once both sides have been set up, the Attacker launches a Preliminary Bombardment (pg 31).

FIRST TURN

The Defender has the first turn.

PLANT THE FLAG

Once the Attacker's army controls an objective marker, it remains under their control for the remainder of the game, even if the unit that was controlling it moves away or is destroyed, and the Defender can never regain control of it. Note that whilst the Attacker continues to control the objective marker, the unit itself does not.

SUSTAINED ASSAULT

The Attacker uses the Sustained Assault rules (pg 31). Each time one of the Attacker's replacement units arrives, roll a D6: on a 1-5, set up the unit so that it is wholly within 6" of the Attacker's battlefield edge. On a 6, set up the unit wholly within 6" of any battlefield edge.

BATTLE LENGTH

The players should use the Random Battle Length rules (pg 31) to determine how long the battle lasts.

VICTORY CONDITIONS

At the end of the battle, the Attacker wins a major victory if they control all the objective markers on the battlefield. Any other result is a major victory for the Defender.

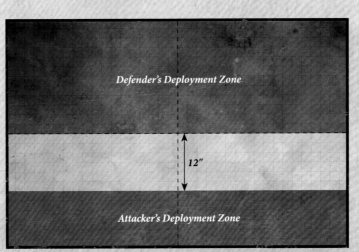

Defender's Deployment Zone

12"

Attacker's Deployment Zone

Attacker's Battlefield Edge

THUNDER RUN

The attacker aims to demoralise the defenders by way of an imposing incursion along the city's main thoroughfare. However, if the defenders prove uncowed they may be able to mount a counter-attack, perhaps striking a critical blow to the attacker's strength.

THE ARMIES

The players must first decide who will be the Attacker and who will be the Defender. Both players then select a Battle-forged army. Neither army can include any Fortifications. This mission works especially well when both forces have a roughly equal Power Level, or when the Attacker's Power Level is slightly higher than the Defender's. This mission works best with ground-based armies that contain few, if any, units that can **FLY**.

After choosing their army, the Attacker must select 1-3 of their units to be Thunder Run units: these units are attempting to advance down the city's thoroughfare. Thunder Run units cannot move into ruins or Sector Mechanicus structures for any reason.

THE BATTLEFIELD

Create a battlefield using the deployment map below and then set up terrain as described on page 27. Ensure that the two short edges of the battlefield are connected by a street or road that is sparsely littered with obstacles.

DEPLOYMENT

After terrain has been set up, the Defender sets up their army using the Concealed Deployment rules (pg 31) and then the Attacker sets up their army. A player's models must be set up wholly within their deployment zone. Thunder Run units must be set up on streets or roads.

LET THEM SEE OUR ADVANCE, LET THEM TREMBLE

The Attacker cannot use any abilities or Stratagems that allow their Thunder Run units to be set up off the battlefield and arrive as reinforcements later. Thunder Run units cannot embark onto **TRANSPORTS**.

FIRST TURN

After both sides have deployed, the Defender rolls a D6: on a 6 the Defender has the first turn, otherwise the Attacker has the first turn.

VICTORY ROUTE

Any Thunder Run unit can move off the battlefield edge labelled 'Victory Route' so long as all of its models can move off the board in the same phase. Any units that do so have successfully completed their Thunder Run – they are removed from the battlefield and take no further part in the battle.

BATTLE LENGTH

The players should use the Random Battle Length rules (pg 31) to determine how long the battle lasts.

VICTORY CONDITIONS

At the end of the battle, the Attacker wins a major victory if any of their Thunder Run units complete their Thunder Run. Any other result is a major victory for the Defender.

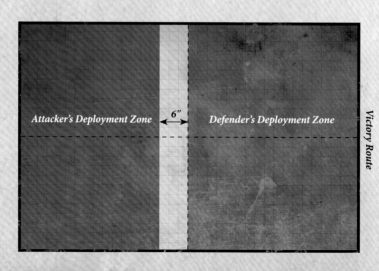

Attacker's Deployment Zone ← 6" → Defender's Deployment Zone · Victory Route

CITIES OF DEATH NARRATIVE PLAY
DECAPITATION

A small, fast-moving attack force has infiltrated deep within hostile territory. Their mission is to destroy the enemy command structure and swiftly exfiltrate the battlefield, severing the head of the opposing army and leaving their foes reeling in confusion.

THE ARMIES

The players must first decide who will be the Attacker and who will be the Defender. Both players then select a Battle-forged army. Neither army can include any Fortifications. This mission works especially well when the Defender's Power Level is at least twice that of the Attacker.

THE BATTLEFIELD

Create a battlefield using the deployment map below and then set up terrain as described on page 27.

DEPLOYMENT

After terrain has been set up, the Defender sets up their Warlord and up to one third of their remaining units using the rules for Concealed Deployment (pg 31). The remainder of the Defender's army starts in Reserve (pg 31). The Attacker then sets up their army wholly within their deployment zone.

FIRST TURN

After both sides have deployed, the Defender rolls a D6: on a 6 the Defender has the first turn, otherwise the Attacker has the first turn.

TIMED STRIKE

At the start of the first battle round, the Attacker chooses whether or not the Dawn Raid rules (pg 31) will be used in the battle.

TARGET SIGHTED

In this mission, the Attacker can use the Master Snipers Stratagem (pg 34) for free (i.e. it costs 0 CPs).

DELAYED REINFORCEMENTS

The Defender must subtract 1 from all Reserve rolls they make in this mission. When the Defender's units arrive from Reserves, they are set up wholly within 6" of any battlefield edge (units may still use any abilities they may have that allow them to arrive elsewhere, such as 'Teleport Strike').

BATTLE LENGTH

The players should use the Random Battle Length rules (pg 31) to determine how long the battle lasts.

VICTORY CONDITIONS

At the end of the battle, if the Defender's Warlord has been destroyed, the Attacker wins a major victory. Any other result is a major victory for the Defender.

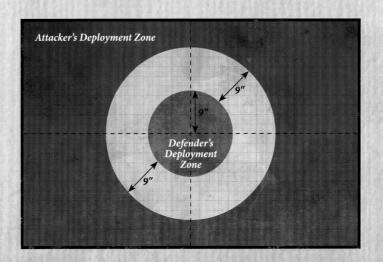

MATCHED PLAY

'TRUST NOT THE XENOS, FOR
THEY WISH TO TAKE WHAT IS
OURS. TRUST NOT IN FLESH, FOR
IT IS WEAK AND CORRUPTIBLE.
PERFORM WELL THE RITES TO
GUARD AGAINST MALFUNCTION
AND PUT THY TRUST IN THE
MACHINE GOD. ONLY THROUGH
HIS DIVINE WEAPONRY MAY OUR
SALVATION BE OBTAINED.'

- Excerpt from Litnus Aeternitas

NEW BATTLEFRONTS

Pitting two Battle-forged armies against one another, matched play missions are as level a playing field as you can get in your Warhammer 40,000 games. Victory will go to the commander who has fortune, strategy and cunning on their side, and each new mission you play is an opportunity to master all three.

The matched play missions available in the *Warhammer 40,000* rulebook give players a wide range of strategic challenges, from the tightly controlled scenarios of Eternal War, to the rapidly shifting battlefield challenges of Maelstrom of War. Every warlord worth their name relishes new strategic challenges, however. Tried and tested tactics must be revised, or whole new routes to victory found. Units that seemed, at first glance, to lack the utility you desired suddenly come into their own as their abilities on the tabletop are proved invaluable. On the following pages you will find just such a range of exciting new opportunities to crush your foes.

PLAYING NEW MISSIONS

This section includes twelve new matched play missions: six Eternal War missions and six Maelstrom of War missions. You can agree with your opponent which set of matched play missions to use, or you can roll off, and whoever rolls highest can choose which set to use, be it one from this book or the *Warhammer 40,000* rulebook.

Having decided the set you wish to use, you can either select one of its six missions, or roll a D6 to randomly select one using the appropriate table. The table for the matched play missions in this book is below.

D6	ETERNAL WAR MISSION	MAELSTROM OF WAR MISSION
1	Vital Intelligence (pg 48)	Disruptive Signals (pg 54)
2	Narrow the Search (pg 49)	Decapitation Strike (pg 55)
3	Cut Off the Head (pg 50)	Strategic Gamble (pg 56)
4	The Four Pillars (pg 51)	Tactical Cascade (pg 57)
5	Supplies from Above (pg 52)	Visions of Victory (pg 58)
6	Beachhead (pg 53)	Scars of Battle (pg 59)

MATCHED PLAY MISSION RULES

The following rules apply to all matched play games:

Battle Brothers

All of the units in each Detachment in your Battle-forged army must have at least one Faction keyword in common. In addition, this keyword cannot be CHAOS, IMPERIUM, AELDARI, YNNARI or TYRANIDS, unless the Detachment in question is a Fortification Network. This has no effect on your Army Faction.

Boots on the Ground

When determining which player controls an objective marker, exclude all units that have the Flyer Battlefield Role – these units can never control objective markers.

Limits of Command

You cannot use the Command Re-roll Stratagem to affect Mission dice rolls. Mission dice rolls include any dice rolls that are made before the battle begins (such as those that determine who chooses deployment zones or who gets the first turn), those that must be made at the end of a battle round (such as rolls that determine if the battle ends) or any rolls that determine how many victory points are awarded to a player.

Psychic Focus

With the exception of *Smite*, each psychic power can be attempted only once per turn, rather than once per psyker per turn. In addition, unless the psyker attempting to manifest *Smite* has either the Brotherhood of Psykers (see *Codex: Grey Knights*) or the Brotherhood of Sorcerers ability (see *Codex: Thousand Sons*), you must add 1 to the warp charge value of *Smite* for each attempt (whether successful or not) that has been made to manifest *Smite* during a given Psychic phase, to a maximum warp charge value of 11.

For example, if an ORK psyker attempts to manifest *Smite* during a Psychic phase in which two other psykers have already attempted to manifest *Smite*, then the warp charge value of *Smite* is 7 for that attempt (note that if the psyker's psychic test is more than 10, it still inflicts D6 mortal wounds instead of D3 as normal).

Strategic Discipline

The same Stratagem cannot be used by the same player more than once during any single phase. This does not affect Stratagems that are not used during a phase, such as those used 'before the battle begins' or 'at the end of a battle round'.

Targeting Characters

An enemy CHARACTER with a Wounds characteristic of less than 10 can only be chosen as a target in the Shooting phase if it is both visible to the firing model and it is the closest enemy unit to the firing model. Ignore other enemy CHARACTERS with a Wounds characteristics of less than 10 when determining if the target is the closest enemy unit to the firing model.

This means that if any other enemy units (excluding other CHARACTERS with a Wounds characteristic of less than 10) are closer, whether they are visible or not, then the enemy CHARACTER cannot be targeted.

Understrength Support

Understrength units can only be included in Auxiliary Support Detachments.

ETERNAL WAR
VITAL INTELLIGENCE

Important tactical information must be captured. Several key data-terminals have been detected, but they have been damaged in the fighting and you cannot reliably tell when each will be processing the intelligence you need.

THE ARMIES

Each player selects a Battle-forged army to an agreed points limit.

THE BATTLEFIELD

The players first place five objective markers as follows: the first objective marker is placed in the centre of the battlefield. Next, four imaginary lines are drawn between the centre of the battlefield and each corner of the battlefield: another objective marker is placed halfway along each of these lines, until there are five objective markers on the battlefield in total. The players then roll off and the winner individually numbers the objective markers 1 through 5.

Once all the objective markers have been placed and numbered, the players then create the rest of the battlefield and set up terrain.

DEPLOYMENT

The players roll off and the winner determines which of the standard deployment maps is used in the battle (see the *Warhammer 40,000* rulebook) and picks one of the deployment zones for their army. Their opponent uses the other deployment zone.

The player who did not pick their deployment zone then deploys their entire army first. Their opponent then deploys their entire army. A player's models must be set up wholly within their deployment zone.

FIRST TURN

The player who finished setting up their army first chooses who takes the first turn. If they decide to take the first turn, their opponent can roll a dice: on a 6 they seize the initiative, and they get the first turn instead.

ACCEPTABLE CASUALTIES

The matched play rules for Sudden Death are not in use in this mission.

BATTLE LENGTH

At the end of battle round 5, the player who had the first turn rolls a D6. On a 3+, the game continues, otherwise the game is over. At the end of battle round 6, the player who had the second turn rolls a D6. This time the game continues on a 4+, otherwise the game is over. The battle automatically ends at the end of battle round 7.

VICTORY CONDITIONS

At the end of the game, the player with the most victory points is the winner. If both players have the same, the game is a draw. Victory points are scored for the following:

Capture the Data: At the start of each battle round, the player who had the first turn rolls a D6 (this cannot be re-rolled for any reason). On a 6, all objective markers are active for that battle round. On any other result, the objective marker which corresponds to the number rolled is active for that battle round. At the end of the battle round, each player scores a number of victory points equal to the number of objective markers they control. Each objective marker is worth 1 victory point; active objective markers are worth 2 victory points instead. In this mission, a player controls an active objective marker if they have more models within 3" of it than their opponent does.

Slay the Warlord: If the enemy Warlord has been slain during the battle, you score 1 victory point.

First Strike: You score 1 victory point if any units from your opponent's army were destroyed during the first battle round.

Linebreaker: If, at the end of the battle, you have at least one model within the enemy's deployment zone, you score 1 victory point.

KNOWLEDGE IS POWER;
POWER CORRUPTS.

+++

ETERNAL WAR
NARROW THE SEARCH

Orbital scanners are locating a powerful relic. You must secure the area while they narrow their scans to its exact location, for it is hidden by a disruptive null field. The enemy is hunting it too, however, and must be driven away from the final location.

THE ARMIES

Each player selects a Battle-forged army to an agreed points limit.

THE BATTLEFIELD

Create the battlefield and set up terrain. The players then place one objective marker in the centre of the battlefield.

DEPLOYMENT

The players roll off and the winner determines which of the standard deployment maps is used in the battle (see the *Warhammer 40,000* rulebook) and picks one of the deployment zones for their army. Their opponent uses the other deployment zone.

The player who did not pick their deployment zone then deploys their entire army first. Their opponent then deploys their entire army. A player's models must be set up wholly within their deployment zone.

FIRST TURN

The player who finished setting up their army first chooses who takes the first turn. If they decide to take the first turn, their opponent can roll a dice: on a 6, they seize the initiative, and they get the first turn instead.

ACCEPTABLE CASUALTIES

The matched play rules for Sudden Death are not in use in this mission.

NULL FIELD

Invulnerable saving throws cannot be made for units that are within 12" of the objective marker.

BATTLE LENGTH

At the end of battle round 5, the player who had the first turn rolls a D6. On a 3+, the game continues, otherwise the game is over. At the end of battle round 6, the player who had the second turn rolls a D6. This time the game continues on a 4+, otherwise the game is over. The battle automatically ends at the end of battle round 7.

VICTORY CONDITIONS

At the end of the game, the player with the most victory points is the winner. If both players have the same, the game is a draw. Victory points are scored for the following:

Zeroing In: At the end of each battle round, the player who controls the objective marker scores 1 victory point. A player controls the objective marker if they have more models within the specified distance of it than their opponent does. At the end of battle round 1, this distance is 18", and it shrinks by 3" at the end of each battle round, to a minimum of 3". So the player with the most models within 15" of the centre of the objective marker at the end of battle round 2, within 12" at the end of battle round 3, and so on, controls the objective marker.

Slay the Warlord: If the enemy Warlord has been slain during the battle, you score 1 victory point.

First Strike: You score 1 victory point if any units from your opponent's army were destroyed during the first battle round.

Linebreaker: If, at the end of the battle, you have at least one model within the enemy's deployment zone, you score 1 victory point.

ETERNAL WAR
CUT OFF THE HEAD

Your commanders were gathering for a crucial tactical meeting when battle was joined. Your leaders must survive to preserve the information they carry, or else transmit it back to headquarters, whilst preventing the enemy commanders from doing so.

THE ARMIES

Each player selects a Battle-forged army to an agreed points limit.

Each player then allocates 3 Intel Points, as evenly as possible, between the **Characters** in their army, and notes this down on their army roster. If your army has no **Characters**, 1 Intel Point is instead allocated to your Warlord.

THE BATTLEFIELD

Create the battlefield and set up terrain. The players then place one objective marker in the centre of the battlefield.

DEPLOYMENT

The players roll off and the winner determines which of the standard deployment maps is used in the battle (see the *Warhammer 40,000* rulebook) and picks one of the deployment zones for their army. Their opponent uses the other deployment zone.

The player who did not pick their deployment zone then deploys their entire army first. Their opponent then deploys their entire army. A player's models must be set up wholly within their deployment zone.

FIRST TURN

The player who finished setting up their army first chooses who takes the first turn. If they decide to take the first turn, their opponent can roll a dice: on a 6, they seize the initiative, and they get the first turn instead.

ACCEPTABLE CASUALTIES

The matched play rules for Sudden Death are not in use in this mission.

BATTLE LENGTH

At the end of battle round 5, the player who had the first turn rolls a D6. On a 3+, the game continues, otherwise the game is over. At the end of battle round 6, the player who had the second turn rolls a D6. This time the game continues on a 4+, otherwise the game is over. The battle automatically ends at the end of battle round 7.

VICTORY CONDITIONS

At the end of the game, the player with the most victory points is the winner. If both players have the same, the game is a draw. Victory points are scored for the following:

Crucial Intel: At the end of the third battle round, and at the end of each battle round thereafter, each player adds up the number of Intel Points allocated to models from their army that are currently on the battlefield, or that are currently embarked within a **Transport** that is on the battlefield; this is the number of victory points that player scores.

Transmit Intel: Starting from the second battle round, a player scores 1 victory point if they control the objective marker at the start of their turn. A player controls this objective marker if they have more **Characters** that have had Intel Points allocated to them within 3" of the objective marker than their opponent does (other units cannot control objective markers; ignore them when determining who controls the objective marker in this mission).

Slay the Warlord: If the enemy Warlord has been slain during the battle, you score 1 victory point.

First Strike: You score 1 victory point if any units from your opponent's army were destroyed during the first battle round.

Linebreaker: If, at the end of the battle, you have at least one model within the enemy's deployment zone, you score 1 victory point.

+++

BY SHOWING THE ENEMY THE SEVERED HEAD OF THEIR LEADER, YOU SHOW THEM ALSO THE STRENGTH OF THE EMPEROR.

+++

ETERNAL WAR
THE FOUR PILLARS

Strange and ancient alien pillars dominate this battlefield. While these are in your possession, their energies can be siphoned off and stored to power weapons of unimaginable destruction.

THE ARMIES

Each player selects a Battle-forged army to an agreed points limit.

THE BATTLEFIELD

First the players place four objective markers as follows. Draw imaginary lines from the centre of the battlefield towards each corner of the battlefield and place an objective marker 15" from the centre of the battlefield along each of these lines.

Once all the objective markers have been placed, the players then create the rest of the battlefield and set up terrain.

DEPLOYMENT

The players roll off and the winner determines which of the standard deployment maps is used in the battle (see the *Warhammer 40,000* rulebook) and picks one of the deployment zones for their army. Their opponent uses the other deployment zone.

The player who did not pick their deployment zone then deploys their entire army first. Their opponent then deploys their entire army. A player's models must be set up wholly within their deployment zone.

FIRST TURN

The player who finished setting up their army first chooses who takes the first turn. If they decide to take the first turn, their opponent can roll a dice: on a 6, they seize the initiative, and they get the first turn instead.

ACCEPTABLE CASUALTIES

The matched play rules for Sudden Death are not in use in this mission.

BATTLE LENGTH

At the end of battle round 5, the player who had the first turn rolls a D6. On a 3+, the game continues, otherwise the game is over. At the end of battle round 6, the player who had the second turn rolls a D6. This time the game continues on a 4+, otherwise the game is over. The battle automatically ends at the end of battle round 7.

VICTORY CONDITIONS

At the end of the game, the player with the most victory points is the winner. If both players have the same, the game is a draw. Victory points are scored for the following:

Siphon Power: At the end of each battle round, if one player controls more objective markers than their opponent, they score 1 victory point. If they control all four objective markers, they score 3 victory points instead. A player controls an objective marker if they have more models with the Troops Battlefield Role within 3" of it than their opponent does (other units cannot control objective markers; ignore them when determining who controls each objective marker in this mission).

No Prisoners: At the end of each battle round, a player scores 1 victory point if more units from their opponent's army were destroyed during that battle round than from their own army.

Slay the Warlord: If the enemy Warlord has been slain during the battle, you score 1 victory point.

First Strike: You score 1 victory point if any units from your opponent's army were destroyed during the first battle round.

Linebreaker: If, at the end of the battle, you have at least one model within the enemy's deployment zone, you score 1 victory point.

+++

ABSOLUTE TYRANNY IS
A SMALL PRICE TO PAY
FOR VICTORY.

+++

ETERNAL WAR
SUPPLIES FROM ABOVE

Valuable supplies are being delivered in slow-fall drop canisters. You must secure the landing sites, although these are hard to judge from the ground, so your forces must be ready to react and secure them while driving the enemy away from these locations.

THE ARMIES

Each player selects a Battle-forged army to an agreed points limit.

THE BATTLEFIELD

Create the battlefield and set up terrain. The players then roll off and, starting with the winner, alternate placing objective markers until four have been placed. Each objective marker can be placed anywhere on the battlefield, as long as each is more than 12" from any other objective marker and more than 6" from the edge of the battlefield.

DEPLOYMENT

The players roll off again and the winner determines which of the standard deployment maps is used in the battle (see the *Warhammer 40,000* rulebook) and picks one of the deployment zones for their army. Their opponent uses the other deployment zone.

The player who did not pick their deployment zone then deploys their entire army first. Their opponent then deploys their entire army. A player's models must be set up wholly within their deployment zone.

FIRST TURN

The player who finished setting up their army first chooses who takes the first turn. If they decide to take the first turn, their opponent can roll a dice: on a 6, they seize the initiative, and they get the first turn instead.

DRIFTING ON THE WIND

At the start of each battle round, starting with the player who has the first turn, alternate picking objective markers; for each objective marker, each player rolls a D6. The player who scores highest can move that objective marker up to 3" (they can be moved over models and terrain, but they cannot end the move on top of models, and cannot leave the battlefield – if they would, reduce the distance they are moved by the minimum amount necessary). If the results are tied, that marker is not moved this battle round. The players should

then repeat this process for each of the other objective markers.

ACCEPTABLE CASUALTIES

The matched play rules for Sudden Death are not in use in this mission.

BATTLE LENGTH

At the end of battle round 5, the player who had the first turn rolls a D6. On a 3+, the game continues, otherwise the game is over. At the end of battle round 6, the player who had the second turn rolls a D6. This time the game continues on a 4+, otherwise the game is over. The battle automatically ends at the end of battle round 7.

VICTORY CONDITIONS

At the end of the game, the player with the most victory points is the winner. If both players have the same, the game is a draw. Victory points are scored for the following:

Secure Supplies: Starting from the second battle round, each player scores 1 victory point for each objective marker they control at the start of their turn. A player controls an objective marker if they have more models within 3" of it than their opponent does. However, if only one player has models that can **FLY** (excluding those with the Flyer Battlefield Role) within 3" of the objective marker, they control it, regardless of the number of nearby enemy models.

Slay the Warlord: If the enemy Warlord has been slain during the battle, you score 1 victory point.

First Strike: You score 1 victory point if any units from your opponent's army were destroyed during the first battle round.

Linebreaker: If, at the end of the battle, you have at least one model within the enemy's deployment zone, you score 1 victory point.

ETERNAL WAR
BEACHHEAD

You must capture a key point in enemy territory while securing your own borders against their attacks. If you seize the enemy's territory but lose your own, there is no advantage gained.

THE ARMIES

Each player selects a Battle-forged army to an agreed points limit.

THE BATTLEFIELD

Create the battlefield and set up terrain. Next, the players place one objective marker in the centre of the battlefield.

DEPLOYMENT

The players roll off and the winner determines which of the standard deployment maps is used in the battle (see the *Warhammer 40,000* rulebook), then picks one of the deployment zones for their army and sets up an additional objective marker within it. Their opponent uses the other deployment zone, and likewise sets up an additional objective marker within it. Neither of these objective markers can be set up within 8" of any battlefield edge or within 12" of any other objective marker.

The player who did not pick their deployment zone then deploys their entire army first. Their opponent then deploys their entire army. A player's models must be set up wholly within their deployment zone.

FIRST TURN

The player who finished setting up their army first chooses who takes the first turn. If they decide to take the first turn, their opponent can roll a dice: on a 6, they seize the initiative, and they get the first turn instead.

ACCEPTABLE CASUALTIES

The matched play rules for Sudden Death are not in use in this mission.

BATTLE LENGTH

At the end of battle round 5, the player who had the first turn rolls a D6. On a 3+, the game continues, otherwise the game is over. At the end of battle round 6, the player who had the second turn rolls a D6. This time the game continues on a 4+, otherwise the game is over. The battle automatically ends at the end of battle round 7.

VICTORY CONDITIONS

At the end of the game, the player with the most victory points is the winner. If both players have the same, the game is a draw. Victory points are scored for the following:

Push Them Back: Starting from the second battle round, each player scores a number of victory points for each objective marker they control at the start of their turn. A player scores 1 victory point if they control the objective marker in their own deployment zone, 2 victory points if they control the objective marker in the centre of the battlefield, and 3 victory points if they control the objective marker in their opponent's deployment zone. A player controls an objective marker if they have more models within 3" of it than their opponent does.

Slay the Warlord: If the enemy Warlord has been slain during the battle, you score 1 victory point.

First Strike: You score 1 victory point if any units from your opponent's army were destroyed during the first battle round.

Linebreaker: If, at the end of the battle, you have at least one model within the enemy's deployment zone, you score 1 victory point.

+++

+++

MAELSTROM OF WAR
DISRUPTIVE SIGNALS

In the chaos of battle, orders will often be disrupted by the enemy, misinterpreted, or undelivered, leaving even the soundest strategy at risk of failure – an experienced commander knows never to rely on a single plan.

THE ARMIES

Each player selects a Battle-forged army to an agreed points limit.

THE BATTLEFIELD

Create the battlefield and set up terrain. The players place six objective markers, as detailed in the Tactical Objectives section of the *Warhammer 40,000* rulebook.

DEPLOYMENT

The players roll off and the winner determines which of the standard deployment maps is used in the battle (see the *Warhammer 40,000* rulebook) and picks one of the deployment zones for their army. Their opponent uses the other deployment zone.

The player who did not pick their deployment zone then deploys their entire army first. Their opponent then deploys their entire army. A player's models must be set up wholly within their deployment zone.

FIRST TURN

The player who finished setting up their army first chooses who takes the first turn. If they decide to take the first turn, their opponent can roll a dice: on a 6, they seize the initiative, and they get the first turn instead.

TACTICAL OBJECTIVES

This mission uses Tactical Objectives. If, at the start of a player's turn, they have fewer than 4 active Tactical Objectives, they must generate Tactical Objectives until they have 4.

REFINED STRATEGY

Before the battle begins, each player selects up to 6 of their Tactical Objectives (inform your opponent of your choice). If they are using Tactical Objective cards, remove the selected cards from their deck; otherwise, if that player generates one of the selected Tactical Objectives during the battle by rolling dice, they must immediately generate a new Tactical Objective to replace it.

ACCEPTABLE CASUALTIES

The matched play rules for Sudden Death are not in use in this mission.

STRATAGEM
Players can use the following Stratagem:

1CP
SIGNAL INTERRUPT
Maelstrom of War Stratagem
Use this Stratagem after your opponent generates Tactical Objectives. Select one of their active Tactical Objectives – it can't be achieved this turn.

BATTLE LENGTH

At the end of battle round 5, the player who had the first turn rolls a D6. On a 3+, the game continues, otherwise the game is over. At the end of battle round 6, the player who had the second turn rolls a D6. This time the game continues on a 4+, otherwise the game is over. The battle automatically ends at the end of battle round 7.

VICTORY CONDITIONS

At the end of the game, the player with the most victory points is the winner. If both players have the same, the game is a draw. In addition to achieving Tactical Objectives, victory points are scored for the following:

Slay the Warlord: If the enemy Warlord has been slain during the battle, you score 1 victory point.

First Strike: You score 1 victory point if any units from your opponent's army were destroyed during the first battle round.

Linebreaker: If, at the end of the battle, you have at least one model within the enemy's deployment zone, you score 1 victory point.

+++

THERE WILL ALWAYS BE SHADOWS, BUT NO DARKNESS CAN SURVIVE THE BLINDING LIGHT OF THE EMPEROR'S HATE.

+++

MAELSTROM OF WAR
DECAPITATION STRIKE

If you want to disrupt your opponent's plans, kill their leaders. For each commander you slay, a portion of the enemy's strategy crumbles away, until your forces sweep them aside.

THE ARMIES

Each player selects a Battle-forged army to an agreed points limit.

THE BATTLEFIELD

Create the battlefield and set up terrain. The players place six objective markers, as detailed in the Tactical Objectives section of the *Warhammer 40,000* rulebook.

DEPLOYMENT

The players roll off and the winner determines which of the standard deployment maps is used in the battle (see the *Warhammer 40,000* rulebook) and picks one of the deployment zones for their army. Their opponent uses the other deployment zone.

The player who did not pick their deployment zone then deploys their entire army first. Their opponent then deploys their entire army. A player's models must be set up wholly within their deployment zone.

FIRST TURN

The player who finished setting up their army first chooses who takes the first turn. If they decide to take the first turn, their opponent can roll a dice: on a 6, they seize the initiative, and they get the first turn instead.

TACTICAL OBJECTIVES

This mission uses Tactical Objectives. At the start of a player's turn, they must generate 3 Tactical Objectives. A player cannot have more than 6 active Tactical Objectives at any one time (stop generating new Tactical Objectives if a player reaches this limit).

REFINED STRATEGY

Before the battle begins, each player selects up to 6 of their Tactical Objectives (inform your opponent of your choice). If they are using Tactical Objective cards, remove the selected cards from their deck; otherwise, if that player generates one of the selected Tactical Objectives during the battle by rolling

dice, they must immediately generate a new Tactical Objective to replace it.

HIGH VALUE TARGETS

Each time a CHARACTER is slain, the controlling player must randomly select one of their active Tactical Objectives and discard it. If a Warlord is slain, the controlling player must instead randomly select D3 of their active Tactical Objectives and discard all of them.

ACCEPTABLE CASUALTIES

The matched play rules for Sudden Death are not in use in this mission.

BATTLE LENGTH

At the end of battle round 5, the player who had the first turn rolls a D6. On a 3+, the game continues, otherwise the game is over. At the end of battle round 6, the player who had the second turn rolls a D6. This time the game continues on a 4+, otherwise the game is over. The battle automatically ends at the end of battle round 7.

VICTORY CONDITIONS

At the end of the game, the player with the most victory points is the winner. If both players have the same, the game is a draw. In addition to achieving Tactical Objectives, victory points are scored for the following:

Slay the Warlord: If the enemy Warlord has been slain during the battle, you score 1 victory point.

First Strike: You score 1 victory point if any units from your opponent's army were destroyed during the first battle round.

Linebreaker: If, at the end of the battle, you have at least one model within the enemy's deployment zone, you score 1 victory point.

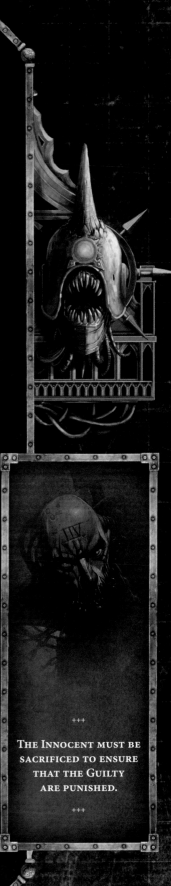

+++

THE INNOCENT MUST BE
SACRIFICED TO ENSURE
THAT THE GUILTY
ARE PUNISHED.

+++

MAELSTROM OF WAR
STRATEGIC GAMBLE

Often success in battle will come down to being in the right place at the right time, and hardened veterans know well that a daring manoeuvre can turn the tide of an entire war.

THE ARMIES

Each player selects a Battle-forged army to an agreed points limit.

THE BATTLEFIELD

Create the battlefield and set up terrain. The players place six objective markers, as detailed in the Tactical Objectives section of the *Warhammer 40,000* rulebook.

DEPLOYMENT

The players roll off and the winner determines which of the standard deployment maps is used in the battle (see the *Warhammer 40,000* rulebook) and picks one of the deployment zones for their army. Their opponent uses the other deployment zone.

The player who did not pick their deployment zone then deploys their entire army first. Their opponent then deploys their entire army. A player's models must be set up wholly within their deployment zone.

FIRST TURN

The player who finished setting up their army first chooses who takes the first turn. If they decide to take the first turn, their opponent can roll a dice: on a 6, they seize the initiative, and they get the first turn instead.

TACTICAL OBJECTIVES

This mission uses Tactical Objectives. If, at the start of a player's turn, they have fewer than 3 active Tactical Objectives, they must generate Tactical Objectives until they have 3.

REFINED STRATEGY

Before the battle begins, each player selects up to 6 of their Tactical Objectives (inform your opponent of your choice). If they are using Tactical Objective cards, remove the selected cards from their deck; otherwise, if that player generates one of the selected Tactical Objectives during the battle by rolling dice, they must immediately generate a new Tactical Objective to replace it.

TAKE A CHANCE

At the start of each player's turn, after they have generated new Tactical Objectives (if any), that player can choose to discard 2 of their Tactical Objectives to generate a new one. If that player is able to achieve the newly generated Tactical Objective by the end of this turn, they score double the number of victory points for that Tactical Objective.

ACCEPTABLE CASUALTIES

The matched play rules for Sudden Death are not in use in this mission.

BATTLE LENGTH

At the end of battle round 5, the player who had the first turn rolls a D6. On a 3+, the game continues, otherwise the game is over. At the end of battle round 6, the player who had the second turn rolls a D6. This time the game continues on a 4+, otherwise the game is over. The battle automatically ends at the end of battle round 7.

VICTORY CONDITIONS

At the end of the game, the player with the most victory points is the winner. If both players have the same, the game is a draw. In addition to achieving Tactical Objectives, victory points are scored for the following:

Slay the Warlord: If the enemy Warlord has been slain during the battle, you score 1 victory point.

First Strike: You score 1 victory point if any units from your opponent's army were destroyed during the first battle round.

Linebreaker: If, at the end of the battle, you have at least one model within the enemy's deployment zone, you score 1 victory point.

HOPE IS WORTHLESS. WHAT IS REQUIRED IS RESOLUTION.

MAELSTROM OF WAR
TACTICAL CASCADE

Victories can often lead to overconfidence. For every success, more responsibility will be placed upon your shoulders. You will need to adapt to this greater responsibility, or be buried by it.

THE ARMIES

Each player selects a Battle-forged army to an agreed points limit.

THE BATTLEFIELD

Create the battlefield and set up terrain. The players place six objective markers, as detailed in the Tactical Objectives section of the *Warhammer 40,000* rulebook.

DEPLOYMENT

The players roll off and the winner determines which of the standard deployment maps is used in the battle (see the *Warhammer 40,000* rulebook) and picks one of the deployment zones for their army. Their opponent uses the other deployment zone.

The player who did not pick their deployment zone then deploys their entire army first. Their opponent then deploys their entire army. A player's models must be set up wholly within their deployment zone.

FIRST TURN

The player who finished setting up their army first chooses who takes the first turn. If they decide to take the first turn, their opponent can roll a dice: on a 6, they seize the initiative, and they get the first turn instead.

REFINED STRATEGY

Before the battle begins, each player selects up to 6 of their Tactical Objectives (inform your opponent of your choice). If they are using Tactical Objective cards, remove the selected cards from their deck; otherwise, if that player generates one of the selected Tactical Objectives during the battle by rolling dice, they must immediately generate a new Tactical Objective to replace it.

TACTICAL OBJECTIVES

This mission uses Tactical Objectives. At the start of a player's first turn, they must choose 2 Tactical Objectives – they automatically generate these Tactical Objectives. At the start of each of their turns after their first,

they must generate 2 Tactical Objectives for each Tactical Objective they achieved in the previous battle round; a player cannot generate more than 6 a turn.

ACCEPTABLE CASUALTIES

The matched play rules for Sudden Death are not in use in this mission.

BATTLE LENGTH

The battle ends immediately once a player has achieved their 25th Tactical Objective. Otherwise, at the end of battle round 5, the player who had the first turn rolls a D6. On a 3+, the game continues, otherwise the game is over. At the end of battle round 6, the player who had the second turn rolls a D6. This time the game continues on a 4+, otherwise the game is over. The battle automatically ends at the end of battle round 7.

VICTORY CONDITIONS

At the end of the game, the player with the most victory points is the winner. If both players have the same, the game is a draw. In addition to achieving Tactical Objectives, victory points are scored for the following:

Burden of Command: Each player loses 1 victory point for every 3 active Tactical Objectives they still have (rounding down) at the end of the battle.

Slay the Warlord: If the enemy Warlord has been slain during the battle, you score 1 victory point.

First Strike: You score 1 victory point if any units from your opponent's army were destroyed during the first battle round.

Linebreaker: If, at the end of the battle, you have at least one model within the enemy's deployment zone, you score 1 victory point.

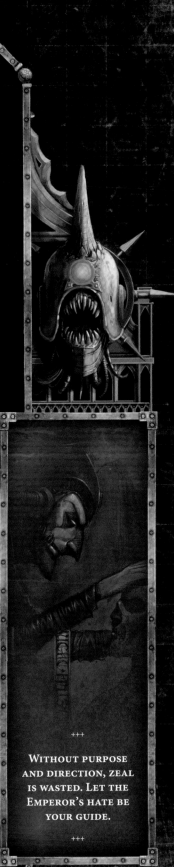

+++

WITHOUT PURPOSE AND DIRECTION, ZEAL IS WASTED. LET THE EMPEROR'S HATE BE YOUR GUIDE.

+++

MAELSTROM OF WAR
VISIONS OF VICTORY

Communications have broken down. Unable to reach any higher authority, you must rely on the advice of your ambitious subordinates to best direct your forces. You can only hope that their advice is well informed.

IN AN HOUR OF DARKNESS A BLIND MAN IS THE BEST GUIDE. IN AN AGE OF INSANITY LOOK TO THE MADMAN TO SHOW THE WAY.

+++

THE ARMIES
Each player selects a Battle-forged army to an agreed points limit.

THE BATTLEFIELD
Create the battlefield and set up terrain. The players place six objective markers, as detailed in the Tactical Objectives section of the *Warhammer 40,000* rulebook.

DEPLOYMENT
The players roll off and the winner determines which of the standard deployment maps is used in the battle (see the *Warhammer 40,000* rulebook) and picks one of the deployment zones for their army. Their opponent uses the other deployment zone.

The player who did not pick their deployment zone then deploys their entire army first. Their opponent then deploys their entire army. A player's models must be set up wholly within their deployment zone.

FIRST TURN
The player who finished setting up their army first chooses who takes the first turn. If they decide to take the first turn, their opponent can roll a dice: on a 6, they seize the initiative, and they get the first turn instead.

TACTICAL OBJECTIVES
This mission uses Tactical Objectives. If, at the start of a player's turn, they have fewer than 4 active Tactical Objectives, they must generate Tactical Objectives until they have 4.

REFINED STRATEGY
Before the battle begins, each player selects up to 6 of their Tactical Objectives. If they are using Tactical Objective cards, remove the selected cards from their deck; otherwise, if that player generates one of the selected Tactical Objectives during the battle by rolling dice, they must immediately generate a new Tactical Objective to replace it.

UNRELIABLE ADVICE
Whenever a player is required to generate a Tactical Objective, they must instead generate two Tactical Objectives and their opponent selects which one they must keep. The other one is discarded, but can potentially be generated again later in the battle.

ACCEPTABLE CASUALTIES
The matched play rules for Sudden Death are not in use in this mission.

BATTLE LENGTH
At the end of battle round 5, the player who had the first turn rolls a D6. On a 3+, the game continues, otherwise the game is over. At the end of battle round 6, the player who had the second turn rolls a D6. This time the game continues on a 4+, otherwise the game is over. The battle automatically ends at the end of battle round 7.

VICTORY CONDITIONS
At the end of the game, the player with the most victory points is the winner. If both players have the same, the game is a draw. In addition to achieving Tactical Objectives, victory points are scored for the following:

Slay the Warlord: If the enemy Warlord has been slain during the battle, you score 1 victory point.

First Strike: You score 1 victory point if any units from your opponent's army were destroyed during the first battle round.

Linebreaker: If, at the end of the battle, you have at least one model within the enemy's deployment zone, you score 1 victory point.

MAELSTROM OF WAR
SCARS OF BATTLE

The battle has raged long and hard. Your communications are unreliable, vital equipment has been lost and even the warriors under your command are fatigued beyond measure. Despite this, a vital opportunity to defeat the foe has arisen. Seize it!

THE ARMIES

Each player selects a Battle-forged army to an agreed points limit.

THE BATTLEFIELD

Create the battlefield and set up terrain. The players place six objective markers, as detailed in the Tactical Objectives section of the *Warhammer 40,000* rulebook.

DEPLOYMENT

The players roll off and the winner determines which of the standard deployment maps is used in the battle (see the *Warhammer 40,000* rulebook) and picks one of the deployment zones for their army. Their opponent uses the other deployment zone.

The player who did not pick their deployment zone then deploys their entire army first. Their opponent then deploys their entire army. A player's models must be set up wholly within their deployment zone.

FIRST TURN

The player who finished setting up their army first chooses who takes the first turn. If they decide to take the first turn, their opponent can roll a dice: on a 6, they seize the initiative, and they get the first turn instead.

TACTICAL OBJECTIVES

This mission uses Tactical Objectives. If, at the start of a player's turn, they have fewer than 3 active Tactical Objectives, they must generate Tactical Objectives until they have 3.

LOST COMMUNICATIONS

At the start of the first battle round, but before the first turn begins, each player rolls a D6. On a 1, that player cannot generate Tactical Objectives numbered 11-16 in this mission, on a 2 that player cannot generate Tactical Objectives numbered 21-26, and so on. If a player is using Tactical Objective cards, remove these cards from their deck; otherwise, if that player generates one of the selected Tactical Objectives during the battle by rolling dice, immediately generate a new Tactical Objective to replace it.

REFINED STRATEGY

Before the battle begins, each player selects up to 6 of their Tactical Objectives. If they are using Tactical Objective cards, remove the selected cards from their deck; otherwise, if that player generates one of the selected Tactical Objectives during the battle by rolling dice, they must immediately generate a new Tactical Objective to replace it.

ACCEPTABLE CASUALTIES

The matched play rules for Sudden Death are not in use in this mission.

BATTLE LENGTH

At the end of battle round 5, the player who had the first turn rolls a D6. On a 3+, the game continues, otherwise the game is over. At the end of battle round 6, the player who had the second turn rolls a D6. This time the game continues on a 4+, otherwise the game is over. The battle automatically ends at the end of battle round 7.

VICTORY CONDITIONS

At the end of the game, the player with the most victory points is the winner. If both players have the same, the game is a draw. In addition to achieving Tactical Objectives, victory points are scored for the following:

Slay the Warlord: If the enemy Warlord has been slain during the battle, you score 1 victory point.

First Strike: You score 1 victory point if any units from your opponent's army were destroyed during the first battle round.

Linebreaker: If, at the end of the battle, you have at least one model within the enemy's deployment zone, you score 1 victory point.

+++

THE EMPEROR WILL NOT JUDGE YOU BY YOUR MEDALS AND DIPLOMAS; HE WILL JUDGE YOU BY YOUR SCARS.

+++

APPENDIX

In this section you will find a collection of supplementary content that you can use in any of your games of Warhammer 40,000.

Battlefield Terrain

This section provides rules for a range of terrain pieces that can be used to transform your gaming table into an interactive, thematic battlefield. Rules for Sector Mechanicus and Sector Imperialis terrain allow you to lace your battlefields with thrumming wonders of arcane technology, while those for Death World Forests enable you to add sprawling thickets of lethal plant life to your games, forcing warriors to battle their way through grasping tendrils and weather salvoes of toxic spines as they do battle with one another.

Codex: Adepta Sororitas

Here you will find a beta codex replete with the history and background of the Adepta Sororitas, an elite sisterhood of warriors who wield faith and fire to destroy their enemies. Within this section you will find all the datasheets needed to forge your Adepta Sororitas Citadel Miniatures into an army, alongside a suite of Detachment rules such as Stratagems, Warlord Traits and relics. You will also find points values for fielding a Sisters of Battle army in your matched play games.

Index: Renegade Knights

Containing background, datasheets and Detachment rules – including Stratagems, a Relic and a Warlord Trait – this section allows you to field the terrifyingly devastating walkers known as Renegade Knights on the battlefields of the 41st Millennium.

The Eight

This section describes the most famed heroes of the Farsight Enclaves – the Eight – and provides you with rules for using them in your battles. These legendary individuals are an army in their own right, offering T'au Empire collectors a fantastic opportunity to build and play with a completely different style of army.

'NO SERVANT OF THE
EMPEROR HAS PROVEN
THEIR FAITH UNTIL
THEY HAVE GIVEN
THEIR LIFE IN SERVICE
OF HIS WILL.'

*- From the writings of
Arch-Cardinal Judhens*

Battle-forged Armies

In this section of the Appendix, you will find useful tools to help you keep track of the details of your Battle-forged armies.

Once you have a suitably impressive collection of Citadel Miniatures, it is always satisfying to add up their points as an army, either simply to figure out how much your army is worth, or to fine-tune it to a specific points value ready to play games with other hobbyists.

However, while many people enjoy the process of adding up their army's points and designing the perfect army list to take to battle, it helps to be able to keep track of that information so that all you need to do each time you start a game is crack open your case, place your models on the table, and get playing. The Detachment and army rosters in the Appendix allow you to do just this, with space to record details of each of your units – including their wargear options, Battlefield Role and points values – as well as each Detachment in your army, for easy reference in your games. They are also essential if you are playing campaigns incorporating the Battle Honours section of this book, giving you a handy place to keep track of each unit's experience points, rank and new abilities (pg 20-25).

Updated Points Values

The points values we give to each unit allow players to organise their armies based on the strength of each element, and are a great tool when collecting a force for the tabletop.

With each new publication, we review the points values we have given to each unit, and update them if necessary. Here you will find lists of all the updated points values for such units, including several from the Forge World range.

Updated Datasheets

Datasheets are essential to playing games of Warhammer 40,000, describing the characteristics, wargear and abilities of the models in a unit. With each new publication, we review the datasheets within that book and, where appropriate, make changes to better reflect that unit's models, options and background. Since those publications, several new model kits have been released with new options not accounted for by the current datasheet. There have also been a few instances where rules have changed for a datasheet following extensive feedback from the community. As a result, this final section contains several updated datasheets that reflect the latest rules and options for such units.

BATTLEFIELD TERRAIN

In this section you will find expanded terrain rules, including rules for recently released terrain features. If rules for a terrain feature that has rules in the *Warhammer 40,000* rulebook appear here, they update and replace those in the rulebook.

CRATERS

Many worlds bear the scars of heavy, sustained bombardment.

INFANTRY units that are entirely within a crater receive the benefit of cover.

Models are slowed when charging across craters. If, when a unit charges, one or more of its models move across a crater, you must subtract 2" from the unit's charge distance.

BARRICADES

Makeshift barricades make excellent defensive positions.

When a model targets an enemy **INFANTRY** unit that has all of its models within 1" of a barricade, the target unit receives the benefit of cover if the shooting model is closer to the barricade than it is to the target and the target is at least partially obscured from the point of view of the shooting model. In addition, enemy units can Fight across a barricade, even though the physical distance is sometimes more than 1". When resolving Fights between units on opposite sides of a barricade, units can be chosen to Fight and can make their attacks if the enemy is within 2" instead of the normal 1".

GALVANIC SERVOHAULERS

These hydraulic machines litter the industrial zones of the Imperium.

When a model targets an enemy **INFANTRY** unit that has all of its models within 3" of a Galvanic Servohauler, the target unit receives the benefit of cover if the shooting model is closer to the Galvanic Servohauler than it is to the target and the target is at least partially obscured from the point of view of the shooting model.

WOODS

Twisted woodlands grow on many a corpse-strewn battlefield.

INFANTRY units that are entirely on the base of a wood receive the benefit of cover. If your wood is not on a base, discuss with your opponent what the boundary of the wood is before the battle begins. Other units only receive the benefit of cover if at least 50% of every model is obscured from the point of view of the shooting model.

Models are slowed when charging through woods. If, when a unit charges, one or more of its models move across a wood's base, you must subtract 2" from the unit's charge distance.

RUINS

The galaxy is littered with the remains of once-proud cities.

Only **INFANTRY**, **BEASTS**, **SWARMS** and units that can **FLY** can be set up or end their move on the upper floors of ruins (any unit can do so on the ground floor). **INFANTRY** are assumed to be able to scale walls and traverse through windows, doors and portals readily. These models can therefore move through the floors and walls of a ruin without further impediment.

INFANTRY units that are entirely on or within a ruin receive the benefit of cover. Other units that are entirely on or within a ruin only receive the benefit of cover if at least 50% of every model is obscured from the point of view of the shooting model.

MUNITORUM ARMOURED CONTAINERS

These vast steel containers are sometimes fitted with defensive weapons to protect the cargo within.

Units do not receive the benefit of cover when they are on top of a Munitorum Armoured Container – their position is too exposed.

If an **INFANTRY** unit is on top of a Munitorum Armoured Container that has one or more storm bolters, up to two models in that unit can each fire them each time their unit shoots instead of firing any of their own weapons. Storm bolters are Rapid Fire 2 weapons, with a Range of 24", a Strength of 4, AP0 and Damage 1.

THERMIC PLASMA CONDUITS

These conduits channel hot plasma and make for dangerous cover.

Thermic Plasma Conduits follow all the rules for Barricades, but they also have the Hazardous Cover ability (see Haemotrope Reactors).

HAEMOTROPE REACTORS

These reactors are objects of cover for the brave only.

When a model targets an enemy unit that has all of its models within 3" of a Haemotrope Reactor, the target unit receives the benefit of cover if at least 25% of every model is obscured by it from the point of view of the shooting model.

Hazardous Cover: Roll a D6 each time you make a saving throw of 7+ (such as a roll of 6, plus 1 for being in cover) for a model within 3" of any terrain features with this ability in the Shooting phase. On a 1, the model's unit suffers 1 mortal wound.

OBSTACLES

The advance of many armies has been thwarted by obstacles.

There are two kinds of obstacles: tank traps, which are obstacles to **Vehicles** and **Monsters**, and tanglewire, which is an obstacle to everything else. Units are slowed when they attempt to move over obstacles. If, when a unit Advances or charges, one or more of its models move over an obstacle, you must halve the unit's Advance or charge distance, as appropriate (rounding up). **Titanic** models are not slowed by obstacles.

SECTOR MECHANICUS

Sectors Mechanicus are a common sight throughout the galaxy, their gantries and girders thrumming with automated industry.

Sector Mechanicus structures follow all the rules for ruins with the following difference:

Unless they can **Fly**, **Infantry**, **Beasts** and **Swarms** must scale ladders, girders or walls to ascend or descend between the different levels of a Sector Mechanicus structure. **Infantry** are also assumed to be able to traverse around girders, buttresses and hanging chains, and so move through them without impediment.

IMPERIAL STATUARY

The heroes of the Imperium are immortalised in stone effigies.

When a model targets an enemy **Infantry** unit that has all of its models within 3" of Imperial Statuary, the target unit receives the benefit of cover if the shooting model is closer to the Imperial Statuary than it is to the target and the target is at least partially obscured from the point of view of the shooting model. In addition, **Imperium** units add 1 to their Leadership characteristic whilst they are within 3" of any Imperial Statuary.

THERMIC PLASMA REGULATORS

These ancient machines thrum with lethal plasma energy.

Thermic Plasma Regulators follow all the rules for Sector Mechanicus structures, but they also have the Hazardous Cover ability (see Haemotrope Reactors).

DEATH WORLD FORESTS

Razor-sharp walls of crystalline growths, remnants of ancient civilisations long since overgrown and sentient flora that ensnare and consume the unwary are but a few of the dangers that can be found lurking in the perilous alien forests of the galaxy.

A Death World Forest consists of one or more of the following terrain pieces in any combination: Shardwrack Spines, Eldritch Ruins, Barbed Venomgorse or Grapple Weeds. Each piece of Death World Forest terrain is a separate model.

When a model targets an enemy **INFANTRY** unit that has all of its models within 1" of a Death World Forest terrain piece, the target unit receives the benefit of cover if the shooting model is closer to the terrain piece than it is to the target and the target is at least partially obscured from the point of view of the shooting model. In addition, subtract 1 from hit rolls for models that make close combat attacks within 3" of a Death World Forest terrain piece – this represents limbs being entangled by sentient roots or minds being fogged by eldritch energies.

Each of the four Death World Forest terrain pieces has an additional ability, as described opposite.

GRAPPLE WEED

These lethal plants uproot themselves to seek out their prey.

Roll a D6 each time a model moves within 3" of any Grapple Weed terrain pieces whilst Advancing or charging – on a roll of 1, that model's unit suffers D3 mortal wounds. In addition, at the start of each battle round, each Grapple Weed terrain piece moves 2D6" in a straight line towards the nearest visible unit, provided there are any within 12". If two or more units are equidistant, roll off to see which one it moves towards. When moving a Grapple Weed terrain piece, it will stop 1" away from any units or any other battlefield terrain. After all Grapple Weed terrain pieces have moved, roll a D6 for each unit within 3" of one or more of them. On a 4+, that unit suffers 1 mortal wound.

SHARDWRACK SPINE

This deadly flora shoots piercing spines at its prey.

Roll a D6 each time a model moves within 6" of any Shardwrack Spine terrain piece whilst Advancing or charging – on a roll of 1, the model's unit suffers 1 mortal wound.

ELDRITCH RUIN

An aura of arcane power surrounds these ancient ruins.

You can add 1 to Psychic tests and Deny the Witch tests you make for **PSYKERS** that are within 3" of any Eldritch Ruin terrain pieces.

BARBED VENOMGORSE

The throttling limbs of barbed venomgorse are swift and strong.

Roll a D6 each time a model moves within 3" of any Barbed Venomgorse terrain piece whilst Advancing or charging – on a roll of 1 or 2, that model's unit suffers 1 mortal wound.

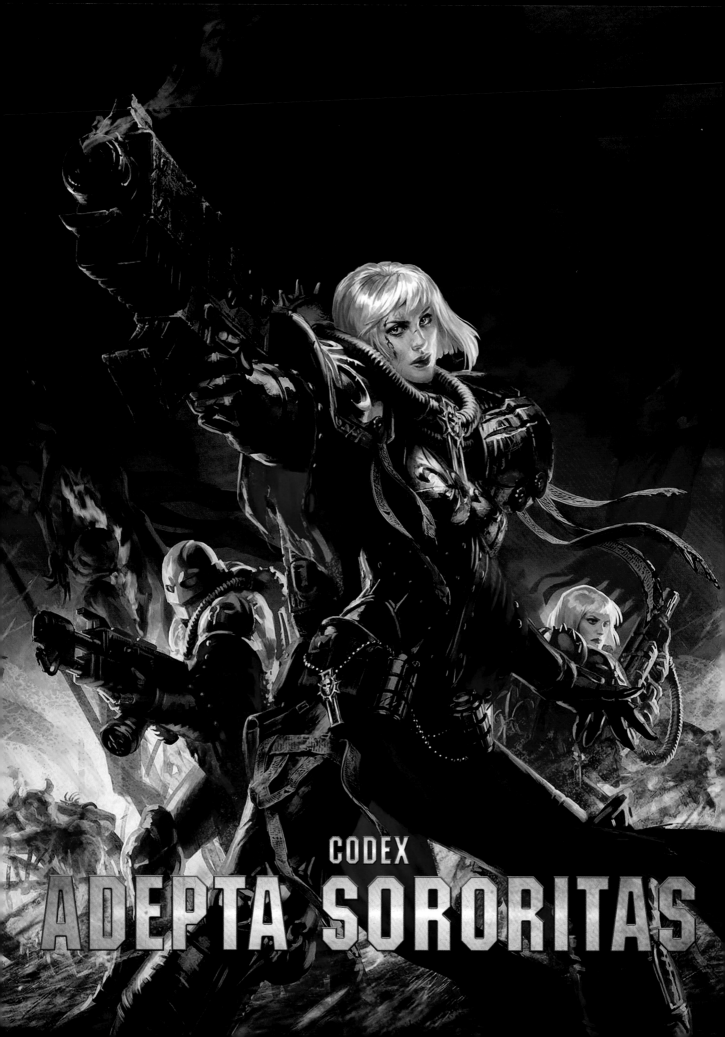

CODEX
ADEPTA SORORITAS

INTRODUCTION

This section describes the history of the Sisters of Battle and gives an overview of how these warriors organise themselves and fight in battle. It also provides you with the rules required to assemble your collection of Adepta Sororitas miniatures into a powerful army in your games of Warhammer 40,000.

The Adepta Sororitas, also known as the Sisters of Battle, are an elite sisterhood of warriors raised from infancy to believe unquestioningly in the supreme power of the Emperor of Mankind. The perfervid, unshakeable nature of their faith is a potent weapon indeed, manifesting as divine inspiration that drives the Sisters of Battle to incredible feats of martial prowess. Their fanatical devotion and unwavering purity are a bulwark against corruption, heresy and alien attack, and once battle has been joined they will stop at nothing until their enemies are utterly crushed.

Beta Codex

This section of *Chapter Approved* forms what we are calling a beta codex. At time of writing, we are busy sculpting a new range for the Adepta Sororitas and are in the initial stages of writing a new *Codex: Adepta Sororitas*. However, it will be some time before this project reaches completion, and we didn't want to leave Sisters of Battle players without a greater selection of the expanded rules – Stratagems, Relics, etc. – that are available to other Factions. This beta codex is therefore designed to provide Sisters of Battle players with a set of these rules that they can make use of until the full *Codex: Adepta Sororitas* is released alongside the new miniatures range.

As this is a beta codex, we want to take this opportunity to invite players to give us feedback on the rules found within. What worked well? What could be improved? What points values should be changed (and to what)? Please get in touch with us at 40kfaq@gwplc.com and let us know (please make the subject of your e-mail 'Beta Codex: Adepta Sororitas feedback'). This feedback will then help to inform the final rules in the full *Codex: Adepta Sororitas*.

It is worth highlighting that we have made some changes for the Adepta Sororitas in this beta codex from the rules within *Index: Imperium 2*. Mostly these take the form of small changes to characteristics or abilities,

but more significantly we have completely overhauled the Acts of Faith ability that is common to much of the army. We are particularly interested to hear your feedback on this rule in comparison to that presented in *Index: Imperium 2*. We have also removed Imagifiers as a unit – instead, models within certain Adepta Sororitas units can now carry a Simulacrum Imperialis, and this ties in to how the proposed new Acts of Faith ability works.

Finally, whilst this beta codex has been designed to be used in all types of games, including matched play games, if you intend to use them at organised events then it is ultimately up to the event organiser as to whether these rules will be allowed or not (as is the case with all our beta rules).

> **Designer's Note – Hand Flamers:** *Whilst writing this beta codex we felt that the profile for a hand flamer did not do this fearsome weapon justice, and learnt that it was often overlooked in favour of other sidearms. As a result, we have improved the hand flamer's Type from Pistol D3 to Pistol D6. We will errata this profile in all our other books wherever it appears. Burn the heretic!*

> **Designer's Note – Crusaders:** *The Crusaders datasheet appears both in this beta codex and in* Codex: Astra Militarum. *The biggest difference between the two arises from the revised Acts of Faith ability. As noted, this is one of the rules we would most like to get your feedback on; as such, if you are using Crusaders as part of an Astra Militarum army, please use the datasheet and all rules for them as presented in this beta codex until the full* Codex: Adepta Sororitas *is published, whereupon we will also make any necessary updates to* Codex: Astra Militarum.

ADEPTA SORORITAS

The Adepta Sororitas are the elite fighting arm of the Ecclesiarchy. Wielding the holy trinity of bolter, melta and flamer, the Sisters are renowned throughout the Imperium as the scourge of the traitor, the mutant and the witch. None may question their devotion to their cause.

The Adeptus Ministorum – commonly known as the Ecclesiarchy – is a vast organisation within the Imperium that is dedicated to the worship of the Emperor. It is they who preach the Imperial Creed, the only accepted religion within the empire of Mankind. The Adepta Sororitas – often referred to as the Sisters of Battle – are the Ecclesiarchy's standing army.

Clad in ceramite power armour and trained to the pinnacle of human ability, the Sisters of Battle stand amongst Mankind's most formidable warriors. From their infancy, the Sisters learn to revere the Emperor and to adhere to the strictest of disciplines. Their fanatical devotion and the unwavering purity of their belief lends the Adepta Sororitas divine aid in battle. Not even injuries or death can stay their zeal, for the blood of martyrs spurs them on to great acts of heroism.

First amongst the duties of the Adepta Sororitas is the safeguarding of the property of the Ecclesiarchy, for they are rich in power and holdings. The Sisters of Battle are called upon to defend shrines, fortress-cathedrals, the burial tombs of fallen saints, and more. It is not property alone they safeguard, for the Adepta Sororitas also serve as bodyguards to all hierarchs – from the Arch-Cardinals to important preachers of the Imperial Creed or any number of wandering figures, such as Missionaries or Preachers.

In addition to defending what is theirs, the Ecclesiarchy calls upon the Sisters of Battle to prosecute its many wars. There are lost relics to recover, xenos to be eradicated, and missionaries to protect. It is the Ministorum's duty to punish heretics, and should the Ecclesiarch call a War of Faith, the militant backbone of such an operation will be provided by the Sisters of Battle.

When not actively prosecuting the Ecclesiarchy's wars, the Sisters of Battle divide their time between training and devotional activities. To the Adepta Sororitas, the disciplines are inseparable, for whilst combat drills and the study of tactical acumen hone the body and mind, only prayer to the Emperor can bolster the spirit – and all three are required to defeat the Imperium's many foes.

While the enormous wealth of the Ecclesiarchy has ensured the Sisters of Battle are outfitted with the best arms and armour riches can buy, their greatest weapon remains their faith. The power of combat doctrine married with prayer is most evident upon the field of battle, where the Sisterhood loudly proclaim their faith in hymns and verses. This chanting is not only done on the march; even in the whirling maelstrom of combat they will continue to venerate the Emperor, and call upon him to aid in the fight against his enemies.

Even unbelievers and heretics cannot deny some supernatural force grants the Adepta Sororitas power, driving them to otherwise unachievable feats of prowess. Gripped with holy fervour, Sisters of Battle shrug off mortal wounds, summon superhuman strength with which to smite their foes, or emerge unscathed from explosions that by rights should have incinerated them many times over. To the Sisters themselves, such acts of faith are inescapable proof of the divine.

ORIGINS

The Adepta Sororitas were founded in the 36th Millennium, during the Age of Apostasy. It was a time of great political upheaval. After centuries of turmoil the Ecclesiarchy had risen to the zenith of its power, and could impose its will over all other branches of the Imperium.

With a military coup, the High Lord Goge Vandire took control over both the Adeptus Administratum and the Adeptus Ministorum. His cruel leadership of these organisations would drive the Imperium to its bitterest period of civil war since the Horus Heresy.

Through deception, Vandire took command of an all-female Ministorum cult – the Daughters of the Emperor. He convinced them that he was pious and chosen by the Emperor to lead Mankind, and thus did he win over the Daughters as his own bodyguard.

Under Vandire's leadership began a time known as the Reign of Blood, in which hundreds of millions were persecuted for disagreeing with his whims. To execute his increasing demands, the Ecclesiarchal armies grew in size, absorbing more power with every passing day.

Rising up against the injustice of the times was a new cult, the Confederation of Light, led by the preacher Sebastian Thor. Swayed by his powerful oratory, entire worlds joined his rebellion against the oppressions of Vandire.

At the head of a crusading army, Sebastian Thor dared to close in on Terra and to attack the Ecclesiarchal Palace itself. By that time Thor's armies were buoyed by many Chapters of Space Marines and armies of the Adeptus Mechanicus – most of whom had previously remained strictly defensive or kept clear of the civil war altogether.

The battle was fierce, and only ended when the commander of the Adeptus Custodes – the elite protectors of the Emperor – sought out Alicia Dominica, the leader of Vandire's bodyguard, and ushered her and her closest Sisters before the Golden Throne. No formal history records what transpired there, yet it was evident some great truth was revealed to Dominica. When they emerged from the throne room, the leader of the Daughters of the Emperor could barely control her fury. She marched into Vandire's chamber, interrupting one of his insane tirades. Pausing only to condemn his crimes, Dominica beheaded Vandire, ending the Reign of Blood with a single stroke.

REFORMATION

In the wake of the war, Sebastian Thor was named Ecclesiarch and the rebuilding of the Imperium began. One of the first commands of the reformed High Lords of Terra was the Decree Passive – a new law which forbade the Adeptus Ministorum from ever controlling 'men under arms'.

As an all-female order, the Daughters of the Emperor did not break this new commandment. They became the founding members of the Adepta Sororitas, and were ordained as the ultimate defenders of the faith. Since that time they have loyally enforced the dogma of the Ecclesiarchy across the galaxy.

ARMIES OF FAITH AND STEEL

Foremost amongst the fanatical warriors of the Ecclesiarchy stand the Sisters of the Adepta Sororitas. With bolt, flame and faith they guard the Adeptus Ministorum against the vile threat of Chaos, the insidious menace of heretics and the inhuman assaults of loathsome xenos.

The Sisters of Battle are organised into orders, split between the Convent Prioris on Holy Terra and the Convent Sanctorum on Ophelia VII. Both Convents are massive fortresses housing tens of thousands of sisters. By far the greater proportion of the Sisterhood's members belong to the Orders Militant, of which the largest and most active are the original four, and the two created in mid M38. Since their founding, numerous other Orders Militant – the Orders Minoris – have been formed across the Imperium. Each has its own traditions, doctrines, livery, and titles. The Orders Minoris vary in size, but all are elite military forces dedicated to destroying the Ecclesiarch's foes.

LEADERS OF FAITH

At the head of each order is a Canoness, a shining example of purity and dedication. Each Canoness is charged with overseeing every aspect of her order, as well as leading her force in battle. To rise so high a Canoness must display leadership, tactical genius, and acts of pure faith that impress her own Sisterhood.

A Canoness might be accompanied by advisors from the non-militant orders, such as from the Orders Dialogus – skilled orators whose amplified voices can embolden nearby troops – and the Orders Hospitaller, healers who aid those wounded in battle.

THE SISTERHOOD

The core of an Adepta Sororitas army is made up of Battle Sisters Squads. Led by a veteran officer known as a Sister Superior, a Battle Sisters Squad bears boltguns as standard armament, although they are also given training in the use of special and heavy weaponry, most particularly the flamer. Battle Sisters Squads are equally adept at attack and defence. Sometimes one of the squad will carry a Simulacrum Imperialis – a relic that inspires the faithful. The Celestian Squads are similarly equipped to the Battle Sisters Squads, but are composed of the finest and noblest warriors of the order. They often act as guardians of their order's leaders upon the battlefield.

The Seraphim are the elite shock troops of the Orders Militant. They are trained in the use of jump packs, and they strike like avenging angels, descending into battle with twin bolt pistols spitting death. For heavier infantry support the Sisters of Battle deploy Dominion and Retributor Squads. Often used as the vanguard of an assault, Dominions are Sisters equipped with special weapons. They use hails of storm bolter shots, melta beams or searing flames to destroy the enemy. Retributor Squads bear heavy weaponry which is used to counter enemy armour or whittle down larger hordes.

Those who fall short of the Adepta Sororitas' rigorous codes are subject to punishment, and in serious cases might be exiled from their order. These warriors – the Sisters Repentia – band together to seek redemption in battle. Each Sister Repentia bears a two-handed chainblade known as an eviscerator. They are often led to battle by a Mistress of Repentance, and it is her duty to observe her fallen Sisters and judge if they have atoned for their sins. Those that fall completely from grace are bound within monstrous bipedal battle machines known as Penitent Engines.

The Sisters of Battle employ the sturdy Rhino as a main transport. The Immolator can also carry troops but its primary purpose is to bear an immolation flamer to sweep the battlefield with cleansing flames. The ornate Exorcist is a mobile weapon that unleashes volleys of explosive judgement.

Imbued with divine power, the mysterious but powerful Living Saints are known to aid the Adepta Sororitas in times of need. Saint Celestine is one such being, and she is often accompanied by her bodyguards – the Geminae Superia.

ECCLESIARCHAL FORCES

Priests of the Ecclesiarchy often join the Orders Militant in battle. Their titles are many, but in war all have a similar goal – to stoke the troops' faith and encourage them to smite the Emperor's foes. Some Priests have gained great fame, such as Uriah Jacobus, a tireless Missionary with a talent for bringing lost worlds back to the Imperium's fold.

Ecclesiarchy Priests often bring with them conclaves of warriors. These are purposefully small in number to avoid drawing attention to the violation of the 'men under arms' prohibition. These can consist of Crusaders – ideal champions – Death Cult Assassins, who live to kill for the Emperor, or Arco-flagellants – heretics turned into living weapons through horrific augmentative surgery as punishment for their crimes.

ORDER OF THE VALOROUS HEART

This order's first leader, now known as Saint Lucia, was the most penitent of Dominica's companions. To this day, the order seeks atonement for the unwitting sedition of their forebears during the Reign of Blood. They take especial pleasure in hunting down and destroying false prophets.

ORDER OF OUR MARTYRED LADY

Originally founded as the Order of the Fiery Heart, the name was changed after their patron's death to the Witch-cult of Mnestteus. For many centuries the order wore only black to honour Saint Katherine, but red was adopted into their livery following the Third War for Armageddon.

ORDER OF THE BLOODY ROSE

Created two and a half millennia after the founding of the Adepta Sororitas, the Order of the Bloody Rose was formed from Sisters who venerated Saint Mina. She had been the most aggressive of Dominica's comrades, and this order has adopted this trait, and is known for the ferocity of its assaults.

ORDER OF THE EBON CHALICE

The oldest of the Orders Militant, the Order of the Ebon Chalice still bear the colours of the Daughters of the Emperor. The symbol of the order is the flaming, skull-filled chalice representing the terrible knowledge passed on to Dominica when she was brought before the Golden Throne.

ORDER OF THE ARGENT SHROUD

The Sisters of the Argent Shroud rarely speak, preferring to let their actions do so for them. Their first leader was Sister Silvana who was martyred and sainted soon after their founding, The order took their name and symbol from the silvery impression of Silvana's skull upon her death shroud.

ORDER OF THE SACRED ROSE

Dedicated to Arabella, the Sisters of Order of the Sacred Rose are known for their discipline and even temper. Yet like their patron Saint, they are resolute warriors beneath their guise of serenity. No matter the foe, no matter the odds, the Sisters of the Sacred Rose hold their ground with cold efficiency.

KEEPERS OF THE FAITH

Clad in ceramite, the Sisters of Battle fight the Emperor's foes with unmatched zeal. These pages showcase the Citadel Miniatures range for the Adepta Sororitas in all its righteous pageantry, as painted by the 'Eavy Metal team. Behold their glory, and suffer not the heretic to live!

Canoness of the Order of the Sacred Rose with bolt pistol

Canoness of the Order of Our Martyred Lady with power sword and bolt pistol

Mistress of Repentance

Canoness with power sword and bolt pistol

Dialogus

Hospitaller

Led by Saint Celestine and her Geminae Superia, a Sisters of Battle army of the Order of Our Martyred Lady prepares to deliver merciless judgement to the despised warriors of the T'au Empire. Those who deny the right of the Emperor of Mankind to rule the stars must be cleansed from the galaxy with bolt and flame.

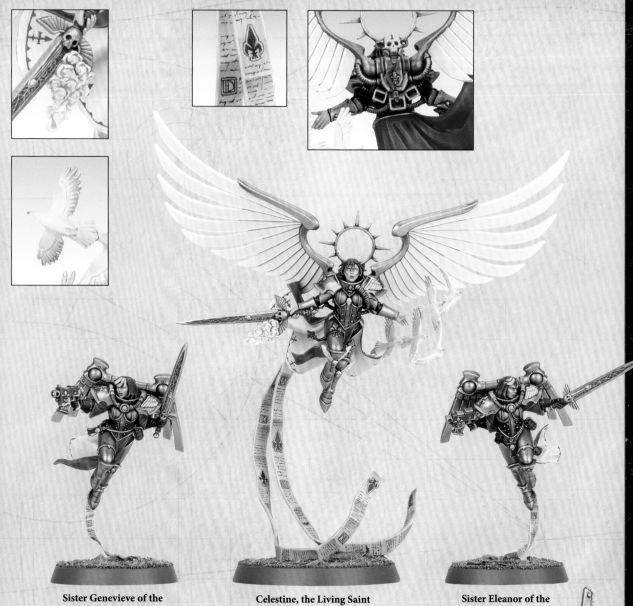

Sister Genevieve of the Geminae Superia

Celestine, the Living Saint

Sister Eleanor of the Geminae Superia

Seraphim with two bolt pistols

Seraphim Superior with bolt pistol and power sword

Seraphim Superior with plasma pistol and chainsword

While an Exorcist bombards the Asuryani constructs, the remaining Sisters of Battle advance, unleashing a hail of bolter-fire. Although reduced to ruins in the fighting, the shrine world remains holy ground, and the presence of the xenos unbelievers can not be tolerated.

**Battle Sister of the
Order of the Sacred Rose**

**Battle Sister of the
Order of the Ebon Chalice**

**Battle Sister of the
Order of the Valorous Heart**

**Battle Sister of the
Order of the Argent Shroud**

**Battle Sister of the
Order of Our Martyred Lady**

**Battle Sister of the
Order of the Bloody Rose**

WARRIORS OF THE FAITH

This section contains the datasheets you need to fight battles with your Adepta Sororitas miniatures. Each datasheet includes the characteristics profiles of the unit it describes, and any wargear and abilities it may have. Some rules are common to several units – these are described below and referenced on the datasheets.

KEYWORDS

Throughout this section you will come across a keyword that is within angular brackets, specifically <Order>. This is shorthand for a keyword of your own choosing, as described below.

<Order>

All members of the Adepta Sororitas belong to an order and have the <Order> keyword. When you include such a unit in your army, you must nominate which order that unit is from. You then simply replace the <Order> keyword in every instance on that unit's datasheet with the name of your chosen order. You can use any of the orders that you have read about, or make up your own.

For example, if your army included a Canoness from the Order of the Bloody Rose, her <Order> Faction keyword is changed to Order of the Bloody Rose, and her Lead the Righteous ability would say 'Re-roll hit rolls of 1 for friendly Order of the Bloody Rose units whilst they are within 6" of this model.'

ABILITIES

The following abilities are common to several units in this section:

Acts of Faith

The Sisters of Battle can call upon the Emperor for divine assistance.

If your army includes any models with this ability, you will start the battle with 3 Faith Points, plus 1 additional Faith Point for every 10 models with this ability in your army (rounding down). These can be spent to attempt the Acts of Faith listed below. Each can only be attempted once per battle round, and you must spend one Faith Point each time you do so (if you have no Faith Points remaining, you cannot attempt an Act of Faith). To attempt an Act of Faith, select a unit in your army that has the Acts of Faith ability and then choose the Act of Faith you wish to attempt. Then make a Test of Faith for the unit by rolling a D6; if the result is less than that Act of Faith's devotion value, or is an unmodified roll of 1, the test fails and nothing happens. Otherwise the test is successful and the Act of Faith takes effect.

Hand of the Emperor
Devotion value 4
Use this Act of Faith at the start of your Movement phase. If successful, add 3" to the selected unit's Move characteristic until the end of that phase.

Spirit of the Martyr
Devotion value 3
Use this Act of Faith at the start of your Movement phase. If successful, one model in the selected unit regains D3 lost wounds, or, if there are no wounded models and any models in the unit have been slain, you can return one slain model to the unit with 1 wound remaining (this model is set up in unit coherency and cannot be set up within 1" of any enemy models – if it is not possible to place this model, it is not returned to the unit).

Aegis of the Emperor
Devotion value 3
Use this Act of Faith at the start of your opponent's Psychic phase. If successful,

then until the end of that phase, roll a D6 each time the selected unit suffers a mortal wound. On a 4+ that mortal wound is ignored.

Divine Guidance
Devotion value 4
Use this Act of Faith at the start of your Shooting phase. If successful, add 1 to hit rolls for attacks made with this unit's ranged weapons until the end of the phase.

The Passion
Devotion value 5
Use this Act of Faith at the start of your Fight phase. If successful, the selected unit can be chosen to fight with twice in that phase.

Light of the Emperor
Devotion value 3
Use this Act of Faith at the start of the Morale phase. If successful, the selected unit automatically passes Morale tests that phase.

SHIELD OF FAITH
Conviction is the greatest armour.

Models in this unit have a 6+ invulnerable save. In addition, units with this ability can attempt to deny one psychic power in each enemy Psychic phase in the same manner as a PSYKER. When they do so, first select a model in the unit – measure range, visibility, etc. from this model. When making this attempt, only roll a single D6 instead of 2D6; the psychic power is resisted if the roll is greater than the result of the Psychic test that manifested the power.

ZEALOT
With righteous fervour, the Emperor's faithful deliver his furious judgement.

You can re-roll failed hit rolls for this unit in a turn in which it made a charge move, was charged or performed a Heroic Intervention.

ADEPTA SORORITAS WARGEAR LISTS

Many of the units you will find on the following pages reference one or more of the following wargear lists (e.g. Ranged Weapons). When this is the case, the unit may take any item from the appropriate list below. The profiles for the weapons in these lists can be found on page 92.

RANGED WEAPONS
- Boltgun
- Combi-flamer
- Combi-melta
- Combi-plasma
- Condemnor boltgun
- Storm bolter

SPECIAL WEAPONS
- Storm bolter
- Flamer
- Meltagun

PISTOLS
- Bolt pistol
- Plasma pistol
- Inferno pistol

MELEE WEAPONS
- Chainsword
- Power maul
- Power sword

HEAVY WEAPONS
- Heavy bolter
- Heavy flamer
- Multi-melta

CELESTINE

NAME	M	WS	BS	S	T	W	A	Ld	Sv
Celestine	12"	2+	2+	3	3	6	6	9	2+

Celestine is a single model armed with the Ardent Blade. Only one of this unit may be included in your army.

WEAPON	RANGE	TYPE	S	AP	D	ABILITIES
The Ardent Blade (shooting)	8"	Assault D6	5	-1	1	This weapon automatically hits its target.
The Ardent Blade (melee)	Melee	Melee	+4	-3	2	-

ABILITIES	
	Acts of Faith, Shield of Faith (pg 78-79)

Healing Tears: At the start of your Movement phase, you can pick a friendly **GEMINAE SUPERIA** unit within 3" of Celestine that has suffered one or more wounds, or a casualty. If you do, a single model in that unit regains all her lost wounds. If the unit contains no wounded models, then a single slain **GEMINAE SUPERIA** is instead returned to the unit with all lost wounds regained (this model is set up in unit coherency and cannot be set up within 1" of any enemy models – if it is not possible to place her, she is not returned to the unit).

The Armour of Saint Katherine: Celestine has a 4+ invulnerable save.

Saintly Blessings: The invulnerable save friendly **ADEPTA SORORITAS** units receive from the Shield of Faith ability is improved by 1 whilst they are within 6" of Celestine (it is improved by 2 instead if it is a **GEMINAE SUPERIA** unit), to a maximum of 3+. In addition, friendly **ADEPTUS MINISTORUM** and **ASTRA MILITARUM** units have a 6+ invulnerable save whilst they are within 6" of Celestine.

Miraculous Intervention: The first time Celestine is reduced to 0 wounds, roll a D6. On a 2+, set her up again at the end of the phase, as close as possible to her previous position and more than 1" from any enemy models, with all lost wounds regained.

FACTION KEYWORDS	**IMPERIUM, ADEPTUS MINISTORUM, ADEPTA SORORITAS**
KEYWORDS	**CHARACTER, INFANTRY, JUMP PACK, FLY, CELESTINE**

Descending out of a blinding flash come Saint Celestine and the Geminae Superia. From on high they bring the Emperor's swift justice to those found wanting. To heretics and unbelievers they bring only death.

CANONESS

NAME	M	WS	BS	S	T	W	A	Ld	Sv
Canoness	6"	2+	2+	3	3	5	4	9	3+

A Canoness is a single model armed with a bolt pistol, frag grenades and krak grenades.

WEAPON	RANGE	TYPE	S	AP	D	ABILITIES
Bolt pistol	12"	Pistol 1	4	0	1	-
Frag grenade	6"	Grenade D6	3	0	1	-
Krak grenade	6"	Grenade 1	6	-1	D3	-

WARGEAR OPTIONS
- This model may replace its bolt pistol with a weapon from the *Ranged Weapons* or *Pistols* list.
- This model may take a weapon from the *Melee Weapons* list.

ABILITIES

Acts of Faith, **Shield of Faith** (pg 78-79)

Rosarius: This model has a 4+ invulnerable save.

Lead the Righteous: Re-roll hit rolls of 1 for friendly <ORDER> units whilst they are within 6" of this model.

FACTION KEYWORDS IMPERIUM, ADEPTUS MINISTORUM, ADEPTA SORORITAS, <ORDER>

KEYWORDS CHARACTER, INFANTRY, CANONESS

URIAH JACOBUS

NAME	M	WS	BS	S	T	W	A	Ld	Sv
Uriah Jacobus	6"	3+	3+	3	3	5	4	8	6+

Uriah Jacobus is a single model armed with the Redeemer, a bolt pistol, chainsword, frag grenades and krak grenades. Only one of this model may be included in your army.

WEAPON	RANGE	TYPE	S	AP	D	ABILITIES
Bolt pistol	12"	Pistol 1	4	0	1	-
The Redeemer	18"	Assault 2	4	-1	1	If the target is within half range, add 1 to this weapon's Strength.
Chainsword	Melee	Melee	User	0	1	Each time the bearer fights, it can make 1 additional attack with this weapon.
Frag grenade	6"	Grenade D6	3	0	1	-
Krak grenade	6"	Grenade 1	6	-1	D3	-

ABILITIES

Shield of Faith, **Zealot** (pg 79)

Word of the Emperor: Roll a D6 each time an ADEPTUS MINISTORUM model flees whilst its unit is within 6" of any friendly models with this ability. On a 4+, that model does not flee.

Banner of Sanctity: Add 1 to the Leadership characteristic of friendly ADEPTUS MINISTORUM and ASTRA MILITARUM units whilst they are within 6" of Uriah Jacobus.

Rosarius: Uriah Jacobus has a 4+ invulnerable save.

War Hymns: Add 1 to the Attacks characteristic of ADEPTUS MINISTORUM INFANTRY and ASTRA MILITARUM INFANTRY units whilst they are within 6" of any friendly MINISTORUM PRIESTS.

Lone Mission: You can only include a single MISSIONARY in each Detachment in a Battle-forged army.

FACTION KEYWORDS IMPERIUM, ADEPTUS MINISTORUM

KEYWORDS CHARACTER, INFANTRY, MINISTORUM PRIEST, MISSIONARY, URIAH JACOBUS

MISSIONARY

NAME	M	WS	BS	S	T	W	A	Ld	Sv
Missionary	6"	4+	4+	3	3	4	3	7	6+

A Missionary is a single model armed with an autogun, laspistol, chainsword, frag grenades and krak grenades.

WEAPON	RANGE	TYPE	S	AP	D	ABILITIES
Autogun	24"	Rapid Fire 1	3	0	1	-
Laspistol	12"	Pistol 1	3	0	1	-
Chainsword	Melee	Melee	User	0	1	Each time the bearer fights, it can make 1 additional attack with this weapon.
Frag grenade	6"	Grenade D6	3	0	1	-
Krak grenade	6"	Grenade 1	6	-1	D3	-

ABILITIES	
Zealot (pg 79) **Rosarius:** This model has a 4+ invulnerable save. **Word of the Emperor:** Roll a D6 each time an **ADEPTUS MINISTORUM** model flees whilst its unit is within 6" of any friendly models with this ability. On a 4+, that model does not flee.	**War Hymns:** Add 1 to the Attacks characteristic of **ADEPTUS MINISTORUM INFANTRY** and **ASTRA MILITARUM INFANTRY** units whilst they are within 6" of any friendly **MINISTORUM PRIESTS**. **Lone Mission:** You can only include a single **MISSIONARY** in each Detachment in a Battle-forged army.

FACTION KEYWORDS	IMPERIUM, ADEPTUS MINISTORUM
KEYWORDS	**CHARACTER, INFANTRY, MINISTORUM PRIEST, MISSIONARY**

BATTLE SISTERS SQUAD

NAME	M	WS	BS	S	T	W	A	Ld	Sv
Battle Sister	6"	4+	3+	3	3	1	1	7	3+
Sister Superior	6"	4+	3+	3	3	1	2	8	3+

This unit contains 1 Sister Superior and 4 Battle Sisters. It may contain up to 5 additional Battle Sisters (**Power Rating +2**) or up to 10 additional Battle Sisters (**Power Rating +4**). Each model is armed with a bolt pistol, boltgun, frag grenades and krak grenades.

WEAPON	RANGE	TYPE	S	AP	D	ABILITIES
Bolt pistol	12"	Pistol 1	4	0	1	-
Boltgun	24"	Rapid Fire 1	4	0	1	-
Frag grenade	6"	Grenade D6	3	0	1	-
Krak grenade	6"	Grenade 1	6	-1	D3	-

WARGEAR OPTIONS	
• One Battle Sister may replace her boltgun with a weapon from the *Special Weapons* list. • One Battle Sister may replace her boltgun with a weapon from the *Special Weapons* or *Heavy Weapons* list. • One Battle Sister who has not replaced her boltgun with a weapon from the *Special Weapons* or *Heavy Weapons* list may take a Simulacrum Imperialis. • The Sister Superior may either replace her boltgun with a weapon from the *Ranged Weapons* or *Melee Weapons* list, or take a weapon from the *Melee Weapons* list in addition to her other wargear. • The Sister Superior may replace her bolt pistol with a weapon from the *Pistols* list.	

ABILITIES	
Acts of Faith, **Shield of Faith** (pg 78-79) **Simulacrum Imperialis:** Add 1 to the result of Tests of Faith for a unit whilst it includes a model with a Simulacrum Imperialis.	

FACTION KEYWORDS	IMPERIUM, ADEPTUS MINISTORUM, ADEPTA SORORITAS, <ORDER>
KEYWORDS	**INFANTRY, BATTLE SISTERS SQUAD**

GEMINAE SUPERIA

NAME	M	WS	BS	S	T	W	A	Ld	Sv
Geminae Superia	12"	3+	3+	3	3	2	3	9	3+

This unit contains 1 Geminae Superia. It can include 1 additional Geminae Superia (**Power Rating +1**). Each model is armed with a bolt pistol, power sword, frag grenades and krak grenades. Only one of this unit may be included in your army.

WEAPON	RANGE	TYPE	S	AP	D	ABILITIES
Bolt pistol	12"	Pistol 1	4	0	1	-
Power sword	Melee	Melee	User	-3	1	-
Frag grenade	6"	Grenade D6	3	0	1	-
Krak grenade	6"	Grenade 1	6	-1	D3	-

ABILITIES	Acts of Faith, Shield of Faith (pg 78-79)	**Lifewards:** Roll a D6 each time **CELESTINE** loses a wound whilst she is within 3" of this unit; on a 2+ Celestine does not lose a wound but this unit suffers 1 mortal wound.
	Divine Guardians: If your army is Battle-forged, this unit does not take up a slot in a Detachment that includes **CELESTINE**. Geminae Superia can never have a Warlord Trait.	

FACTION KEYWORDS	IMPERIUM, ADEPTUS MINISTORUM, ADEPTA SORORITAS
KEYWORDS	CHARACTER, INFANTRY, JUMP PACK, FLY, GEMINAE SUPERIA

Descending from the heavens upon gilded wings, Saint Celestine brings fire and ruin to the servants of Chaos.

REPENTIA SQUAD

NAME	M	WS	BS	S	T	W	A	Ld	Sv
Sister Repentia	6"	3+	3+	3	3	1	2	8	7+

This unit contains 3 Sisters Repentia. It may contain up to 3 additional Sisters Repentia (**Power Rating +2**) or up to 6 additional Sisters Repentia (**Power Rating +4**). Each model is armed with a penitent eviscerator.

WEAPON	RANGE	TYPE	S	AP	D	ABILITIES
Penitent eviscerator	Melee	Melee	x2	-2	2	When attacking with this weapon, you must subtract 1 from the hit roll.

ABILITIES	Acts of Faith, Shield of Faith (pg 78-79)
FACTION KEYWORDS	IMPERIUM, ADEPTUS MINISTORUM, ADEPTA SORORITAS, <ORDER>
KEYWORDS	INFANTRY, REPENTIA SQUAD

MISTRESS OF REPENTANCE

NAME	M	WS	BS	S	T	W	A	Ld	Sv
Mistress of Repentance	6"	3+	3+	3	3	4	3	8	3+

A Mistress of Repentance is a single model armed with neural whips, frag grenades and krak grenades.

WEAPON	RANGE	TYPE	S	AP	D	ABILITIES
Neural whips	Melee	Melee	User	-2	1	Add 1 to the wound rolls for attacks made with this weapon if the target unit's highest Leadership characteristic is less than 8 (other than VEHICLES).
Frag grenade	6"	Grenade D6	3	0	1	-
Krak grenade	6"	Grenade 1	6	-1	D3	-

ABILITIES	Acts of Faith, Shield of Faith (pg 78-79) **Driven Onwards:** You can re-roll Advance, charge and hit rolls for friendly <ORDER> REPENTIA SQUAD units that are within 6" of this model when the dice are rolled.	**Mistress of the Penitent:** If your army is Battle-forged, this model does not take up slots in a Detachment that includes any <ORDER> REPENTIA SQUAD units.

FACTION KEYWORDS	IMPERIUM, ADEPTUS MINISTORUM, ADEPTA SORORITAS, <ORDER>
KEYWORDS	CHARACTER, INFANTRY, MISTRESS OF REPENTANCE

CELESTIAN SQUAD

NAME	M	WS	BS	S	T	W	A	Ld	Sv
Celestian	6"	3+	3+	3	3	1	2	8	3+
Celestian Superior	6"	3+	3+	3	3	1	3	9	3+

This unit contains 1 Celestian Superior and 4 Celestians. It may contain up to 5 additional Celestians (**Power Rating +2**). Each model is armed with a bolt pistol, boltgun, frag grenades and krak grenades.

WEAPON	RANGE	TYPE	S	AP	D	ABILITIES
Bolt pistol	12"	Pistol 1	4	0	1	-
Boltgun	24"	Rapid Fire 1	4	0	1	-
Frag grenade	6"	Grenade D6	3	0	1	-
Krak grenade	6"	Grenade 1	6	-1	D3	-

WARGEAR OPTIONS	• One Celestian may replace her boltgun with a weapon from the *Special Weapons* list. • One Celestian may replace her boltgun with a weapon from the *Special Weapons* or *Heavy Weapons* list. • One Celestian who has not replaced her boltgun with a weapon from the *Special Weapons* or *Heavy Weapons* list may take a Simulacrum Imperialis. • The Celestian Superior may either replace her boltgun with a weapon from the *Ranged Weapons* or *Melee Weapons* list, or take a weapon from the *Melee Weapons* list in addition to her other wargear. • The Celestian Superior may replace her bolt pistol with a weapon from the *Pistols* list.
ABILITIES	**Acts of Faith**, **Shield of Faith** (pg 78-79) **Bodyguard:** You can roll a D6 each time a friendly <Order> Character loses a wound whilst they are within 3" of this unit; on a 2+ a model from this unit intercepts that hit – the character does not lose a wound but this unit suffers 1 mortal wound. **Simulacrum Imperialis:** Add 1 to the result of Tests of Faith for a unit whilst it includes a model with a Simulacrum Imperialis.
FACTION KEYWORDS	IMPERIUM, ADEPTUS MINISTORUM, ADEPTA SORORITAS, <ORDER>
KEYWORDS	INFANTRY, CELESTIAN SQUAD

PREACHER

NAME	M	WS	BS	S	T	W	A	Ld	Sv
Preacher	6"	4+	4+	3	3	4	3	7	6+

A Preacher is a single model armed with a laspistol and chainsword.

WEAPON	RANGE	TYPE	S	AP	D	ABILITIES
Laspistol	12"	Pistol 1	3	0	1	-
Chainsword	Melee	Melee	User	0	1	Each time the bearer fights, it can make 1 additional attack with this weapon.

ABILITIES	**Zealot** (pg 79) **Rosarius:** This model has a 4+ invulnerable save. **Icon of the Ecclesiarchy:** Subtract 1 from the Leadership characteristic of CHAOS units whilst they are within 3" of any enemy models with this ability.	**War Hymns:** Add 1 to the Attacks characteristic of ADEPTUS MINISTORUM INFANTRY and ASTRA MILITARUM INFANTRY units whilst they are within 6" of any friendly MINISTORUM PRIESTS.
FACTION KEYWORDS	IMPERIUM, ADEPTUS MINISTORUM	
KEYWORDS	CHARACTER, INFANTRY, MINISTORUM PRIEST, PREACHER	

2 POWER

HOSPITALLER

NAME	M	WS	BS	S	T	W	A	Ld	Sv
Hospitaller	6"	4+	3+	3	3	4	2	8	3+

A Hospitaller is a single model armed with chirurgeon's tools.

WEAPON	RANGE	TYPE	S	AP	D	ABILITIES
Chirurgeon's tools	Melee	Melee	User	-1	1	-

ABILITIES	Acts of Faith, Shield of Faith (pg 78-79)
	Medicus Ministorum: At the end of your Movement phase a Hospitaller can attempt to heal or revive a single model. Select a friendly **ADEPTUS MINISTORUM INFANTRY** unit within 3" of the Hospitaller and roll a D6. On a roll of 4+, one model in the unit regains D3 lost wounds; if the chosen unit contains no wounded models but one or more of its models have been slain during the battle, then a single slain model is returned to the unit with 1 wound remaining (this model is set up in unit coherency and cannot be set up within 1" of any enemy models – if it is not possible to place it, it is not returned to the unit). A unit can only be the target of the Medicus Ministorum ability once in each turn.

FACTION KEYWORDS	IMPERIUM, ADEPTUS MINISTORUM, ADEPTA SORORITAS
KEYWORDS	CHARACTER, INFANTRY, HOSPITALLER

2 POWER

DIALOGUS

NAME	M	WS	BS	S	T	W	A	Ld	Sv
Dialogus	6"	4+	3+	3	3	4	2	8	6+

A Dialogus is a single model armed with a Dialogus staff.

WEAPON	RANGE	TYPE	S	AP	D	ABILITIES
Dialogus staff	Melee	Melee	+1	0	1	-

ABILITIES	Acts of Faith, Shield of Faith (pg 78-79)
	Laud Hailer: Add 1 to the Leadership characteristic of **ADEPTA SORORITAS** units whilst they are within 6" of any friendly models with this ability. In addition, you can re-roll failed Tests of Faith for **ADEPTA SORORITAS** units whilst they are within 6" of any friendly models with this ability.

FACTION KEYWORDS	IMPERIUM, ADEPTUS MINISTORUM, ADEPTA SORORITAS
KEYWORDS	CHARACTER, INFANTRY, DIALOGUS

2 POWER

ARCO-FLAGELLANTS

NAME	M	WS	BS	S	T	W	A	Ld	Sv
Arco-flagellant	7"	3+	-	4	3	2	2	7	7+

This unit contains 3 Arco-flagellants. It may contain up to 3 additional Arco-flagellants (**Power Rating +2**) or up to 6 additional Arco-flagellants (**Power Rating +4**). Each Arco-flagellant is armed with arco-flails.

WEAPON	RANGE	TYPE	S	AP	D	ABILITIES
Arco-flails	Melee	Melee	+1	-1	1	Make D3 hit rolls for each attack made with this weapon.

ABILITIES	Zealot (pg 79)	**Ecclesiarchy Battle Conclave:** If your army is Battle-forged, this unit does not take up slots in a Detachment that includes any **MINISTORUM PRIESTS**.
	Berserk Killing Machines: Each time a model with this ability loses a wound, roll a D6; on a 5+, the model does not lose that wound.	

FACTION KEYWORDS	IMPERIUM, ADEPTUS MINISTORUM
KEYWORDS	INFANTRY, ECCLESIARCHY BATTLE CONCLAVE, ARCO-FLAGELLANTS

CRUSADERS

1 POWER

NAME	M	WS	BS	S	T	W	A	Ld	Sv
Crusader	6"	3+	4+	3	3	1	2	7	4+

This unit contains 2 Crusaders. It may contain up to 2 additional Crusaders (**Power Rating +1**), up to 4 additional Crusaders (**Power Rating +2**), up to 6 additional Crusaders (**Power Rating +4**) or up to 8 additional Crusaders (**Power Rating +5**). Each Crusader is armed with a power sword and storm shield.

WEAPON	RANGE	TYPE	S	AP	D	ABILITIES
Power sword	Melee	Melee	User	-3	1	-

ABILITIES	**Acts of Faith**, **Shield of Faith**, **Zealot** (pg 78-79)	**Ecclesiarchy Battle Conclave:** If your army is Battle-forged, this unit does not take up slots in a Detachment that includes any **Ministorum Priests**.
	Storm Shield: Models in this unit have a 3+ invulnerable save.	

FACTION KEYWORDS	**Imperium, Adeptus Ministorum, Astra Militarum**
KEYWORDS	**Infantry, Ecclesiarchy Battle Conclave, Crusaders**

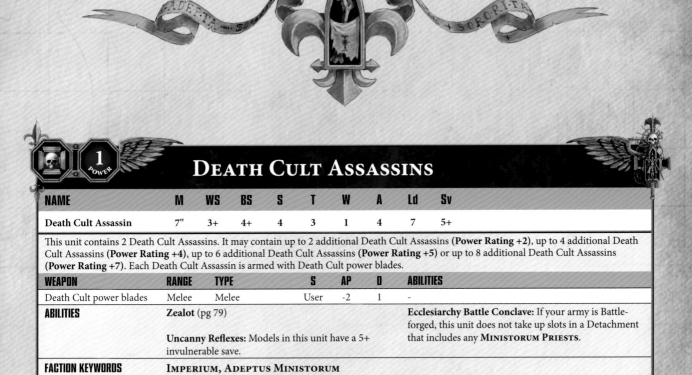

DEATH CULT ASSASSINS

1 POWER

NAME	M	WS	BS	S	T	W	A	Ld	Sv
Death Cult Assassin	7"	3+	4+	4	3	1	4	7	5+

This unit contains 2 Death Cult Assassins. It may contain up to 2 additional Death Cult Assassins (**Power Rating +2**), up to 4 additional Death Cult Assassins (**Power Rating +4**), up to 6 additional Death Cult Assassins (**Power Rating +5**) or up to 8 additional Death Cult Assassins (**Power Rating +7**). Each Death Cult Assassin is armed with Death Cult power blades.

WEAPON	RANGE	TYPE	S	AP	D	ABILITIES
Death Cult power blades	Melee	Melee	User	-2	1	-

ABILITIES	**Zealot** (pg 79)	**Ecclesiarchy Battle Conclave:** If your army is Battle-forged, this unit does not take up slots in a Detachment that includes any **Ministorum Priests**.
	Uncanny Reflexes: Models in this unit have a 5+ invulnerable save.	

FACTION KEYWORDS	**Imperium, Adeptus Ministorum**
KEYWORDS	**Infantry, Ecclesiarchy Battle Conclave, Death Cult Assassins**

SERAPHIM SQUAD

4 POWER

NAME	M	WS	BS	S	T	W	A	Ld	Sv
Seraphim	12"	3+	3+	3	3	1	1	7	3+
Seraphim Superior	12"	3+	3+	3	3	1	2	8	3+

This unit contains 1 Seraphim Superior and 4 Seraphim. It can include up to 5 additional Seraphim (**Power Rating +2**). Each model is armed with two bolt pistols, frag grenades and krak grenades.

WEAPON	RANGE	TYPE	S	AP	D	ABILITIES
Bolt pistol	12"	Pistol 1	4	0	1	-
Hand flamer	6"	Pistol D6	3	0	1	This weapon automatically hits its target.
Inferno pistol	6"	Pistol 1	8	-4	D6	If the target is within half range of this weapon, roll two dice when inflicting damage with it and discard the lowest result.
Frag grenade	6"	Grenade D6	3	0	1	-
Krak grenade	6"	Grenade 1	6	-1	D3	-

WARGEAR OPTIONS	
	• Up to two Seraphim may replace both their bolt pistols with two hand flamers or two inferno pistols. • The Seraphim Superior may replace one of her bolt pistols with a chainsword or power sword and/or may replace her other bolt pistol with a plasma pistol.

ABILITIES	
	Acts of Faith, Shield of Faith (pg 78-79) **Sky Strike:** During deployment, you can set up a unit of Seraphim high in the sky instead of placing them on the battlefield. At the end of any of your Movement phases the Seraphim can descend from the sky – set them up anywhere on the battlefield that is more than 9" away from any enemy models. **Angelic Visage:** Improve the invulnerable save this unit receives from the Shield of Faith ability by 1, to a maximum of 3+.

FACTION KEYWORDS	IMPERIUM, ADEPTUS MINISTORUM, ADEPTA SORORITAS, \<ORDER\>
KEYWORDS	INFANTRY, JUMP PACK, FLY, SERAPHIM SQUAD

DOMINION SQUAD

5 POWER

NAME	M	WS	BS	S	T	W	A	Ld	Sv
Dominion	6"	4+	3+	3	3	1	1	7	3+
Dominion Superior	6"	4+	3+	3	3	1	2	8	3+

This unit contains 1 Dominion Superior and 4 Dominions. It can include up to 5 additional Dominions (**Power Rating +2**). Each model is armed with a bolt pistol, boltgun, frag grenades and krak grenades.

WEAPON	RANGE	TYPE	S	AP	D	ABILITIES
Bolt pistol	12"	Pistol 1	4	0	1	-
Boltgun	24"	Rapid Fire 1	4	0	1	-
Frag grenade	6"	Grenade D6	3	0	1	-
Krak grenade	6"	Grenade 1	6	-1	D3	-

WARGEAR OPTIONS	
	• Up to four Dominions may replace their boltgun with a weapon from the *Special Weapons* list. • One Dominion who has not replaced her boltgun with a weapon from the *Special Weapons* list may take a Simulacrum Imperialis. • The Dominion Superior may either replace her boltgun with a weapon from the *Ranged Weapons* or *Melee Weapons* list, or take a weapon from the *Melee Weapons* list in addition to her other wargear. • The Dominion Superior may replace her bolt pistol with a weapon from the *Pistols* list.

ABILITIES	
	Acts of Faith, Shield of Faith (pg 78-79) **Vanguard:** Once both sides are deployed but before the first player takes their turn, this unit can move as if it were their Movement phase. This unit cannot end this move within 9" of any enemy models. If both players have units that can do this, the player who is taking the first turn moves their units first. If all of the models embarked on a transport have this ability, then the transport can make the move instead. **Simulacrum Imperialis:** Add 1 to the result of Tests of Faith for a unit whilst it includes a model with a Simulacrum Imperialis.

FACTION KEYWORDS	IMPERIUM, ADEPTUS MINISTORUM, ADEPTA SORORITAS, \<ORDER\>
KEYWORDS	INFANTRY, DOMINION SQUAD

EXORCIST

7 POWER

NAME	M	WS	BS	S	T	W	A	Ld	Sv
Exorcist	✱	6+	✱	7	8	12	✱	7	3+

An Exorcist is a single model equipped with an Exorcist missile launcher.

DAMAGE
Some of this model's characteristics change as it suffers damage, as shown below:

REMAINING W	M	BS	A
7-12+	12"	3+	3
4-6	6"	4+	D3
1-3	4"	5+	1

WEAPON	RANGE	TYPE	S	AP	D	ABILITIES
Exorcist missile launcher	48"	Heavy D6	8	-4	D6	-
Hunter-killer missile	48"	Heavy 1	8	-2	D6	This weapon can only be fired once per battle.
Storm bolter	24"	Rapid Fire 2	4	0	1	-

WARGEAR OPTIONS	
	• This model may take a storm bolter. • This model may take a hunter-killer missile.

ABILITIES	
	Shield of Faith (pg 79) **Explodes:** If this model is reduced to 0 wounds, roll a D6 before removing it from the battlefield. On a 6 it explodes, and each unit within 6" suffers D3 mortal wounds.	**Smoke Launchers:** Once per game, instead of shooting any weapons in the Shooting phase, this model can use its smoke launchers; until your next Shooting phase your opponent must subtract 1 from all hit rolls for ranged weapons that target this vehicle.

FACTION KEYWORDS	**IMPERIUM, ADEPTUS MINISTORUM, ADEPTA SORORITAS, <ORDER>**
KEYWORDS	**VEHICLE, EXORCIST**

RETRIBUTOR SQUAD

5 POWER

NAME	M	WS	BS	S	T	W	A	Ld	Sv
Retributor	6"	4+	3+	3	3	1	1	7	3+
Retributor Superior	6"	4+	3+	3	3	1	2	8	3+

This unit contains 1 Retributor Superior and 4 Retributors. It can include up to 5 additional Retributors (**Power Rating +2**). Each model is armed with a bolt pistol, a boltgun, frag grenades and krak grenades.

WEAPON	RANGE	TYPE	S	AP	D	ABILITIES
Bolt pistol	12"	Pistol 1	4	0	1	-
Boltgun	24"	Rapid Fire 1	4	0	1	-
Frag grenade	6"	Grenade D6	3	0	1	-
Krak grenade	6"	Grenade 1	6	-1	D3	-

WARGEAR OPTIONS	
	• Up to four Retributors may replace their boltgun with a weapon from the *Heavy Weapons* list. • One Retributor who has not replaced her boltgun with a weapon from the *Heavy Weapons* list may take a Simulacrum Imperialis. • The Retributor Superior may either replace her boltgun with a weapon from the *Ranged Weapons* or *Melee Weapons* list, or take a weapon from the *Melee Weapons* list in addition to her other wargear. • The Retributor Superior may replace her bolt pistol with a weapon from the *Pistols* list.

ABILITIES	
	Acts of Faith, Shield of Faith (pg 78-79) **Simulacrum Imperialis:** Add 1 to the result of Tests of Faith for a unit whilst it includes a model with a Simulacrum Imperialis.

FACTION KEYWORDS	**IMPERIUM, ADEPTUS MINISTORUM, ADEPTA SORORITAS, <ORDER>**
KEYWORDS	**INFANTRY, RETRIBUTOR SQUAD**

PENITENT ENGINES

NAME	M	WS	BS	S	T	W	A	Ld	Sv
Penitent Engine	7"	3+	5+	5	6	7	4	8	4+

This unit contains 1 Penitent Engine. It can include 1 additional Penitent Engine (**Power Rating +5**) or 2 additional Penitent Engines (**Power Rating +10**). Each Penitent Engine is equipped with penitent buzz-blades and two heavy flamers.

WEAPON	RANGE	TYPE	S	AP	D	ABILITIES
Heavy flamer	8"	Heavy D6	5	-1	1	This weapon automatically hits its target.
Penitent buzz-blades	Melee	Melee	x2	-3	3	-

ABILITIES	**Zealot** (pg 79)	**Berserk Killing Machines:** Each time a model with this ability loses a wound, roll a D6; on a 5+, the model does not lose that wound.
	Desperate for Redemption: This unit can fight twice in each Fight phase, instead of only once.	

FACTION KEYWORDS	**IMPERIUM, ADEPTUS MINISTORUM**

KEYWORDS	**VEHICLE, PENITENT ENGINES**

In brutal close combat the pilot of a Penitent Engine seeks to gain absolution through the act of slaughtering heretics and traitors.

SORORITAS RHINO

DAMAGE
Some of this model's characteristics change as it suffers damage, as shown below:

REMAINING W	M	BS	A
6-10+	12"	3+	3
3-5	6"	4+	D3
1-2	3"	5+	1

NAME	M	WS	BS	S	T	W	A	Ld	Sv
Sororitas Rhino	✱	6+	✱	6	7	10	✱	8	3+

A Sororitas Rhino is a single model equipped with a storm bolter.

WEAPON	RANGE	TYPE	S	AP	D	ABILITIES
Hunter-killer missile	48"	Heavy 1	8	-2	D6	This weapon can only be fired once per battle.
Storm bolter	24"	Rapid Fire 2	4	0	1	-

WARGEAR OPTIONS	• This model may take a hunter-killer missile. • This model may take an additional storm bolter.

ABILITIES	**Shield of Faith** (pg 79) **Smoke Launchers:** Once per game, instead of shooting any weapons in the Shooting phase, this model can use its smoke launchers; until your next Shooting phase your opponent must subtract 1 from all hit rolls for ranged weapons that target this vehicle.	**Self-repair:** Roll a D6 at the start of each of your turns; on a 6, this model regains one lost wound. **Explodes:** If this model is reduced to 0 wounds, roll a D6 before removing it from the battlefield and before any embarked models disembark. On a 6 it explodes, and each unit within 6" suffers D3 mortal wounds.

TRANSPORT	This model can transport 10 **ADEPTUS MINISTORUM INFANTRY** models. It cannot transport **JUMP PACK** models and can only transport **ADEPTA SORORITAS** models if they have the **<ORDER>**, **DIALOGUS** or **HOSPITALLER** keyword.

FACTION KEYWORDS	**IMPERIUM, ADEPTUS MINISTORUM, ADEPTA SORORITAS, <ORDER>**

KEYWORDS	**VEHICLE, TRANSPORT, RHINO, SORORITAS RHINO**

IMMOLATOR

DAMAGE
Some of this model's characteristics change as it suffers damage, as shown below:

REMAINING W	M	BS	A
6-10+	12"	3+	3
3-5	6"	4+	D3
1-2	3"	5+	1

NAME	M	WS	BS	S	T	W	A	Ld	Sv
Immolator	✱	6+	✱	6	7	10	✱	8	3+

An Immolator is a single model equipped with a immolation flamer.

WEAPON	RANGE	TYPE	S	AP	D	ABILITIES
Hunter-killer missile	48"	Heavy 1	8	-2	D6	This weapon can only be fired once per battle.
Immolation flamer	12"	Assault 2D6	5	-1	1	This weapon automatically hits its target.
Storm bolter	24"	Rapid Fire 2	4	0	1	-
Twin heavy bolter	36"	Heavy 6	5	-1	1	-
Twin multi-melta	24"	Heavy 2	8	-4	D6	If the target is within half range of this weapon, roll two dice when inflicting damage with it and discard the lowest result.

WARGEAR OPTIONS	• This model may replace its immolation flamer with a twin heavy bolter or twin multi-melta. • This model may take a storm bolter. • This model may take a hunter-killer missile.

ABILITIES	**Shield of Faith** (pg 79) **Explodes:** If this model is reduced to 0 wounds, roll a D6 before removing it from the battlefield and before any embarked models disembark. On a 6 it explodes, and each unit within 6" suffers D3 mortal wounds.	**Smoke Launchers:** Once per game, instead of shooting any weapons in the Shooting phase, this model can use its smoke launchers; until your next Shooting phase your opponent must subtract 1 from all hit rolls for ranged weapons that target this vehicle.

TRANSPORT	This model can transport 6 **ADEPTUS MINISTORUM INFANTRY** models. It cannot transport **JUMP PACK** models and can only transport **ADEPTA SORORITAS** models if they have the **<ORDER>**, **DIALOGUS** or **HOSPITALLER** keyword.

FACTION KEYWORDS	**IMPERIUM, ADEPTUS MINISTORUM, ADEPTA SORORITAS, <ORDER>**

KEYWORDS	**VEHICLE, TRANSPORT, IMMOLATOR**

WEAPONS OF FAITH

The forces of the Adepta Sororitas carry a wide variety of weapons to war, but most revolve around the holy trinity of bolt weapons, flame weapons and melta weapons. From the simple bolt pistol to the ornate and deadly Exorcist missile launcher, all are deadly tools in the hands of the faithful.

RANGED WEAPONS

WEAPON	RANGE	TYPE	S	AP	D	ABILITIES
The Ardent Blade (shooting)	8"	Assault D6	5	-1	1	This weapon automatically hits its target.
Autogun	24"	Rapid Fire 1	3	0	1	-
Bolt pistol	12"	Pistol 1	4	0	1	-
Boltgun	24"	Rapid Fire 1	4	0	1	-
Combi-flamer	When attacking with this weapon, choose one or both of the profiles below. If you choose both, subtract 1 from all hit rolls for this weapon.					
- Boltgun	24"	Rapid Fire 1	4	0	1	-
- Flamer	8"	Assault D6	4	0	1	This weapon automatically hits its target.
Combi-melta	When attacking with this weapon, choose one or both of the profiles below. If you choose both, subtract 1 from all hit rolls for this weapon.					
- Boltgun	24"	Rapid Fire 1	4	0	1	-
- Meltagun	12"	Assault 1	8	-4	D6	If the target is within half range of this weapon, roll two dice when inflicting damage with it and discard the lowest result.
Combi-plasma	When attacking with this weapon, choose one or both of the profiles below. If you choose both, subtract 1 from all hit rolls for this weapon.					
- Boltgun	24"	Rapid Fire 1	4	0	1	-
- Plasma gun	24"	Rapid Fire 1	7	-3	1	This weapon can be supercharged by the bearer before firing. If they do so, increase the Strength and Damage of the weapon by 1 this turn. On any hit rolls of 1 when firing supercharge, the bearer is slain after all of the weapon's shots have been resolved.
Condemnor boltgun	24"	Rapid Fire 1	4	0	1	When attacking a **Psyker**, this weapon has a Damage characteristic of D3.
Exorcist missile launcher	48"	Heavy D6	8	-4	D6	-
Flamer	8"	Assault D6	4	0	1	This weapon automatically hits its target.
Frag grenade	6"	Grenade D6	3	0	1	-
Hand flamer	6"	Pistol D6	3	0	1	This weapon automatically hits its target.
Heavy bolter	36"	Heavy 3	5	-1	1	-
Heavy flamer	8"	Heavy D6	5	-1	1	This weapon automatically hits its target.
Hunter-killer missile	48"	Heavy 1	8	-2	D6	This weapon can only be fired once per battle.
Immolation flamer	12"	Assault 2D6	5	-1	1	This weapon automatically hits its target.
Inferno pistol	6"	Pistol 1	8	-4	D6	If the target is within half range of this weapon, roll two dice when inflicting damage with it and discard the lowest result.
Krak grenade	6"	Grenade 1	6	-1	D3	-
Laspistol	12"	Pistol 1	3	0	1	-
Meltagun	12"	Assault 1	8	-4	D6	If the target is within half range of this weapon, roll two dice when inflicting damage with it and discard the lowest result.
Multi-melta	24"	Heavy 1	8	-4	D6	If the target is within half range of this weapon, roll two dice when inflicting damage with it and discard the lowest result.
Plasma pistol	When attacking with this weapon, choose one of the profiles below.					
- Standard	12"	Pistol 1	7	-3	1	-
- Supercharge	12"	Pistol 1	8	-3	2	On a hit roll of 1, the bearer is slain.
The Redeemer	18"	Assault 2	4	-1	1	When resolving shots at targets within half range, add 1 to this weapon's Strength characteristic.
Storm bolter	24"	Rapid Fire 2	4	0	1	-
Twin heavy bolter	36"	Heavy 6	5	-1	1	-
Twin multi-melta	24"	Heavy 2	8	-4	D6	If the target is within half range of this weapon, roll two dice when inflicting damage with it and discard the lowest result.

MELEE WEAPONS

WEAPON	RANGE	TYPE	S	AP	D	ABILITIES
Arco-flails	Melee	Melee	+1	-1	1	Make D3 hit rolls for each attack made with this weapon.
The Ardent Blade (melee)	Melee	Melee	+4	-3	2	-
Chainsword	Melee	Melee	User	0	1	Each time the bearer fights, it can make 1 additional attack with this weapon.
Chirurgeon's tools	Melee	Melee	User	-1	1	-
Death Cult power blades	Melee	Melee	User	-2	1	-
Dialogus staff	Melee	Melee	+1	0	1	-
Neural whips	Melee	Melee	User	-2	1	Add 1 to the wound rolls for attacks made with this weapon if the target unit's highest Leadership characteristic is less than 8 (other than **Vehicles**).
Penitent buzz-blades	Melee	Melee	x2	-3	3	-
Penitent eviscerator	Melee	Melee	x2	-2	2	When attacking with this weapon, you must subtract 1 from the hit roll.
Power maul	Melee	Melee	+2	-1	1	-
Power sword	Melee	Melee	User	-3	1	-

POINTS VALUES

If you are playing a matched play game, or a game that uses a points limit, you can use the following lists to determine the total points cost of your army. Simply add together the points costs of all your models and the wargear they are equipped with to determine your army's total points value.

HQ

UNIT	MODELS PER UNIT	POINTS PER MODEL (Does not include wargear)
Canoness	1	45
Missionary	1	35

TROOPS

UNIT	MODELS PER UNIT	POINTS PER MODEL (Does not include wargear)
Battle Sisters Squad	5-15	9

ELITES

UNIT	MODELS PER UNIT	POINTS PER MODEL (Does not include wargear)
Arco-flagellants	3-9	15
Celestian Squad	5-10	11
Crusaders	2-10	9
Death Cult Assassins	2-10	17
Dialogus	1	30
Geminae Superia	1-2	21
Hospitaller	1	30
Mistress of Repentance	1	35
Preacher	1	25
Repentia Squad	3-9	15

FAST ATTACK

UNIT	MODELS PER UNIT	POINTS PER MODEL (Does not include wargear)
Dominion Squad	5-10	10
Seraphim Squad	5-10	11

HEAVY SUPPORT

UNIT	MODELS PER UNIT	POINTS PER MODEL (Does not include wargear)
Exorcist	1	125
Penitent Engines	1-3	72
Retributor Squad	5-10	9

DEDICATED TRANSPORT

UNIT	MODELS PER UNIT	POINTS PER MODEL (Does not include wargear)
Immolator	1	68
Sororitas Rhino	1	73

NAMED CHARACTERS

UNIT	MODELS PER UNIT	POINTS PER MODEL (Including wargear)
Celestine	1	160
Uriah Jacobus	1	50

RANGED WEAPONS

WEAPON	POINTS PER WEAPON
Autogun	0
Bolt pistol	0
Boltgun	0
Combi-flamer	8
Combi-melta	15
Combi-plasma	11
Condemnor boltgun	1
Exorcist missile launcher	0
Flamer	6
Frag grenade	0
Hand flamer	3
Heavy bolter	10
Heavy flamer	14
Hunter-killer missile	6
Immolation flamer	30
Inferno pistol	7
Krak grenade	0
Laspistol	0
Meltagun	14
Multi-melta	22
Plasma pistol	5
Storm bolter	2
Twin heavy bolter	17
Twin multi-melta	40

MELEE WEAPONS

WEAPON	POINTS PER WEAPON
Arco-flails	0
Chainsword	0
Chirurgeon's tools	0
Death Cult power blades	0
Dialogus staff	0
Neural whips	0
Penitent buzz-blades	0
Penitent eviscerator	0
Power maul	4
Power sword	4

OTHER WARGEAR

ITEM	POINTS PER ITEM
Simulacrum Imperialis	10
Storm shield	0

FURY OF THE RIGHTEOUS

In this section you will find rules for Battle-forged armies that include Adepta Sororitas Detachments – that is, any Detachment which includes only Adepta Sororitas units (as defined below). These rules include the abilities below and a series of Stratagems that can only be used by the Adepta Sororitas. This section also contains unique Warlord Traits and Relics for the faithful.

ADEPTA SORORITAS UNITS

In the rules described in this section we sometimes refer to 'Adepta Sororitas units'. This is shorthand for units with one of the following keywords: **ADEPTA SORORITAS**, **MINISTORUM PRIEST**, **PENITENT ENGINE** or **ECCLESIARCHY BATTLE CONCLAVE**.

ABILITIES

Adepta Sororitas Detachments gain the following abilities:

ORDER CONVICTIONS

Each order of the Adepta Sororitas has developed its own specialised combat philosophy, suited to the unique skills and traits of its Sisters.

If your army is Battle-forged, all **<ORDER> INFANTRY** units in an Adepta Sororitas Detachment gain an Order Conviction, so long as every unit in that Detachment is from the same order. The Order Conviction gained depends upon the order they are drawn from, as shown in the table opposite. For example, an **ORDER OF THE EBON CHALICE** unit with the Order Convictions ability gains the Daughters of the Emperor conviction.

If your order does not have an associated Order Conviction, you may pick the conviction that you feel best represents the fighting style and strategies of the warriors in your army.

STRENGTH OF FAITH

The warriors of the Ecclesiarchy have an unshakeable faith, and never doubt the righteousness of their cause. While a single believer stands, the Imperial Creed will be spread through word and fire.

If your army is Battle-forged, all Troops units in Adepta Sororitas Detachments gain this ability. Such a unit that is within range of an objective marker (as specified in the mission) controls the objective marker even if there are more enemy models within range of that objective marker. If an enemy unit within range of the same objective marker has a similar ability, then the objective marker is controlled by the player who has the most models within range of it as normal.

Designer's Note: *The Stratagems, Warlord Traits and Relics found in this section replace those presented in the Adepta Sororitas Faction rules found in* Chapter Approved: 2017 Edition.

THE PIOUS AND THE PENITENT

The units found in this codex and listed below can be included in an Adepta Sororitas Detachment without preventing other units in that Detachment from gaining an Order Conviction. Note that the units listed below can never themselves benefit from an Order Conviction.

- Celestine
- Geminae Superia
- Hospitaller
- Dialogus
- Penitent Engines
- **MINISTORUM PRIEST** models
- **ECCLESIARCHY BATTLE CONCLAVE** models

ORDER	ORDER CONVICTION
Valorous Heart	**Stoic Endurance:** *Like their patron Saint Lucia, those of the Order of the Valorous Heart are willing to bear any agony in the name of atonement. Such is their willingness to suffer for their cause that they can shrug off seemingly mortal wounds without breaking stride.* Each time a model with this conviction loses a wound, roll a D6; on a 6 the wound is not lost.
Our Martyred Lady	**The Blood of Martyrs:** *So dedicated are the Sisters of the Order of Our Martyred Lady that nothing can keep them from fulfilling their Emperor-given duty. When the fighting is fiercest and the casualties highest, these holy warriors fight with renewed conviction and purpose, inspired by their desire to avenge the deaths of their fallen.* Each time a unit with this conviction from your army is destroyed, you gain 1 Faith Point.
Ebon Chalice	**Daughters of the Emperor:** *The Order of the Ebon Chalice is the oldest of the Orders Militant, and it is said that they above all others bear the blessing of the Emperor's divine grace.* Add 1 to the result of Tests of Faith for units with this conviction.
Argent Shroud	**Deeds, Not Words:** *It is the strong belief of those within the Order of the Argent Shroud that one's conviction is best shown through bold action. Thus is battle the best way to prove their unquenchable faith, for there they may smite the Emperor's foes and demonstrate the depths of their devotion.* Each time an enemy unit is destroyed by a unit with this conviction, roll a D6. On a 4+ you gain a Faith Point.
Bloody Rose	**Quick to Anger:** *Once their battle fury is roused, none prosecute the wars of the Adeptus Ministorum with greater fervour than do those warriors who belong to Order of the Bloody Rose.* Add 1 to the Strength and Attacks characteristics of a model with this conviction during any turn in which it made a charge move, was charged or performed a Heroic Intervention.
Sacred Rose	**Devout Serenity:** *The Sisters of the Order of the Sacred Rose are renowned for their calm and implacable resolve in battle. Even in the face of overwhelming odds, the heirs of Saint Arabella stand unyielding.* A unit with this conviction can never lose more than a single model as the result of any single failed Morale test. In addition, when a model with this conviction fires Overwatch, a 5 or 6 is required for a successful hit roll, irrespective of the firing model's Ballistic Skill or any modifiers.

STRATAGEMS

If your army is Battle-forged and includes any Adepta Sororitas Detachments (excluding Auxiliary Support Detachments), you have access to the Stratagems shown below, meaning you can spend Command Points to activate them. These help to reflect the holy crusades and strategies used by the Sisters of Battle on the battlefield.

OPEN THE RELIQUARIES
1CP/3CP

Adepta Sororitas Stratagem

In the direst circumstances, even the most sacred of the Ministorum's holy artefacts are brought forth to aid the faithful.

Use this Stratagem before the battle. Your army can have one extra Relic of the Ecclesiarchy for 1 CP, or two extra Relics of the Ecclesiarchy for 3 CPs. All of the Relics of the Ecclesiarchy that you include must be different and be given to different **ADEPTA SORORITAS CHARACTERS**. You can only use this Stratagem once per battle.

BURNING DESCENT
1CP

Adepta Sororitas Stratagem

Seraphim arrive on the battlefield in a blaze of glory, spreading fire from on high to scour the foe as they descend.

Use this Stratagem after a **SERAPHIM SQUAD** unit from your army is set up on the battlefield using its Sky Strike ability. You can immediately shoot with that unit as if it were your Shooting phase, and for those attacks, the range of that unit's hand flamers is increased to 12". This does not prevent it from shooting again in the following Shooting phase.

VESSEL OF THE EMPEROR'S WILL
3CP

Adepta Sororitas Stratagem

The Emperor's grace extends from his chosen leaders to those that follow them into battle.

Use this Stratagem after a successful Test of Faith roll is made for an **ADEPTA SORORITAS CHARACTER** from your army. The Act of Faith used on that character affects all friendly **ADEPTA SORORITAS** units within 6" of the character (this does not cost any additional Faith Points and no additional Tests of Faith are required).

SUFFER NOT THE WITCH
1CP

Adepta Sororitas Stratagem

Those who would wield sorcery against the righteous often find themselves facing the full fury of the Ecclesiarchy.

Use this Stratagem at the start of any Shooting or Fight phase. Choose an **ADEPTA SORORITAS** unit from your army. Until the end of the phase, you can re-roll failed wound rolls for attacks made by that unit that target enemy **PSYKER** units.

EXTREMIS TRIGGER WORD
2CP

Adepta Sororitas Stratagem

Arco-flagellants are conditioned with sacred trigger words that release their cerebral inhibitors and unleash the full fury of their killing rage.

Use this Stratagem in the Fight phase when you pick an **ARCO-FLAGELLANTS** unit to fight. Until the end of that phase, replace that unit's arco-flails' ability with 'Make 3 hit rolls for each attack made with this weapon.' At the end of that phase, roll a number of D6 equal to the number of models in that unit. For each roll of 6, one model in the unit is slain.

FINAL REDEMPTION
1CP

Adepta Sororitas Stratagem

Even the most grievous wound cannot stop a Sister Repentia in her quest to earn redemption in the eyes of the Emperor.

Use this Stratagem at the start of the Fight phase. Pick a **REPENTIA SQUAD** unit from your army. Until the end of the phase, roll a D6 each time a model in that unit is slain. On a 4+ the enemy unit that slew that model suffers 1 mortal wound after the unit has resolved all of its attacks.

BLESSED BOLTS
1CP

Adepta Sororitas Stratagem

It takes an artificer a lifetime to produce just one of these blessed bolts, which are said to be imbued with the Emperor's divine vengeance.

Use this Stratagem before shooting with an **ADEPTA SORORITAS INFANTRY** unit from your army in the Shooting phase. Until the end of the phase, change the AP characteristic of storm bolters that models in that unit are armed with to -2, and their Damage characteristic to 2.

FAITH AND FURY
1CP

Adepta Sororitas Stratagem

With the Emperor watching over them, the righteous zeal of the Sisters of Battle burns ever brighter, fuelling their attacks.

Use this Stratagem after a successful Test of Faith roll is made for an **ADEPTA SORORITAS** unit from your army. You can re-roll wound rolls of 1 for that unit until the end of the phase.

SACRED BANNER OF THE ORDER MILITANT
1CP

Adepta Sororitas Stratagem

Each of the Orders Militant possesses a single ancient banner, an irreplaceable holy relic.

Use this Stratagem before the battle. Select a model from your army that has a Simulacrum Imperialis; it is upgraded to a Sacred Banner. In addition to its normal ability, the power of the banner can be used once per battle, at the start of any battle round. When used, until the end of the battle round, the invulnerable save this model's unit receives from the Shield of Faith ability is improved by 1, to a maximum of 3+. You can only use this Stratagem once per battle.

RALLY THE FAITHFUL
1CP

Adepta Sororitas Stratagem

Even the most hopeless battle can be turned by a spark of divine inspiration.

Use this Stratagem when an **ADEPTA SORORITAS** unit from your army fails a Morale test. Halve the number of models that flee (rounding down).

PURITY OF FAITH
1CP

Adepta Sororitas Stratagem

The faith of the Ecclesiarchy's warriors steels their hearts and bodies against psychic assaults.

Use this Stratagem when an enemy **PSYKER** manifests a psychic power within 24" of an **ADEPTA SORORITAS** unit from your army. Roll a D6; on a 4+ that psychic power is resisted and its effects are negated.

MARTYRDOM
1CP

Adepta Sororitas Stratagem

The Sisters of Battle do not give in to despair when their leaders are slain. Instead, the blood of these martyred heroes only strengthens their resolve.

Use this Stratagem when an **ADEPTA SORORITAS CHARACTER** from your army is slain. You immediately gain D3 Faith Points; if the slain model was your Warlord, you instead gain 3 Faith Points.

HOLY TRINITY
1CP

Adepta Sororitas Stratagem

With bolter, flamer and melta is the foe purged.

Use this Stratagem before shooting with an **ADEPTA SORORITAS** unit in the Shooting phase. If that unit targets all of its attacks at the same target, and that target is within range of at least one model in the unit firing a bolt weapon, one other model firing a flamer weapon, and one other model firing a melta weapon, add 1 to all wound rolls made for the firing unit until the end of the phase. For the purposes of this Stratagem, a bolt weapon is any weapon profile whose name includes the word 'bolt' (e.g. boltgun), a flamer weapon is any weapon profile whose name includes the word 'flamer' (e.g. hand flamer), and a melta weapon includes inferno pistols and any weapon profile whose name includes the word 'melta' (e.g. meltagun).

SACRED RITES
1CP

Adepta Sororitas Stratagem

The observance of battle-rites and the chanting of blessed psalms stirs the hearts of the faithful.

Use this Stratagem at the start of your Movement phase. Gain 1 Faith Point.

WARLORD TRAITS

From fervent preachers to militant commanders, those who lead the warriors of the Adeptus Ministorum to battle are as varied as they are deeply pious in their devotion to the Emperor.

If an **Adepta Sororitas Character** is your Warlord, they can generate a Warlord Trait from the following table instead of the one in the *Warhammer 40,000* rulebook. You can either roll on the table below to randomly generate a Warlord Trait, or you can select the one that best suits her preferred style of waging war. If a **Ministorum Priest** is your Warlord, they can have the Righteous Rage Warlord Trait from the table below instead of generating a Warlord Trait from the table in the *Warhammer 40,000* rulebook.

D6 RESULT

1 INSPIRING ORATOR

Those who hear this leader's stirring words are inspired to great feats of bravery.

You can re-roll failed Morale tests for friendly <Order> units whilst they are within 6" of this Warlord. In addition, friendly <Order> units can use this Warlord's Leadership characteristic instead of their own whilst they are within 6" of this Warlord.

2 RIGHTEOUS RAGE

With burning indignation, this servant of the divine can barely contain their desire to strike down the unfaithful.

You can re-roll failed charge rolls for this Warlord. In addition, if this Warlord made a charge move, was charged or performed a Heroic Intervention, you can re-roll failed wound rolls made for it until the end of the Fight phase.

3 EXECUTIONER OF HERETICS

This Sister has a fearsome reputation for hunting down the Ecclesiarchy's enemies and slaying them without mercy.

Subtract 1 from the Leadership characteristic of enemy units whilst they are within 6" of your Warlord.

4 BEACON OF FAITH

This Adepta Sororitas leader is a shining beacon of faith, a spiritual as well as a military leader who inspires intense devotion in their warriors.

At the start of your turn, roll a D6 if this Warlord is on the battlefield; on a 4+ you gain 1 Faith Point.

5 INDOMITABLE BELIEF

This chosen champion has such strength of belief that their followers refuse to yield before the Emperor's enemies.

The invulnerable save friendly <Order> units receive from the Shield of Faith ability is improved to 5+ whilst they are within 6" of this Warlord.

6 PURE OF WILL

With a will of adamant, this devout servant's faith can turn aside even the most foul of witchcraft.

Your Warlord can attempt to deny one additional psychic power in each enemy Psychic phase, as described in the Shield of Faith ability. In addition, enemy **Psykers** must subtract 1 from their Psychic tests whilst they are within 12" of this Warlord.

NAMED CHARACTERS

If Celestine is your Warlord, she must be given the Beacon of Faith Warlord Trait. If Uriah Jacobus is your Warlord, he must be given the Righteous Rage Warlord Trait.

RELICS OF THE ECCLESIARCHY

A religious organisation as vast as the Adeptus Ministorum has no shortage of icons, relics, religious artefacts and other paraphernalia. Whilst many of these are fakes, crafted by charlatans to sell to the uninformed masses, those held by the mightiest servants of the Ecclesiarchy are powerful tools of faith.

If your army is led by an **Adepta Sororitas** Warlord, then before the battle you may give one of the following Relics of the Ecclesiarchy to an **Adepta Sororitas Character**. If your army includes any **Ministorum Priests**, you can instead give one of them the Book of St. Lucius. **Geminae Superia**, and named characters such as Celestine, cannot be given any of the following relics.

Note that some weapons replace one of the character's existing weapons. Where this is the case, if you are playing a matched play game or are otherwise using points values, you must still pay the cost of the weapon that is being replaced. Write down any Relics of the Ecclesiarchy your characters may have on your army roster.

BLADE OF ADMONITION

This blessed power sword is the very blade carried into battle by Alicia Dominica – the founding saint of the Adepta Sororitas – and was famously used to cut the head from the traitor Goge Vandire and bring an end to the Reign of Blood. St. Dominica wielded this blade in the decades following the reformation of the Ecclesiarchy, and a thousand more false prophets and heretics were slain upon its razor edge before Alicia's eventual martyrdom.

Model with a power sword only. The Blade of Admonition replaces the bearer's power sword and has the following profile:

WEAPON	RANGE	TYPE	S	AP	D
Blade of Admonition	Melee	Melee	+2	-3	3

BOOK OF ST. LUCIUS

This tome contains the complete writings of St. Lucius of Agathea, the first Arch-confessor. Such was St. Lucius' zeal and devotion that his book was penned with his own blood. Even now, centuries after his death, it is believed that a fraction of his essence still pervades the book's pages, and whoever holds the revered relic speaks with all the deceased Arch-confessor's holy authority.

Increase the range of the bearer's aura abilities by 3".

BRAZIER OF ETERNAL FLAME

The Brazier of Eternal Flame burns above the faithful, its blazing light driving back the darkness and protecting the true servants of the Emperor from foul sorceries.

Roll 2D6 instead of D6 for Deny the Witch tests taken by friendly <Order> units using the Shield of Faith ability whilst they are within 6" of the bearer.

LITANIES OF FAITH

When Sebastian Thor was declared Ecclesiarch in the wake of the Age of Apostasy, his first sermon was transcribed onto scrolls by an army of scribes. Today, only a single original copy remains, kept in a stasis vault beneath the Convent Prioris on Terra and released only with the sanction of the Ecclesiarch himself. This unassuming parchment is one of the holiest relics in the Ministorum's charge, its mere presence enough to fill the hearts of the faithful with righteous fervour.

Roll a D6 each time you successfully pass a Test of Faith for a friendly **Adepta Sororitas** unit whilst it is within 6" of the bearer; on 5+ the Faith Point used to attempt that Act of Faith is immediately refunded.

MANTLE OF OPHELIA

The Mantle of Ophelia was once the badge of office for the Prioress of the Convent Sanctorum, and was worn by Helena the Virtuous, a Living Saint and one of the most revered leaders in the history of the Adepta Sororitas. The mantle is thought to have sacred powers of protection, for Helena was said to have anointed it with the Tears of the Emperor, a phial of blood-like liquid meticulously collected over a century from weeping statues of the Emperor found across the cardinal worlds of the Imperium.

Canoness only. The bearer has a 3+ invulnerable save.

WRATH OF THE EMPEROR

The ornate bolt pistol known as the Wrath of the Emperor fires shells imbued with incendiary charges. Upon detonation, these immolate their unfortunate victims in a flash of holy flame.

Model with a bolt pistol only. The Wrath of the Emperor replaces the bearer's bolt pistol and has the following profile:

WEAPON	RANGE	TYPE	S	AP	D
Wrath of the Emperor	18"	Pistol 3	5	-1	2

INDEX

RENEGADE KNIGHTS

QUESTOR TRAITORIS

This section describes the Renegade Knights, giant engines of war piloted by treacherous nobles who have long since broken their oaths of loyalty in favour of worship to the Chaos Gods. It provides you with the rules required to assemble an army of such terrifying war machines in your games of Warhammer 40,000.

Humanoid war engines that tower over their foes, each Renegade Knight carries an army's worth of firepower upon its weaponised limbs and hulking carapace. At close quarters, their roaring chainswords and crushing thunderstrike gauntlets destroy what their trampling feet cannot, scattering terrified survivors before their unstoppable advance.

The ground shudders beneath the godlike tread of the Renegade Knights. Even one such looming war engine possesses the firepower to annihilate entire regiments of enemy warriors, pick apart armoured columns, and swat squadrons of aircraft from the skies. Chaos Lords and rebellious demagogues will go to great lengths to secure the services of such a lone warrior, sacrificing whatever they must to ensure that this god of destruction fights at their side.

Deployed in great number, the Questor Traitoris are more fearsome still, and have been known to bring entire worlds to heel, scourging them by blade and by flame in the name of the Dark Gods.

CORRUPTING THE INCORRUPTIBLE

Those who pilot Imperial Knights are brave and noble warriors, drawn from ancestral knightly houses. In their eighteenth year, aspirants face the Ritual of Becoming, a strange rite where the mind of the Noble is fused with the Knight's machine spirit, allowing the pilot to occupy the machine's Throne Mechanicum and control it with their thoughts alone. This rite – coupled with psychosuggestive subroutines fed through the Knight's neural jacks – is intended to weed out those who are weak in mind or soul, reinforcing notions of honour and selflessness so that few Knights risk falling to the temptations of Chaos.

No man is beyond the reach of the Dark Gods, however. To believe otherwise is dangerous arrogance. There are many ways that a Knight may stray from the true path laid out in the Code Chivalric, or else be driven from it by force. Most common are those times when Freeblade Knights – those who have already forsworn their knightly houses due to some shame or tragedy – find themselves driven to commit ignoble acts to survive. The ghosts of the Thrones Mechanicum are uncompromising and unforgiving, and the judgemental voices of ancestors long passed will lambaste such a fallen Knight mercilessly. Some pilots take their own lives, or abandon the throne forever – to a Noble pilot, there is little difference between these two terrible ends. Those who do not, or worse, cannot, are driven swiftly mad. It is this insanity that the Dark Gods prey upon, claiming the Nobles' lost souls and twisting the machine spirits of their steeds into ravening beasts. In recent years, covens of Warpsmiths have taken to capturing lone Knights and giving them over for torture until this horrible end is achieved. There are even whispered rumours that some Renegade Knights no longer contain living pilots at all, but are instead the unwilling hosts to parasitic possessor Daemons who clad themselves in the war engine's adamantium plates as a mortal warrior might don a suit of armour.

Rarer and more terrible are those instances when an entire lance, or even a whole knightly house falls into damnation. During the dark days of the Horus Heresy, this was a tragedy that played out many times, most famously with the once glorious House Devine who fell to the temptations of Slaanesh. With the Cicatrix Maledictum splitting the galaxy, such wholesale corruption has become a hazard once again. Here, a compromised Sacristan creeps from one Throne Mechanicum to the next, tainting them with daemonic ichor brewed to drive the Knights to madness and mutation. There a Baron leads a noble crusade to purge a world of Chaos taint, only to become so immersed in blood that he and his followers degenerate into the very berserk beasts they strode out to slay. The Inquisition have gone to great pains in their efforts to suppress reports of traitorous knightly houses, for the mere notion of such loyal warriors turning traitor is every bit as horrifying as the concept of Renegade Space Marines. Yet more Knights fall with every passing year, and their devastating rampages have become difficult to conceal.

RENEGADE KNIGHT

DAMAGE

Some of this model's characteristics change as it suffers damage, as shown below:

REMAINING W	M	WS	BS
13-24+	12"	3+	3+
7-12	9"	4+	4+
1-6	6"	5+	5+

NAME	M	WS	BS	S	T	W	A	Ld	Sv
Renegade Knight	*	*	*	8	8	24	4	9	3+

A Renegade Knight is a single model equipped with a reaper chainsword, thunderstrike gauntlet, heavy stubber and titanic feet.

WEAPON	RANGE	TYPE	S	AP	D	ABILITIES
Avenger gatling cannon	36"	Heavy 12	6	-2	2	-
Heavy flamer	8"	Heavy D6	5	-1	1	This weapon automatically hits its target.
Heavy stubber	36"	Heavy 3	4	0	1	-
Ironstorm missile pod	72"	Heavy D6	5	-1	2	This weapon can target units that are not visible to the bearer.
Meltagun	12"	Assault 1	8	-4	D6	If the target is within half range of this weapon, roll two dice when inflicting damage with it and discard the lowest result.
Rapid-fire battle cannon	72"	Heavy 2D6	8	-2	D3	-
Stormspear rocket pod	48"	Heavy 3	8	-2	D6	-
Thermal cannon	36"	Heavy D6	9	-4	D6	If the target is within half range of this weapon, roll two dice when inflicting damage with it and discard the lowest result.
Twin Icarus autocannon	48"	Heavy 4	7	-1	2	Add 1 to hit rolls made for this weapon against targets that can **FLY**. Subtract 1 from the hit rolls made for this weapon against all other targets.
Reaper chainsword	Melee	Melee	+6	-3	6	-
Thunderstrike gauntlet	Melee	Melee	x2	-4	6	When attacking with this weapon, you must subtract 1 from the hit roll. If a **VEHICLE** or **MONSTER** is slain by this weapon, pick an enemy unit within 9" of the bearer and roll a D6. On a 4+ that unit suffers D3 mortal wounds.
Titanic feet	Melee	Melee	User	-2	D3	Make 3 hit rolls for each attack made with this weapon.

WARGEAR OPTIONS
- This model may take a twin Icarus autocannon, stormspear rocket pod or ironstorm missile pod.
- This model may replace its thunderstrike gauntlet with an avenger gatling cannon and heavy flamer, rapid-fire battle cannon and heavy stubber, or thermal cannon.
- This model may replace its reaper chainsword with an avenger gatling cannon and heavy flamer, rapid-fire battle cannon and heavy stubber, or thermal cannon.
- This model may replace one heavy stubber with a meltagun.

ABILITIES

Ion Shield: This model has a 5+ invulnerable save against ranged weapons.

Explodes: If this model is reduced to 0 wounds, roll a D6 before removing it from the battlefield; on a 6 it explodes, and each unit within 2D6" suffers D6 mortal wounds.

Engine of Destruction: If this model has a reaper chainsword and a thunderstrike gauntlet, its Attacks characteristic is changed to 5 and its Weapon Skill is improved by 1 (e.g. WS 3+ becomes WS 2+).

Super-heavy Walker: This model can Fall Back in the Movement phase and still shoot and/or charge in the same turn. When this model Falls Back, it can move over enemy **INFANTRY** and **SWARM** models, though it must end its move more than 1" from any enemy units. In addition, this model can move and fire Heavy weapons without suffering the penalty to its hit rolls. Finally, this model only gains a bonus to its save for being in cover if at least half of the model is obscured from the firer.

FACTION KEYWORDS | **CHAOS, QUESTOR TRAITORIS**

KEYWORDS | **TITANIC, VEHICLE, RENEGADE KNIGHT**

RENEGADE KNIGHT DOMINUS

DAMAGE

Some of this model's characteristics change as it suffers damage, as shown below:

REMAINING W	M	WS	BS
15-28+	10"	4+	3+
8-14	7"	5+	4+
1-7	4"	6+	5+

NAME	M	WS	BS	S	T	W	A	Ld	Sv
Renegade Knight Dominus	∗	∗	∗	8	8	28	4	9	3+

A Renegade Knight Dominus is a single model equipped with a plasma decimator, volcano lance, two shieldbreaker missiles, two twin meltaguns, two twin siegebreaker cannons and titanic feet.

WEAPON	RANGE	TYPE	S	AP	D	ABILITIES
Conflagration cannon	18"	Heavy 3D6	7	-2	2	This weapon automatically hits its target.
Plasma decimator	When attacking with this weapon, choose one of the profiles below.					
- Standard	48"	Heavy 2D6	7	-3	1	-
- Supercharge	48"	Heavy 2D6	8	-3	2	For each hit roll of 1, the bearer suffers 1 mortal wound after all of this weapon's shots have been resolved.
Shieldbreaker missile	48"	Heavy 1	10	-4	D6	Each shieldbreaker missile can only be fired once per battle, and a model can only fire one each turn. Invulnerable saving throws cannot be made against wounds caused by this weapon.
Twin siegebreaker cannon	48"	Heavy 2D3	7	-1	D3	-
Twin meltagun	12"	Assault 2	8	-4	D6	If the target is within half range of this weapon, roll two dice when inflicting damage with it and discard the lowest result.
Thundercoil harpoon	12"	Heavy 1	16	-6	10	You can re-roll failed hit rolls when targeting **VEHICLE** or **MONSTER** units with this weapon. In addition, if this weapon inflicts any damage, the target unit suffers an additional D3 mortal wounds.
Volcano lance	80"	Heavy D6	14	-5	3D3	You can re-roll failed wound rolls when targeting **TITANIC** units with this weapon.
Titanic feet	Melee	Melee	User	-2	D3	Make 3 hit rolls for each attack made with this weapon.

WARGEAR OPTIONS	
	• This model may replace its plasma decimator and its volcano lance with a conflagration cannon and a thundercoil harpoon.
	• This model may replace one of its twin siegebreaker cannons with two shieldbreaker missiles.

ABILITIES	
	Ion Shield: This model has a 5+ invulnerable save against ranged weapons. **Super-heavy Walker:** This model can Fall Back in the Movement phase and still shoot and/or charge in the same turn. When this model Falls Back, it can move over enemy **INFANTRY** and **SWARM** models, though it must end its move more than 1" from any enemy units. In addition, this model can move and fire Heavy weapons without suffering the penalty to its hit rolls. Finally, this model only gains a bonus to its save for being in cover if at least half of the model is obscured from the firer.
	Dual Plasma Core Explosion: If this model is reduced to 0 wounds, roll 2D6 before removing it from the battlefield. If you roll a 6 on either dice, it explodes, and each unit within 2D6" suffers D6 mortal wounds; if you roll a 6 on both dice, each unit within 3D6" suffers D6 mortal wounds instead.

FACTION KEYWORDS	**CHAOS, QUESTOR TRAITORIS**
KEYWORDS	**TITANIC, VEHICLE, RENEGADE KNIGHT DOMINUS**

INFERNAL QUESTS

When Renegade Knights gather in great number they are compelled to swear grim oaths to the Dark Gods. In a twisted parody of their former nobility, they vow to complete mighty tasks on pain of death and dishonour. Such deeds may include the burning of a cardinal world or other great place of faith, the hunting of some feted Imperial hero, or the wholesale butchery of a star system whose defenders have offended the Dark Gods with their resistance. Once they have set themselves to such an Infernal Quest, Renegade Knights will not relent until either they emerge victorious, or they are slain to the last.

RENEGADE ARMIGER

DAMAGE
Some of this model's characteristics change as it suffers damage, as shown below:

REMAINING W	M	WS	BS
7-12+	14"	3+	3+
4-6	10"	4+	4+
1-3	7"	5+	5+

NAME	M	WS	BS	S	T	W	A	Ld	Sv
Renegade Armiger	*	*	*	6	7	12	4	8	3+

This unit contains 1 Renegade Armiger. It can include 1 additional Renegade Armiger (**Power Rating +9),** or 2 additional Renegade Armigers (**Power Rating +18**). Each Renegade Armiger is equipped with two Armiger autocannons and a heavy stubber.

WEAPON	RANGE	TYPE	S	AP	D	ABILITIES
Armiger autocannon	60"	Heavy 2D3	7	-1	3	Ignore the penalty to hit rolls for moving and firing this Heavy weapon.
Heavy stubber	36"	Heavy 3	4	0	1	-
Meltagun	12"	Assault 1	8	-4	D6	If the target is within half range of this weapon, roll two dice when inflicting damage with it and discard the lowest result.
Thermal spear	30"	Assault D3	8	-4	D6	If the target is within half range of this weapon, roll two dice when inflicting damage with it and discard the lowest result.
Reaper chain-cleaver	When attacking with this weapon, choose one of the profiles below:					
- Strike	Melee	Melee	x2	-3	3	-
- Sweep	Melee	Melee	User	-2	1	Make 2 hit rolls for each attack made with this weapon, instead of 1.

WARGEAR OPTIONS	• Any model may replace both its autocannons with a thermal spear and a reaper chain-cleaver. • Any model may replace its heavy stubber with a meltagun.
ABILITIES	**Ion Shield:** Models in this unit have a 5+ invulnerable save against ranged weapons. **Explodes:** Each time a model in this unit is reduced to 0 wounds, roll a dice before removing it from the battlefield; on a 6 it explodes, and each unit within 6" suffers D3 mortal wounds.	**Vehicle Squadron:** The first time this unit is set up, all of its models must be placed within 6" of each other. From that point onwards, each operates independently and is treated as a separate unit.
FACTION KEYWORDS	**CHAOS, QUESTOR TRAITORIS**
KEYWORDS	**VEHICLE, RENEGADE ARMIGER**

POINTS VALUES

If you are playing a matched play game, or a game that uses a points limit, you can use the following lists to determine the total points cost of your army. Simply add together the points costs of all your models and the wargear they are equipped with to determine your army's total points value.

MELEE WEAPONS

WEAPON	POINTS PER WEAPON
Reaper chain-cleaver	0
Reaper chainsword	30
Thunderstrike gauntlet	35
Titanic feet	0

RANGED WEAPONS

WEAPON	POINTS PER WEAPON
Armiger autocannon	5
Avenger gatling cannon	75
Conflagration cannon	0
Heavy flamer	14
Heavy stubber	2
Ironstorm missile pod	16
Meltagun	14
Plasma decimator	0
Rapid-fire battle cannon	100
Shieldbreaker missile	12
Stormspear rocket pod	45
Thermal cannon	76
Thermal spear	0
Thundercoil harpoon	0
Twin Icarus autocannon	20
Twin meltagun	0
Twin siegebreaker cannon	35
Volcano lance	10

UNITS

UNIT	MODELS PER UNIT	POINTS PER MODEL (Does not include wargear)
Renegade Armiger	1-3	160
Renegade Knight	1	285
Renegade Knight Dominus	1	500

DETACHMENT RULES

On this page you'll find rules for Battle-forged armies that include QUESTOR TRAITORIS Detachments – that is, any Detachment which includes only QUESTOR TRAITORIS units. This includes the Detachment ability below and Stratagems, a Warlord Trait and a Relic that can only be used by the Renegade Knights. Together, these rules help to reflect their character and fighting style in your games of Warhammer 40,000.

ABILITIES

QUESTOR TRAITORIS Detachments (excluding Super-heavy Auxiliary Detachments) gain the following ability:

RENEGADE KNIGHT LANCE

Though they have left their nobility far behind, Renegade Knight houses are still ruled over by despotic lords who lead them with brutal authority.

If your army is Battle-forged, select one model in each QUESTOR TRAITORIS Super-heavy Detachment in your army. Each model you selected gains the **CHARACTER** keyword. However, the Command Benefit of each QUESTOR TRAITORIS Super-heavy Detachment is changed to 'None' if it does not contain at least one QUESTOR TRAITORIS TITANIC unit, and it is changed to '+6 Command Points' if it contains at least three QUESTOR TRAITORIS TITANIC units.

WARLORD TRAIT

If a QUESTOR TRAITORIS TITANIC CHARACTER is your Warlord, you can choose to give them the following Warlord Trait:

INFERNAL QUEST

This warlord has sworn a grim oath to the Dark Gods – they will not relent in spreading carnage across the galaxy until they have honoured it, or they are slain.

If your Warlord is within range of an objective marker (as specified within the mission), it controls that objective marker even if there are more enemy models within range of the same objective marker. If an enemy unit within range of the same objective marker has a similar ability, then the objective marker is controlled by the player who has the most models within range as normal – in this case, however, your Warlord counts as 10 models.

RELIC

If your army is led by a QUESTOR TRAITORIS Warlord, then you may give the following Relic to a QUESTOR TRAITORIS CHARACTER in your army.

THE TRAITOR'S MARK

The fell deeds and blood-stained heraldry of this traitor Knight are recounted across the galaxy, and all know that to confront it is to face a painful death.

Enemy units must subtract 1 from their Leadership characteristic whilst they are within 12" of the bearer. Whilst they are within 6" of the bearer, subtract 2 from their Leadership characteristic instead.

STRATAGEMS

If your army is Battle-forged and includes any QUESTOR TRAITORIS Detachments, you have access to the following Stratagems:

ROTATE ION SHIELDS

1CP/3CP

Questor Traitoris Stratagem

The directional power of an ion shield can be rotated so that its strongest part is facing the enemy, the better to deflect incoming shots.

Use this Stratagem when an enemy unit targets a QUESTOR TRAITORIS VEHICLE unit from your army that has an invulnerable save (this Stratagem costs 3 CPs if the targeted unit is a RENEGADE DOMINUS KNIGHT, otherwise it costs 1 CP). Until the end of the phase, that vehicle's invulnerable save is improved by 1 (to a maximum of 3+).

TRAIL OF DESTRUCTION

2CP

Questor Traitoris Stratagem

When Renegade Knights march to war, they leave only broken bodies and twisted wreckage in their wake.

Use this Stratagem when you choose a QUESTOR TRAITORIS unit from your army to make attacks with in the Shooting or Fight phase. Until the end of the phase, you can re-roll all failed hit rolls for this unit.

THE EIGHT

The Eight are the greatest champions of the Farsight Enclaves, led by none other than Commander Farsight himself. This section details who these legendary warriors are, and provides you with rules for using them in your games of Warhammer 40,000.

The Eight take to the battlefield as one, a band of fearless warriors piloting some of the most powerful battlesuits the T'au have ever created. Dynamic and deadly, the Eight act as Farsight's foremost warriors and advisors alike. They fight in perfect concert with a skill that only decades as comrades in arms can forge.

When Commander Farsight goes to war, he does so in swift, dynamic fashion. He is the master of the Mont'ka, the art of identifying a target of opportunity and striking it with maximum force. Farsight leads each assault in person, typically deploying from an overhead Manta Missile Destroyer. Using his jump jets, Farsight descends to his carefully selected targets – for it is vital that the sudden shock and ferocity of the attack put the enemy in immediate peril. Firing his plasma rifle and crushing enemies beneath the feet of his battlesuit, Commander Farsight lands in a flurry of violence. He swings wide arcs with his sword, the Dawn Blade, an energy-wreathed weapon so potent that it severs ferrocrete as easily as if slicing through water. Before the last of his targets have fallen, Farsight is already in motion, whirling, spinning and chopping until all foes within reach are dead. Activating his jump jets, he leaps into the air, plasma rifle spitting bursts of blue energy that never miss their mark.

Not far behind Commander Farsight come the rest of the Eight, each a whirlwind of devastation, dealing death in their own unique fashion. Yet the Eight fight flawlessly as a team despite their individual modes of battle, each of their number complementing the style and weaponry of the others. Though their choice of armaments and support systems may have changed over time, each warrior has a speciality and way of war that persists and is intimately understood by the others in the team.

Sub-Commander Torchstar sends out sheets of fire even before her battlesuit touches the ground, incinerating those who stand in the Eight's path. Brightsword's twin fusion guns melt away the metal hulls of battle tanks as if made of candle wax. Bravestorm's plasma rifle punches his selected targets off their feet while he closes on a suitable victim for his formidable Onager Gauntlet. Further from the front, Shas'vre Ob'lotai sends forth steady barrages from his high-yield missile pod, his AI enabling him to simultaneously blast multiple targets across the battlefield.

Such long-range tactics are not for Arra'kon, whose battlesuit is bedecked with anti-infantry weapons. With each bounding leap, Arra'kon leaves behind another heap of bodies, the dead falling so thick before his onslaught that they often obscure the ground. Of all the Eight, O'Vesa cuts perhaps the largest swathe of death, his towering XV104 Riptide Battlesuit unleashing prodigious blasts of super-charged energy from its ion accelerator. Shas'o Sha'vastos relays the enemy's movements between delivering volleys from his plasma rifles, allowing the Eight to maintain the relentless pace of their Mont'ka assault and providing the fullest opportunity to bring about the total destruction of their foe.

Despite their rebel status, the Eight are an inspirational embodiment of the T'au warrior spirit, for whom no foe is too great, and no fight so desperate that victory cannot be seized. They are as devoted as any to the supremacy of the T'au race, and it is this conviction that carries Farsight's elite to victory over every foe that stands against them.

'Faith is a powerful force indeed, it is true. We have our own faith – not in one of our number raised to godhood, but in a mutual destiny that cannot be denied.'

- Commander Farsight

HEROES OF THE ENCLAVES

The greatest living legends of the Farsight Enclaves are the Eight. Led by O'Shovah himself, the Eight are warriors beyond compare, the greatest of battlesuit pilots and true masters of the art of war. Farsight could not ask for a more loyal bodyguard.

COMMANDER FARSIGHT

The renegade Fire caste Commander is Shas'o Vior'la Shovah Kais Mont'yr, often shortened to O'Shovah, and even better known as Commander Farsight. Over his unnaturally long lifespan, Farsight has been known by many other names as well, for he was the most exalted of all the protégés of the legendary Commander Puretide. He was also the 'Hero of Vior'la' and 'The Bane of Greenskins' and after he left the Empire, he became known as the 'Great Traitor' or 'He who Renounced the Greater Good'. To the T'au of the Farsight Enclaves, he is their one true leader, a warrior who will take his people to their great destiny.

COMMANDER BRAVESTORM

Commander Bravestorm was entombed in life-support systems after sustaining critical injuries during the battle at Blackthunder Mesa on Dal'yth. Since that fateful day, the scorched and twisted T'au has been confined to a battlesuit, although his core support cocoon has been reinstalled into an XV8-02 Crisis Iridium mantle. Despite his hardships, Bravestorm has lost neither his fervour for the Greater Good, nor his lightning-quick mind. He fights with a battle prowess and bravado that few can equal, for he has passed beyond fear and courted death itself.

COMMANDER BRIGHTSWORD

Few deliver a death blow with such deadly efficiency as Commander Brightsword. With his pair of fusion blasters, Brightsword leads his Rapid Insertion Force from the front, and his war exploits have proven more than worthy. Many famous warriors have previously borne the same name, and the current Brightsword is mindful of the heritage that accompanies the honoured title. In battle, he always chooses the most powerful enemy target to annihilate first, and thus far, none have escaped the blades of energy that form his fusion blades. He has destroyed the most hulking of war engines and monsters, and his aggressive attack style has been modelled upon the tactics of O'Shovah himself.

SHAS'O SHA'VASTOS

Commander Sha'vastos was the first Fire caste warrior to receive a Puretide neurochip. Something went amiss, however, and the prototype chip suffered rapid degeneration. Rather than allow the loyal warrior to suffer a lobotomy, Farsight had him spirited away and placed in stasis until some cure could be discovered. Many decades later, O'Vesa was able to recalibrate the neurochip, and Shas'o Sha'vastos was reawakened. A tactical genius, Commander Sha'vastos leads his cadres to victory after victory, for he always seems to know the enemy's battle plans even before setting foot on the battlefield.

SHAS'O ARRA'KON

Equipped with an XV85 Enforcer battlesuit, and mounting an extensive suite of anti-infantry weapons, Commander Arra'kon can leave even the largest formations of enemy troops in ruins in an instant. Willingly leaving the larger targets to Commander Brightsword, Arra'kon instead seeks out masses of enemy foot soldiers. An analytical warrior, Arra'kon encourages the Eight to review and critique all of their past battles on holo-vid – for it is his constant goal to further hone his battle arts.

BROADSIDE SHAS'VRE OB'LOTAI 9-0

Although it is not known outside of the Eight and their Earth caste attendants, the Broadside battlesuit Ob'lotai 9-0 is not piloted by flesh and blood. Instead, the Broadside is controlled by a late-generation mnemonic AI engram of the original Shas'vre Ob'lotai. Long ago, at the Fire caste training domes, it was Shas'vre Ob'lotai who first taught the piloting arts to the young warrior who would one day become Commander Farsight. Using a velocity tracker and advanced scanfeeds, Ob'lotai 9-0 is a master at supplying the rest of the Eight with deadly accurate supporting fire.

SUB-COMMANDER TORCHSTAR

A defector from the T'au Empire, Sub-Commander Torchstar is the youngest and most impetuous of the Eight. Bearing twin flamers, the Vior'lan borders on reckless as she bounds headlong into battle.

O'VESA

The final member of the Eight is O'Vesa. He is, in fact, not a shas'vre at all, being an old Earth caste colleague of Farsight, kept alive by microdrones of his own invention. Given that Commander Farsight is a diehard Fire caste traditionalist, it speaks to the bond between the two that he allows a member of any other caste the great honour of piloting a battlesuit, much less a powerful XV104 Riptide. Many AI suites that O'Vesa invented are integrated into the Riptide's piloting array – his technological genius offering him great aid in targeting and compensating for his lack of a lifetime's worth of intense training and experience in battle.

USING THE EIGHT IN BATTLE

This section details the rules that allow you to field the Eight in your battles, including the datasheet for these mighty heroes and the rules required to include them in your army. You will also find a summary of the weapons they wield here, along with abilities that are common to several of their number.

INCLUDING THE EIGHT IN YOUR ARMY

The datasheet for the Eight can be found on pages 116-117. If your army is Battle-forged, you can only include this datasheet in a Super-heavy Auxiliary Detachment; if you do the Command Benefits of that Detachment are changed to '-3 Command Points', you cannot give any model in your army a Signature System. This is to take account of the Signature Systems that are always equipped on various members of the Eight (effectively, the Emergency Dispensation Stratagem has automatically been used to give the Eight the various Signature Systems they require).

Matched Play Rules

The Matched Play Rule presented in *Codex: T'au Empire* that restricts COMMANDERS to one per Detachment does not apply to the Eight's Detachment.

Commander Farsight

If you include the Eight in your army then you cannot also include the Commander Farsight datasheet from *Codex: T'au Empire*. Furthermore, if you include the Eight in your army, Commander Farsight must be your army's Warlord, and he has the following Warlord Trait:

Hero of the Enclaves: Your Warlord can perform a Heroic Intervention if they are within 6" of any enemy units after the enemy has completed all their charge moves. Your Warlord can move up to 6" when performing a Heroic Intervention, so long as they end the move closer to the nearest enemy model. In addition, if your Warlord charged, was charged or performed a Heroic Intervention, then until the end of the turn you can re-roll failed hit rolls made for them.

Points Value

If you are playing a matched play game, or a game that uses a points limit, then the points value for the Eight can be found below. Simply add this to the cost of your other models and the wargear they are equipped with to determine your army's total points value.

THE EIGHT		
UNIT	MODELS PER UNIT	POINTS PER UNIT (Including wargear)
The Eight	8 Characters 14 Drones	1120

ABILITIES

The following abilities apply to several of the Eight:

Master of War

Once per battle, at the beginning of your turn, a single COMMANDER from your army can declare either Kauyon or Mont'ka:

Kauyon: Until the end of the turn, you can re-roll failed hit rolls for friendly FARSIGHT ENCLAVES units within 6" of the COMMANDER, but these units cannot move for any reason.

Mont'ka: Friendly FARSIGHT ENCLAVES units within 6" of the COMMANDER can both Advance and shoot as if they hadn't moved this turn.

Unless stated otherwise, you can only use the Master of War ability once per battle, irrespective of how many models in your army have this ability.

Sept Tenet

If your army is Battle-forged, all models in the Eight's Detachment gain the following Sept Tenet:

Devastating Counter-strike: Re-roll wound rolls of 1 for models with this tenet for shooting attacks against enemy units that are within 6" of the firing model.

Enclave Drone Support

When a CHARACTER from the Eight is set up on the battlefield, any accompanying Drones are set up in unit coherency with it. From that point onwards, the Drones are treated as a separate unit with the HQ Battlefield Role, and are considered to have a Power Rating of 0.

Saviour Protocols

If a FARSIGHT ENCLAVES INFANTRY or FARSIGHT ENCLAVES BATTLESUIT unit within 3" of a friendly FARSIGHT ENCLAVES DRONES unit is wounded by an enemy attack, roll a D6. On a 2+ you can allocate that wound to the Drones unit instead of the target. If you do, that Drones unit suffers 1 mortal wound instead of the normal damage.

WEAPONS

WEAPON	RANGE	TYPE	S	AP	D	ABILITIES
Airbursting fragmentation projector	18"	Assault D6	4	0	1	This weapon can target units that are not visible to the bearer.
Cyclic ion blaster	When attacking with this weapon, choose one of the profiles below.					
- Standard	18"	Assault 3	7	-1	1	-
- Overcharge	18"	Assault 3	8	-1	D3	If you roll one of more hit rolls of 1, the bearer's unit suffers 1 mortal wound after all of this weapon's shots have been resolved.
Flamer	8"	Assault D6	4	0	1	This weapon automatically hits its target.
Fusion Blades (ranged)	18"	Assault 2	8	-4	D6	If the target is within half range of this weapon, roll two dice when inflicting damage with it and discard the lowest result.
Fusion blaster	18"	Assault 1	8	-4	D6	If the target is within half range of this weapon, roll two dice when inflicting damage with it and discard the lowest result.
High-intensity plasma rifle	30"	Rapid Fire 1	6	-4	2	-
High-yield missile pod	36"	Heavy 4	7	-1	D3	-
Ion accelerator	When attacking with this weapon, choose one of the profiles below.					
- Standard	72"	Heavy D6	8	-3	D3	-
- Overcharge	72"	Heavy D6	9	-3	3	If you roll one or more hit rolls of 1, the bearer suffers 1 mortal wound after all of this weapon's shots have been resolved.
Markerlight	36"	Heavy 1	-	-	-	Markerlights (see below)
Missile pod	36"	Assault 2	7	-1	D3	-
Plasma rifle	24"	Rapid Fire 1	6	-3	1	-
Pulse carbine	18"	Assault 2	5	0	1	-
Seeker missile	72"	Heavy 1	8	-2	D6	Each seeker missile can only be used once per battle. This weapon only hits on a roll of 6, regardless of the firing model's Ballistic Skill or any modifiers.
Smart missile system	30"	Heavy 4	5	0	1	This weapon can target units that are not visible to the bearer. Units attacked by this weapon do not gain any bonus to their saving throws for cover.
Dawn Blade	Melee	Melee	+3	-4	D3	-
Fusion Blades (melee)	Melee	Melee	8	-4	D6	Each time the bearer fights, it can make two (and only two) attacks with this weapon.
Onager Gauntlet	Melee	Melee	10	-4	D6	Each time the bearer fights, it can make one (and only one) attack with this weapon.

SUPPORT SYSTEMS

SYSTEM	EFFECT
Advanced targeting system	A model equipped with an advanced targeting system increases the AP characteristic of all of its weapons by 1 (e.g. an AP of 0 becomes -1, an AP of -1 becomes -2).
Counterfire defence system	A model equipped with a counterfire defence system re-rolls failed hit rolls when firing Overwatch.
Drone controller	**FARSIGHT ENCLAVES DRONE** units within 6" of any friendly models equipped with a drone controller add one to their hit rolls.
Early warning override	If any enemy units are set up within 12" of a model from your army equipped with an early warning override as the result of an ability that allows them to arrive mid-battle (i.e. teleporting to the battlefield), then at the end of that phase the model may immediately shoot at one of those units as if it were your Shooting phase, but you must subtract 1 from hit rolls when resolving these shots.
Shield generator	A model with a shield generator has a 4+ invulnerable save. You cannot take this support system on a Riptide battlesuit.
Target lock	A model with a target lock does not suffer the penalty for moving and firing Heavy weapons, or for Advancing and firing Assault weapons. The model can also Advance and fire Rapid Fire weapons, but subtracts 1 from its hit rolls when doing so.
Velocity tracker	Add 1 to hit rolls for a model with a velocity tracker when it shoots at a unit that can **FLY**.

MARKERLIGHTS

If a model (other than a VEHICLE) fires a markerlight, it cannot fire any other weapons in that phase. When a unit is hit by a markerlight, place a counter next to it for the remainder of the phase. The table to the right describes the benefits T'AU EMPIRE models receive when shooting at a unit that has markerlight counters. All benefits are cumulative.

MARKERLIGHT TABLE

MARKERLIGHTS	BENEFIT
1	You can re-roll hit rolls of 1 for T'AU EMPIRE models attacking this unit.
2	Destroyer and seeker missiles fired at this unit use the firing model's Ballistic Skill (and any modifiers) rather than only hitting on a 6.
3	The target unit does not gain any bonus to its saving throws for being in cover.
4	T'AU EMPIRE models attacking this unit do not suffer the penalty for moving and firing Heavy weapons or Advancing and firing Assault weapons.
5 or more	Add 1 to hit rolls for T'AU EMPIRE models attacking this unit.

THE EIGHT

DAMAGE

Some of O'Vesa's characteristics change as he suffers damage, as shown below:

REMAINING W	M	BS	A
7-14+	12"	4+	4
4-6	8"	5+	3
1-3	4"	5+	2

NAME	M	WS	BS	S	T	W	A	Ld	Sv
Commander Farsight	8"	2+	2+	5	5	6	4	9	3+
Commander Brightsword	8"	3+	2+	5	5	5	4	9	3+
Commander Bravestorm	8"	3+	2+	5	5	5	4	9	2+
Shas'o Sha'vastos	8"	3+	2+	5	5	5	4	9	3+
Shas'o Arra'kon	8"	3+	2+	5	5	6	4	9	3+
Sub-Commander Torchstar	8"	3+	2+	5	5	5	4	9	3+
Broadside Shas'vre Ob'lotai 9-0	5"	5+	4+	5	5	6	3	8	2+
O'Vesa	*	6+	*	6	7	14	*	8	2+
MV1 Gun Drone	8"	5+	5+	3	4	1	1	6	4+
MV4 Shield Drone	8"	5+	5+	3	4	1	1	6	4+
MV7 Marker Drone	8"	5+	5+	3	4	1	1	6	4+
MV8 Missile Drone	8"	5+	5+	3	4	1	1	6	4+
MV84 Shielded Missile Drone	12"	5+	5+	4	4	1	1	6	4+

Only one of this unit can be included in your army. This unit contains the following eight characters and their accompanying Drones:
- Commander Farsight, equipped with a high-intensity plasma rifle, the Dawn Blade and a shield generator.
- Commander Brightsword, equipped with the Fusion Blades, a target lock and a counterfire defence system. Brightsword is accompanied by 2 MV4 Shield Drones.
- Commander Bravestorm, equipped with a plasma rifle, flamer, Onager Gauntlet, shield generator and advanced targeting system. Bravestorm is also equipped with XV8-02 Iridium armour – his profile already takes this into account. Bravestorm is accompanied by 2 MV1 Gun Drones, each of which is equipped with two pulse carbines.
- Shas'o Sha'vastos, equipped a plasma rifle, flamer, shield generator and drone controller. Sha'vastos is accompanied by 2 MV1 Gun Drones, each of which is equipped with two pulse carbines.
- Shas'o Arra'kon, equipped with an airbursting fragmentation projector, cyclic ion blaster, plasma rifle and counterfire defence system. Arra'kon is accompanied by 2 MV1 Gun Drones, each of which is equipped with two pulse carbines.
- Sub-Commander Torchstar, equipped with two flamers, an advanced targeting system and a drone controller. Torchstar is accompanied by 2 MV7 Marker Drones, each of which is equipped with a markerlight.
- Broadside Shas'vre Ob'lotai 9-0, equipped with two high-yield missile pods, two smart missile systems, a seeker missile and a velocity tracker. Ob'lotai 9-0 is accompanied by 2 MV8 Missile Drones, each of which is equipped with a missile pod.
- O'Vesa, equipped with an ion accelerator, two fusion blasters, a target lock and an early warning override. O'Vesa is accompanied by 2 MV84 Shielded Missile Drones, each of which is equipped with a missile pod.

ABILITIES

For the Greater Good: When an enemy unit declares a charge, a unit with this ability that is within 6" of one of the charging unit's targets may fire Overwatch as if they were also targeted. A unit that does so cannot fire Overwatch again in this turn.

The Eight: During deployment, all models in this unit are deployed at the same time, but they do not need to be placed in unit coherency (see the Enclave Drone Support ability (pg 114) for details on how to place a model's accompanying Drones). Each **CHARACTER** is treated as a separate unit, and each is considered to have a Power Rating of 7. With the exception of O'Vesa, if a **CHARACTER** in this unit can **FLY**, it, and any of its accompanying Drones, can be set up in a Manta hold instead of being placed on the battlefield. At the end of any of your Movement phases any character that does so can use a Manta strike to enter the fray – set them and their accompanying Drones up anywhere on the battlefield that is more than 9" from any enemy models.

ABILITIES (FARSIGHT)	**Master of War** (pg 114)
	Genius of Mont'ka: Once per battle, Commander Farsight can declare Mont'ka even if Kauyon or Mont'ka has already been declared. Mont'ka and Kauyon cannot both be declared in the same turn.
	Way of the Short Blade: You can re-roll hit rolls of 1 for friendly **Farsight Enclaves** units within 6" of Commander Farsight in the Fight phase (or any phase if the target is an **Ork** unit).
ABILITIES (BRIGHTSWORD)	**Master of War** (pg 114)
	Warscaper Drones: If a charge is declared for an enemy unit whilst it is within 12" of either of Brightsword's MV4 Shield Drones, subtract 2 from the roll.
ABILITIES (BRAVESTORM)	**Master of War** (pg 114)
	Advanced Support Cocoon: Roll a D6 each time Bravestorm loses a wound. On a 6, that wound is not lost.
ABILITIES (SHA'VASTOS)	**Master of War** (pg 114)
	Puretide Engram Neurochip: Once per battle, you can re-roll a single hit roll, wound roll or damage roll made for Sha'vastos, or a friendly **Farsight Enclaves** unit within 6" of Sha'vastos. In addition, if your army is Battle-forged and Sha'vastos is on the battlefield, roll a D6 each time you or your opponent use a Stratagem; on a 6 you gain a Command Point.
ABILITIES (ARRA'KON)	**Master of War** (pg 114)
	Repulsor Impact Field: Roll a D6 each time an enemy unit ends a charge move within 1" of Arra'kon; on a 2+ that units suffers 1 mortal wound.
ABILITIES (TORCHSTAR)	**Master of War** (pg 114)
	Neuroweb System Jammer: Enemy units that are set up on the battlefield as reinforcements cannot be set up within 12" of Torchstar. In addition, subtract 1 from hit rolls for ranged weapons that target Torchstar.
ABILITIES (OB'LOTAI 9-0)	**No Longer Flesh and Blood:** Reduce all damage inflicted on Ob'lotai 9-0 by 1 (to a minimum of 1).
	Advanced Scan Feeds: This model does not suffer the penalty to its hit rolls for moving and firing Heavy weapons.
ABILITIES (O'VESA)	**Riptide Shield Generator:** O'Vesa has a 5+ invulnerable save.
	Earth Caste Pilot Array: Re-roll hit rolls of 1 for attacks made with O'Vesa's ranged weapons. In addition, roll a D6 each time O'Vesa uses his Nova Reactor ability. On a 4+, he does not suffer the mortal wound.
	Nova Reactor: In your Movement phase you can choose to use O'Vesa's Nova Reactor. If you do, O'Vesa suffers 1 mortal wound. Choose one of the following effects to last until the beginning of your next turn: • **Nova Shield:** O'Vesa has a 3+ invulnerable save. • **Boost:** O'Vesa can move 2D6" in your charge phase (even if he doesn't declare a charge). • **Nova-charge:** Change O'Vesa's ion accelerator Type (both standard and overcharge) to Heavy 6.
ABILITIES (DRONES)	**Saviour Protocols, Enclave Drone Support** (pg 114)
	Shield Generator: MV4 Shield Drones and MV84 Shielded Missile Drones have a 4+ invulnerable save. In addition, roll a D6 each time an MV4 Shield Drone or MV84 Shielded Missile Drone loses a wound; on a 5+ it does not lose a wound.
FACTION KEYWORDS	T'au Empire, Farsight Enclaves
KEYWORDS (FARSIGHT)	Battlesuit, Character, Jet Pack, Fly, Commander, Farsight
KEYWORDS (BRIGHTSWORD)	Battlesuit, Character, XV8 Crisis, Jet Pack, Fly, Commander, Brightsword
KEYWORDS (BRAVESTORM)	Battlesuit, Character, XV8 Crisis, Jet Pack, Fly, Commander, Bravestorm
KEYWORDS (SHA'VASTOS)	Battlesuit, Character, XV8 Crisis, Jet Pack, Fly, Commander, Shas'o Sha'vastos
KEYWORDS (ARRA'KON)	Battlesuit, Character, XV85 Enforcer, Jet Pack, Fly, Commander, Shas'o Arra'kon
KEYWORDS (TORCHSTAR)	Battlesuit, Character, XV8 Crisis, Jet Pack, Fly, Commander, Torchstar
KEYWORDS (OB'LOTAI 9-0)	Battlesuit, Character, XV88 Broadside Battlesuit, Shas'vre Ob'lotai 9-0
KEYWORDS (O'VESA)	Battlesuit, Character, Monster, Jet Pack, Fly, XV104 Riptide Battlesuit, O'Vesa
KEYWORDS (GUN, SHIELD AND MARKER DRONES)	Drone, Fly, Tactical Drones
KEYWORDS (MISSILE DRONES)	Drone, Fly, MV8 Missile Drones
KEYWORDS (SHIELDED MISSILE DRONES)	Drone, Fly, MV84 Shielded Missile Drones

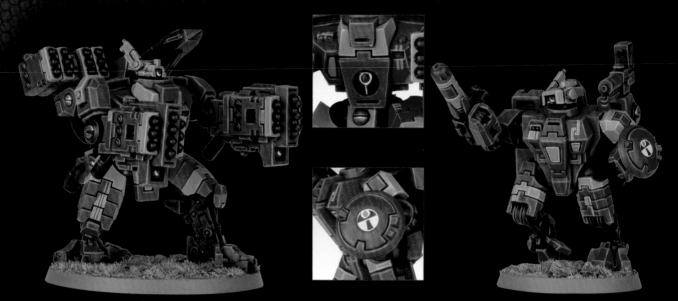

Ob'lotai 9-0

Shas'o Sha'vastos

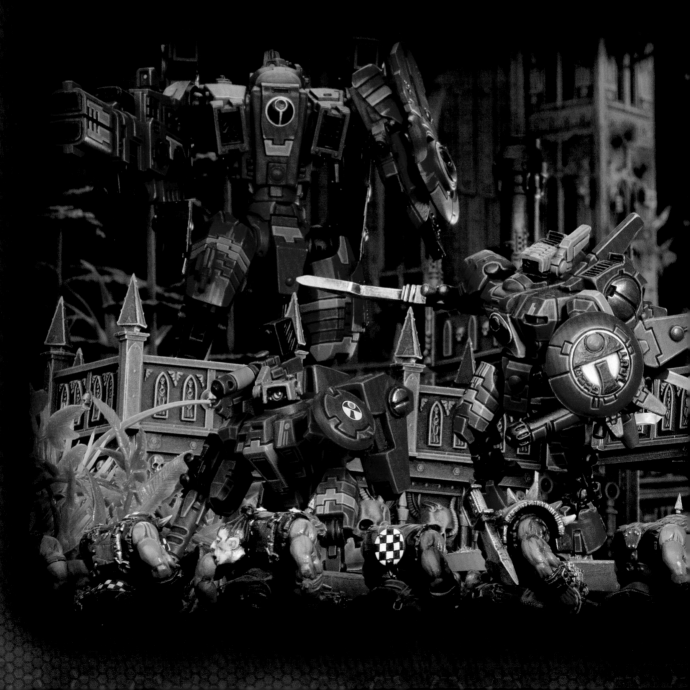

Commander Brightsword

Sub-Commander Torchstar

BATTLE-FORGED ARMIES

When picking a Battle-forged army for matched play, you will need to record the details of your army on a piece of paper (your Army Roster). Here we show one example of how you can do this, using several Detachment Rosters – at least one for each Detachment in your army – and one main Army Roster as a summary. Over the page are blank rosters you can photocopy.

DETACHMENT ROSTERS

Each Detachment Roster details all the units a Detachment includes. Each unit section has room for you to write down the name and type of the unit, its Battlefield Role, the number of models it contains, and the wargear each model is equipped with. Details of how many models make up each unit and what weapons and upgrades each can take can be found on that unit's datasheet.

The points values of each unit's models and each individual weapon is then calculated by referencing the points values in the appropriate codex, and then added together to give a points cost for the unit. The points value of the entire Detachment is simply the sum of the points values of its units. This can be noted down alongside other useful information, such as the number of Command Points (if any) the Detachment gives you (see the *Warhammer 40,000* rulebook for more on Command Points).

Unit Champions

Many units are led by a champion of some kind such as a Sergeant. Unit champions often have better characteristics and weapon options. Unless noted otherwise, unit champions have the same points cost as the other models in their unit.

Understrength Units

Sometimes you may find that you do not have enough models to field a minimum-sized unit; if this is the case, you can still include one unit of that type in your army, with as many models as you have available. An understrength unit still takes up the appropriate slot in a Detachment. In matched play games, you can only include understrength units in Auxiliary Support Detachments, but you only pay the points for the models you actually have (and any wargear they are equipped with).

ARMY ROSTER

Once you have filled in all of your Detachment Rosters, you can then fill out the main Army Roster. The name and points value of each Detachment is noted down here for reference. The total points value of your army is the sum of all the Detachment points values in your army plus any reinforcement points you have chosen to put aside (see below). The points value of your army should not exceed the points limit you are using for the battle.

There are lots of other useful things to write down on your main Army Roster, such as who the army's Warlord is (this should be done at the start of the battle) and the number of Command Points available to your army. Remember that all Battle-forged armies start with 3 Command Points, but certain Detachments, and occasionally certain models, can change this total.

Reinforcement Points

Sometimes an ability will allow you to add units to your army, or replace units that have been destroyed. You must set aside some of your points in order to use these units and record them on your army roster; these are your reinforcement points. Each time a unit is added to an army during battle, subtract the number of points the unit would cost from your pool of reinforcement points.

ARMY ROSTER

PLAYER NAME:	Alex Smith	ARMY FACTION:	Adeptus Astartes
ARMY NAME:	Strike Force Calgar	WARLORD:	Marneus Calgar

DETACHMENT NAME	TYPE	CPS	POINTS
Lords of Macragge	Patrol	0+2	626
4th Battle Demi-company	Battalion	5	931
Ultima Task Force	Vanguard	1	443

WARLORD TRAIT

FILL IN AT SET-UP:

Total Command Points:	11
Reinforcement Points:	0
TOTAL POINTS:	2000

DETACHMENT ROSTER

NAME:	Lords of Macragge	TYPE:	Patrol

UNIT

UNIT TITLE:	BATTLEFIELD ROLE:	NO. OF MODELS:	POINTS (MODELS):
Marneus Calgar	HQ	1	200

WARGEAR:	POINTS (WARGEAR):
Gauntlets of Ultramar and relic blade (all wargear points included in the model's points)	N/A

	TOTAL POINTS (UNIT):	200

UNIT

UNIT TITLE:	BATTLEFIELD ROLE:	NO. OF MODELS:	POINTS (MODELS):
Tactical Squad	Troops	10	130

WARGEAR:	POINTS (WARGEAR):
Chainsword (0), missile launcher (20), plasma gun (11), 7 x boltguns (0), 10 x bolt pistols (0), 10 x frag and krak grenades (0)	31

	TOTAL POINTS (UNIT):	161

UNIT

UNIT TITLE:	BATTLEFIELD ROLE:	NO. OF MODELS:	POINTS (MODELS):
Devastator Squad	Heavy Support	5	65

WARGEAR:	POINTS (WARGEAR):
Combi-plasma (11), 2 x heavy bolters (20), 2 x lascannon (50), 5 x bolt pistols (0), 5 x frag and krak grenades (0), Armorium Cherub (5)	86

	TOTAL POINTS (UNIT):	151

UNIT

UNIT TITLE:	BATTLEFIELD ROLE:	NO. OF MODELS:	POINTS (MODELS):
Dreadnought	Elites	1	60

WARGEAR:	POINTS (WARGEAR):
Assault cannon (22), Dreadnought combat weapon (30), storm bolter (2)	54

	TOTAL POINTS (UNIT):	114

Total Points (Detachment):	626	Command Points:	0+2

NOTES: Detachment has Defenders of Humanity ability.
All units are Ultramarines and so have Codex Discipline Chapter Tactic.
Gain 2 Command Points if Marneus Calgar is the army's Warlord.

ARMY ROSTER

PLAYER NAME:	ARMY FACTION:
ARMY NAME:	WARLORD:

DETACHMENT NAME	TYPE	CPS	POINTS

WARLORD TRAIT

FILL IN AT SET-UP:

Total Command Points:	
Reinforcement Points:	
TOTAL POINTS:	

DETACHMENT ROSTER

NAME: | TYPE:

UNIT

UNIT TITLE:	BATTLEFIELD ROLE:	NO. OF MODELS:	POINTS (MODELS):
Wargear:			POINTS (WARGEAR):
		TOTAL POINTS (UNIT):	

UNIT

UNIT TITLE:	BATTLEFIELD ROLE:	NO. OF MODELS:	POINTS (MODELS):
Wargear:			POINTS (WARGEAR):
		TOTAL POINTS (UNIT):	

UNIT

UNIT TITLE:	BATTLEFIELD ROLE:	NO. OF MODELS:	POINTS (MODELS):
Wargear:			POINTS (WARGEAR):
		TOTAL POINTS (UNIT):	

UNIT

UNIT TITLE:	BATTLEFIELD ROLE:	NO. OF MODELS:	POINTS (MODELS):
Wargear:			POINTS (WARGEAR):
		TOTAL POINTS (UNIT):	

Total Points (Detachment): | Command Points:

NOTES:

UPDATED POINTS VALUES: DECEMBER 2018

Whenever we publish a new edition of *Chapter Approved*, or a new codex, we review, update and fine-tune the points values of all our datasheets. This means that the points values for the units and items of wargear that appear in one of the tables below replace those that appear in books with an earlier publication date, and also take precedence over points-value lists that have no publication date at all. If a unit or item of wargear does not appear in any of the tables below, continue to use the points values for it that are listed within the most recently published book for that Faction – for the Adepta Sororitas, see page 93; for Renegade Knights, see page 105.

Note that sometimes a weapon can appear in several different books, each with different points costs (for example, power fists appear in both *Codex: Space Marines* and *Codex: Astra Militarum*). If such an item of wargear appears in one of the tables below, only apply the change to the appropriate Faction. Note also that some points match the values found in the corresponding codex: some of these are provided to support the updated datasheets found later in this book (pg 140-143), while the others update points values that appeared in the last edition of *Chapter Approved*.

ADEPTUS CUSTODES UNITS

UNIT	MODELS PER UNIT	POINTS PER MODEL (Does not include wargear)
Allarus Custodians	3-10	65
Custodian Wardens	3-10	43
Shield-Captain	1	100
Shield-Captain in Allarus Terminator Armour	1	110
Venerable Contemptor Dreadnought	1	90
Venerable Land Raider	1	217

UNIT	MODELS PER UNIT	POINTS PER MODEL (Including wargear)
Captain-General Trajann Valoris	1	185

ADEPTUS CUSTODES WARGEAR

WARGEAR	POINTS PER ITEM
Salvo launcher	15
Sentinel blade	7
Storm shield (CHARACTERS)	10

ADEPTUS MECHANICUS UNITS

UNIT	MODELS PER UNIT	POINTS PER MODEL (Does not include wargear)
Fulgurite Electro-Priests	5-20	16
Ironstrider Ballistarii	1-6	40
Kataphron Breachers	3-12	20
Kataphron Destroyers	3-12	15
Knight Crusader	1	285
Knight Errant	1	285
Knight Gallant	1	285
Knight Paladin	1	285
Knight Warden	1	285
Onager Dunecrawler	1	70
Servitors	4	5
Sicarian Infiltrators	5-10	12
Sicarian Ruststalkers	5-10	10
Skitarii Rangers	5-10	7
Skitarii Vanguard	5-10	8
Tech-Priest Dominus	1	80
Tech-Priest Enginseer	1	30

ADEPTUS MECHANICUS UNITS

UNIT	MODELS PER UNIT	POINTS PER MODEL (Including wargear)
Belisarius Cawl	1	190

ADEPTUS MECHANICUS WARGEAR

WARGEAR	POINTS PER ITEM
Avenger gatling cannon	75
Cognis flamer	7
Cognis heavy stubber	2
Enhanced data-tether	5
Eradication beamer	30
Eradication ray	10
Heavy arc rifle	6
Heavy flamer	14
Heavy stubber	2
Hydraulic claw	5
Incendine combustor	15
Kastelan fists	25
Meltagun	14
Multi-melta	22
Phosphor blast pistol	3
Phosphor blaster	6
Phosphor serpenta	4
Plasma caliver	11
Plasma cannon	16
Power fist	9
Radium pistol	0
Servo-arm	0
Taser goad	4
Torsion cannon	20
Transonic blades	4
Transuranic arquebus	15
Twin cognis autocannon	20
Twin cognis lascannon	40
Twin Icarus autocannon	20

ASTRA MILITARUM UNITS

UNIT	MODELS PER UNIT	POINTS PER MODEL (Does not include wargear)
Armoured Sentinels	1-3	30
Astropath	1	26
Banehammer	1	370
Banesword	1	370
Chimera	1	60
Commissar	1	15
Conscripts	20-30	4
Deathstrike	1	125
Doomhammer	1	400
Hydras	1-3	85

ASTRA MILITARUM UNITS

UNIT	MODELS PER UNIT	POINTS PER MODEL (Does not include wargear)
Lord Commissar	1	30
Manticore	1	125
Officer of the Fleet	1	20
Ogryn Bodyguard	1	45
Ogryns	3-9	24
Primaris Psyker	1	38
Ratlings	5-10	7
Scout Sentinels	1-3	30
Servitors	4	5
Shadowsword	1	410
Stormlord	1	410
Stormsword	1	370
Tank Commander	1	142
Taurox	1	50
Taurox Prime	1	80
Valkyries	1-3	100
Veterans*	10	5
Wyrdvane Psykers	3-9	7
Wyverns	1-3	95

UNIT	MODELS PER UNIT	POINTS PER MODEL (Including wargear)
Colour Sergeant Kell	1	40
Commissar Yarrick	1	100
Lord Castellan Creed	1	55
Nork Deddog	1	60
Sly Marbo	1	55

* If models in these units form Heavy Weapons Teams, there is no change in the unit's points cost.

ASTRA MILITARUM WARGEAR

WARGEAR	POINTS PER ITEM
Augur array	5
Autocannon	10
Chem cannon	7
Demolisher cannon	20
Eradicator nova cannon	15
Executioner plasma cannon	15
Exterminator autocannon	17
Flamer	6
Force stave	8
Grenade launcher	3
Grenadier gauntlet	5
Heavy flamer	14
Heavy stubber	2
Hellstrike missiles	12
Hot-shot lasgun	0
Hot-shot laspistol	0
Hot-shot volley gun	7
Medi-pack	5
Meltagun (model with a Ballistic Skill of 4+)	10
Meltagun (other models)	14
Missile launcher	15
Multi-laser	5
Multi-melta	15
Multiple rocket pod	8
Plasma cannon	10

ASTRA MILITARUM WARGEAR

WARGEAR	POINTS PER ITEM
Plasma gun (other models)	11
Power fist	8
Servo-arm	0
Storm shield	0
Taurox battle cannon	18
Taurox gatling cannon	20
Taurox missile launcher	30
Tempestus command rod	5
Twin heavy flamer	28
Vanquisher battle cannon	15

BLOOD ANGELS UNITS

UNIT	MODELS PER UNIT	POINTS PER MODEL (Does not include wargear)
Assault Squad with Jump Packs	5-10	15
Attack Bike Squad	1-3	25
Baal Predator	1	90
Bike Squad	3-9	21 (Attack Bike is 25)
Captain in Cataphractii Armour	1	95
Captain in Gravis Armour	1	90
Captain in Terminator Armour	1	95
Cataphractii Terminator Squad	5-10	26
Chaplain in Terminator Armour	1	90
Company Veterans	2-5	14
Contemptor Dreadnought	1	88
Death Company Dreadnought	1	80
Dreadnought	1	60
Drop Pod	1	63
Furioso Dreadnought	1	70
Hunter	1	80
Intercessor Squad	5-10	17
Land Raider	1	200
Land Raider Crusader	1	200
Land Raider Redeemer	1	180
Land Speeders	1-3	50
Librarian Dreadnought	1	110
Librarian in Terminator Armour	1	102
Predator	1	90
Primaris Captain	1	78
Primaris Chaplain	1	77
Redemptor Dreadnought	1	105
Repulsor	1	185
Sanguinary Ancient	1	64
Scout Bike Squad	3-9	21
Servitors	4	5
Sternguard Veteran Squad	5-10	14
Tartaros Terminator Squad	5-10	23
Terminator Assault Squad	5-10	23
Terminator Squad	5-10	23
Vanguard Veteran Squad	5-10	14
Vanguard Veteran Squad with Jump Packs	5-10	17

BLOOD ANGELS UNITS

UNIT	MODELS PER UNIT	POINTS PER MODEL (Including wargear)
Astorath	1	105
Brother Corbulo	1	83
Captain Tycho	1	85
Chief Librarian Mephiston	1	160
Commander Dante	1	175
Lemartes	1	100
The Sanguinor	1	150

BLOOD ANGELS WARGEAR

WARGEAR	POINTS PER ITEM
Astartes grenade launcher	6
Auto bolt rifle	1
Auxiliary grenade launcher	0
Blood talons	35
Bolt pistol	0
Bolt rifle	0
Cerberus launcher	0
Chainfist	11
Chainsword	0
Combi-flamer	8
Combi-grav	13
Combi-melta	15
Combi-plasma	11
Cyclone missile launcher	38
Dreadnought combat weapon	30
Eviscerator	11
Flamer	6
Flamestorm gauntlets	15
Frag cannon	30
Frag grenades	0
Furioso fist (single/pair)	30/40
Grav-gun	12
Grenade harness	0
Heavy flamer	14
Heavy onslaught gatling cannon	30
Heavy plasma cannon	16
Icarus stormcannon	10
Inferno pistol	7
Krak grenades	0
Master-crafted power sword	6
Meltagun	14
Missile launcher	20
Multi-melta	22
Plasma cannon	16
Plasma cutter	5
Plasma gun	11
Plasma pistol	5
Power fist	9
Power sword	4
Reaper autocannon	10
Relic blade	9
Servo-arm	0
Sniper rifle	2
Stalker bolt rifle	0
Storm shield (CHARACTERS)	10
Storm shield (other models)	2

BLOOD ANGELS WARGEAR

WARGEAR	POINTS PER ITEM
Twin heavy plasma cannon	24
Twin lascannon	40
Twin multi-melta	40
Typhoon missile launcher	38
Volkite charger	3
Whirlwind castellan launcher	15
Whirlwind vengeance launcher	20
Wrist-mounted grenade launcher	0

CHAOS BASTION WARGEAR

WARGEAR	POINTS PER ITEM
Heavy bolter	8

CHAOS DAEMONS UNITS

UNIT	MODELS PER UNIT	POINTS PER MODEL (Including weapons)
Be'lakor	1	240
Bloodcrushers	3-12	47
Bloodthirster of Insensate Rage	1	260
Bloodthirster of Unfettered Fury	1	240
The Blue Scribes	1	75
Burning Chariot	1	110
Changecaster	1	65
Daemonettes	10-30	6
Exalted Flamer	1	70
Exalted Seeker Chariot	1	80
Fateskimmer	1	130
Feculent Gnarlmaws	1-3	85
Fiends	1-9	42
Flamers	3-9	25
Flesh Hounds	5-20	15 (Gore Hounds are 24)
Fluxmaster	1	85
Furies	5-20	8
Great Unclean one with:		
- Bilesword and bileblade	1	275
- Bilesword and plague flail	1	285
- Doomsday bell and bileblade	1	295
- Doomsday bell and plague flail	1	305
Hellflayer	1	70
Herald of Slaanesh	1	60
Kairos Fateweaver	1	285
Keeper of Secrets	1	165
Lord of Change	1	270
Lord of Change with baleful sword	1	275
The Masque of Slaanesh	1	65
Plague Drones	3-9	40
Rotigus	1	285
Screamers	3-9	28
Seeker Chariot	1	50
Seekers	5-20	15
Skarbrand	1	330
Skull Cannon	1	90
Skullmaster	1	90

CHAOS DAEMONS UNITS

UNIT	MODELS PER UNIT	POINTS PER MODEL (Including weapons)
Soul Grinder	1	180
Spoilpox Scrivener	1	95
Wrath of Khorne Bloodthirster	1	240

CHAOS DAEMONS WARGEAR

WARGEAR	POINTS PER ITEM
Chanting Horrors (for Burning Chariot and Fateskimmer)	5
Daemonic Icon	15
Instrument of Chaos	10

CHAOS SPACE MARINES UNITS

UNIT	MODELS PER UNIT	POINTS PER MODEL (Does not include wargear)
Chaos Bikers	3-9	21
Chaos Cultists	10-40	5
Chaos Land Raider	1	200
Chaos Lord in Terminator Armour	1	95
Chaos Spawn	1-5	25
Chaos Terminators	5-10	28
Chaos Vindicator	1	125
Chosen	5-10	14
Defiler	1	120
Forgefiend	1	100
Helbrute	1	60
Heldrake	1	120
Khorne Lord of Skulls	1	380
Maulerfiend	1	120
Mutilators	3	35
Plague Marines	5-20	16
Possessed	5-20	20
Raptors	5-15	15
Rubric Marines	5-20	16
Sorcerer in Terminator Armour	1	102
Sorcerer with Jump Pack	1	112
Warp Talons	5-10	12
Warpsmith	1	35

UNIT	MODELS PER UNIT	POINTS PER MODEL (Including weapons)
Daemonettes	10-30	6
Horrors	10-30	
- Blue Horrors		5
- Pairs of Brimstone Horrors		3
- Pink Horrors		7

UNIT	MODELS PER UNIT	POINTS PER MODEL (Including wargear)
Cypher	1	80
Fabius Bile	1	90
Huron Blackheart	1	105
Khârn the Betrayer	1	120
Lucius the Eternal	1	85

CHAOS SPACE MARINES WARGEAR

WARGEAR	POINTS PER ITEM
Autocannon	10
Blight launcher	10
Bubotic axe	5
Chainfist	11
Combi-flamer	8
Combi-melta	15
Combi-plasma	11
Daemonic Icon	15
Doom siren	8
Ectoplasma cannon	20
Flamer	6
Force axe	10
Force stave	8
Force sword	8
Hades autocannon	20
Havoc launcher	6
Heavy flamer	14
Heavy stubber	2
Helbrute fist (single/pair)	30/40
Helbrute hammer	30
Helbrute plasma cannon	16
Icon of Flame	5
Icon of Vengeance	5
Inferno bolt pistol	0
Instrument of Chaos	10
Meltagun	14
Missile launcher	20
Multi-melta	22
Plague belcher	7
Plague spewer	15
Plasma gun	11
Plasma pistol	5
Power fist	9
Power scourge	35
Predator autocannon	40
Reaper autocannon	10
Soulreaper cannon	10
Twin heavy flamer	28
Twin lascannon	40
Warp bolter	3
Warpflame pistol	3
Warpflamer	10

CRAFTWORLDS UNITS

UNIT	MODELS PER UNIT	POINTS PER MODEL (Does not include wargear)
Dark Reapers	3-10	12
Falcon	1	110
Farseer	1	110
Fire Dragons	5-10	10
Night Spinner	1	110
Shining Spears	3-9	24
Spiritseer	1	65
Storm Guardians	8-24	6
Striking Scorpions	5-10	10
Support Weapons (including crew)	1-3	25

CRAFTWORLDS UNITS

UNIT	MODELS PER UNIT	POINTS PER MODEL (Does not include wargear)
Vypers	1-3	40
War Walkers	1-3	40
Warlock	1	55
Warlock Conclave	2-10	45
Wave Serpent	1	120
Windriders	3-9	16
Wraithknight	1	315
Wraithlord	1	85

UNIT	MODELS PER UNIT	POINTS PER MODEL (Including wargear)
Avatar of Khaine	1	220
Eldrad Ulthran	1	135
Fuegan	1	140
Jain Zar	1	115
Karandras	1	125
Prince Yriel	1	70

CRAFTWORLDS WARGEAR

WARGEAR	POINTS PER ITEM
Aeldari missile launcher	20
Avenger shuriken catapult	3
Biting blade	5
D-scythe	20
Death spinner	6
Dragon's breath flamer	14
Firepike	17
Flamer	6
Fusion gun	14
Fusion pistol	7
Scatter laser	7
Scattershield	30
Scorpion's claw	9
Shadow weaver	12
Shimmershield	10
Starcannon	13
Suncannon	60
Twin Aeldari missile launcher	40
Twin scatter laser	12
Twin shuriken catapult	2
Twin starcannon	24
Vibro cannon	15
Wraithcannon	15

DARK ANGELS UNITS

UNIT	MODELS PER UNIT	POINTS PER MODEL (Does not include wargear)
Assault Squad with Jump Packs	5-10	15
Company Veterans	2-5	14
Contemptor Dreadnought	1	88
Deathwing Cataphractii Terminator Squad	5-10	26
Deathwing Knights	5-10	35
Deathwing Tartaros Terminator Squad	5-10	23
Deathwing Terminator Squad	5-10	23
Dreadnought	1	60

DARK ANGELS UNITS

UNIT	MODELS PER UNIT	POINTS PER MODEL (Does not include wargear)
Drop Pod	1	63
Hunter	1	80
Intercessor Squad	5-10	17
Interrogator-Chaplain	1	80
Interrogator-Chaplain in Terminator Armour	1	100
Interrogator-Chaplain with Jump Pack	1	95
Land Raider	1	200
Land Raider Crusader	1	200
Land Raider Redeemer	1	180
Librarian in Terminator Armour	1	102
Master in Cataphractii Armour	1	95
Master in Gravis Armour	1	90
Master in Terminator Armour	1	95
Primaris Chaplain	1	77
Primaris Master	1	78
Ravenwing Attack Bike Squad	1-3	25
Ravenwing Bike Squad	3-9	21 (Ravenwing Attack Bike is 25)
Ravenwing Black Knights	3-10	38
Ravenwing Dark Talon	1	180
Ravenwing Land Speeders	1-5	50
Redemptor Dreadnought	1	105
Repulsor	1	185
Scout Bike Squad	3-9	21
Servitors	4	5
Venerable Dreadnought	1	80

DARK ANGELS WARGEAR

WARGEAR	POINTS PER ITEM
Astartes grenade launcher	6
Auto bolt rifle	1
Auxiliary grenade launcher	0
Bolt pistol	0
Bolt rifle	0
Cerberus launcher	0
Chainfist	11
Chainsword	0
Combi-flamer	8
Combi-grav	13
Combi-melta	15
Combi-plasma	11
Cyclone missile launcher	38
Dreadnought combat weapon	30
Eviscerator	11
Flamer	6
Flamestorm gauntlets	15
Frag grenades	0
Grav-gun	12
Grenade harness	0
Heavy flamer	14
Heavy onslaught gatling cannon	30
Heavy plasma cannon	16

DARK ANGELS WARGEAR

WARGEAR	POINTS PER ITEM
Icarus stormcannon	10
Krak grenades	0
Master-crafted power sword	6
Meltagun	14
Missile launcher	20
Multi-melta	22
Plasma cannon	16
Plasma cutter	5
Plasma gun	11
Plasma pistol	5
Power fist	9
Power sword	4
Reaper autocannon	10
Relic blade	9
Servo-arm	0
Sniper rifle	2
Stalker bolt rifle	0
Storm shield (Characters)	10
Storm shield (other models)	2
Twin heavy plasma cannon	24
Twin lascannon	40
Twin multi-melta	40
Typhoon missile launcher	38
Volkite charger	3
Whirlwind castellan launcher	15
Whirlwind vengeance launcher	20
Wrist-mounted grenade launcher	0

DEATH GUARD UNITS

UNIT	MODELS PER UNIT	POINTS PER MODEL (Does not include wargear)
Biologus Putrifier	1	60
Blightlord Terminators	5-10	34
Chaos Cultists	10-40	5
Chaos Land Raider	1	200
Chaos Lord in Terminator Armour	1	95
Chaos Spawn	1-5	25
Daemon Prince of Nurgle with Wings	1	170
Deathshroud Terminators	3-6	35
Defiler	1	120
Helbrute	1	60
Lord of Contagion	1	95
Myphitic Blight-haulers	1-3	75
Noxious Blightbringer	1	50
Plague Marines	5-20	16
Plague Surgeon	1	54
Plagueburst Crawler	1	100
Possessed	5-20	20
Sorcerer in Terminator Armour	1	102
Tallyman	1	50

UNIT	MODELS PER UNIT	POINTS PER MODEL (Including weapons)
Beasts of Nurgle	1-9	34
Plague Drones	3-9	40

DEATH GUARD WARGEAR

WARGEAR	POINTS PER ITEM
Bile spurt	0
Blight launcher	10
Chainfist	11
Combi-flamer	8
Combi-melta	15
Combi-plasma	11
Entropy cannon	15
Flamer	6
Force axe	10
Force stave	8
Force sword	8
Havoc launcher	6
Heavy flamer	14
Heavy stubber	2
Helbrute fist (single/pair)	30/40
Helbrute hammer	30
Helbrute plasma cannon	16
Meltagun	14
Missile launcher	20
Multi-melta	22
Plague belcher	7
Plague spewer	15
Plaguereaper	20
Plaguespurt gauntlet	0
Plasma gun	11
Plasma pistol	5
Power fist	9
Power scourge	35
Predator autocannon	40
Reaper autocannon	10
Twin heavy flamer	28
Twin lascannon	40

DEATHWATCH UNITS

UNIT	MODELS PER UNIT	POINTS PER MODEL (Does not include wargear)
Bikers	3-6	21
Chaplain in Terminator Armour	1	90
Corvus Blackstar	1	135
Dreadnought	1	60
Drop Pod	1	63
Intercessors	5-10	17
- Aggressors		21
- Hellblasters		18
- Inceptors		25
- Reivers		18
Land Raider	1	200
Land Raider Crusader	1	200
Land Raider Redeemer	1	180
Librarian in Terminator Armour	1	102
Primaris Chaplain	1	77
Primaris Watch Captain	1	78
Redemptor Dreadnought	1	105
Repulsor	1	185
Terminators	5-10	23
Vanguard Veterans	5-10	17

DEATHWATCH UNITS

UNIT	MODELS PER UNIT	POINTS PER MODEL (Does not include wargear)
Venerable Dreadnought	1	80
Watch Captain in Terminator Armour	1	95
Veterans	5-10	14
- Bikers		21
- Black Shield		16
- Terminators		23
- Vanguard Veterans		17

DEATHWATCH WARGEAR

WARGEAR	POINTS PER ITEM
Absolvor bolt pistol	0
Auxiliary grenade launcher	0
Bolt carbine	2
Bolt pistol	0
Chainfist	11
Combi-flamer	9
Combi-grav	14
Combi-melta	16
Combi-plasma	12
Cyclone missile launcher	38
Dreadnought combat weapon	30
Flamer	6
Flamestorm gauntlets	15
Grav-gun	12
Hand flamer	1
Heavy bolt pistol	0
Heavy flamer	14
Heavy onslaught gatling cannon	30
Heavy plasma cannon	16
Inferno pistol	7
Meltagun	14
Missile launcher	20
Multi-melta	22
Plasma gun	11
Plasma pistol	5
Power fist	9
Relic blade	9
Stalker bolt rifle	1
Storm shield (CHARACTERS)	10
Storm shield (other models)	2
Twin lascannon	40

GENESTEALER CULTS UNITS

UNIT	MODELS PER UNIT	POINTS PER MODEL (Does not include wargear)
Purestrain Genestealers	5-20	15

GENESTEALER CULTS WARGEAR

WARGEAR	POINTS PER ITEM
Autocannon	10
Cult icon	20
Eradicator nova cannon	15
Exterminator autocannon	17
Flamer	6
Grenade launcher	3
Heavy flamer	14
Heavy rock saw	14

GENESTEALER CULTS WARGEAR

WARGEAR	POINTS PER ITEM
Heavy seismic cannon	15
Heavy stubber	2
Missile launcher	15
Multi-laser	5
Multi-melta	15
Plasma cannon	10
Power hammer	16
Power maul	4
Power pick	10
Purestrain talons	0
Seismic cannon	10
Vanquisher battle cannon	15

GREY KNIGHTS UNITS

UNIT	MODELS PER UNIT	POINTS PER MODEL (Does not include wargear)
Apothecary	1	75
Brother-Captain	1	110
Brotherhood Ancient	1	90
Brotherhood Champion	1	90
Chaplain	1	105
Dreadnought	1	65
Grand Master	1	130
Grand Master in Nemesis Dreadknight	1	170
Interceptor Squad	5-10	21
Land Raider	1	200
Land Raider Crusader	1	200
Land Raider Redeemer	1	180
Librarian	1	113
Paladin Ancient	1	98
Paladin Squad	3-10	47
Purifier Squad	5-10	19
Razorback	1	70
Servitors	4	5
Stormraven Gunship	1	192
Techmarine	1	55
Terminator Squad	5-10	39
Venerable Dreadnought	1	85

UNIT	MODELS PER UNIT	POINTS PER MODEL (Including wargear)
Brother-Captain Stern	1	105
Castellan Crowe	1	80
Grand Master Voldus	1	153
Lord Kaldor Draigo	1	180

GREY KNIGHTS WARGEAR

WARGEAR	POINTS PER ITEM
Assault cannon	22
Combi-flamer	8
Combi-melta	15
Combi-plasma	11
Dreadnought combat weapon	30
Flamer	6
Heavy flamer	14
Heavy incinerator	19
Heavy plasma cannon	16
Heavy psycannon	24

GREY KNIGHTS WARGEAR

WARGEAR	POINTS PER ITEM
Hurricane bolter	10
Icarus stormcannon	10
Incinerator	9
Incinerator (Terminator)	13
Missile launcher	20
Multi-melta	22
Plasma cannon	16
Plasma cutter	5
Psilencer (Terminator)	8
Psycannon	7
Psycannon (Terminator)	11
Servo-arm	0
Twin assault cannon	44
Twin heavy plasma cannon	24
Twin lascannon	40
Twin multi-melta	40
Typhoon missile launcher	38

HARLEQUINS WARGEAR

WARGEAR	POINTS PER ITEM
Fusion pistol	7

IMPERIAL KNIGHTS WARGEAR

WARGEAR	POINTS PER ITEM
Heavy flamer	14
Heavy stubber	2
Meltagun	14
Multi-laser	5
Twin Icarus autocannon	20

NECRONS UNITS

UNIT	MODELS PER UNIT	POINTS PER MODEL (Does not include wargear)
Annihilation Barge	1	100
Canoptek Wraiths	3-6	48
Catacomb Command Barge	1	124
Deathmarks	5-10	17
Doom Scythe	1	150
Doomsday Ark	1	160
Ghost Ark	1	145
Lord	1	65
Monolith	1	320
Necron Warriors	10-20	11
Night Scythe	1	135
Obelisk	1	380
Tesseract Vault	1	566
Transcendent C'tan	1	200
Triarch Praetorians	5-10	16
Triarch Stalker	1	85

UNIT	MODELS PER UNIT	POINTS PER MODEL (Including wargear)
C'tan Shard of the Nightbringer	1	180
Illuminor Szeras	1	120
Imotekh the Stormlord	1	160
Nemesor Zahndrekh	1	150
Trazyn the Infinite	1	90
Vargard Obyron	1	125

NECRONS WARGEAR

WARGEAR	POINTS PER ITEM
Dispersion shield	6
Gauss blaster	7
Heat ray	40
Heavy gauss cannon	20
Particle shredder	30
Tesla carbine	7
Twin heavy gauss cannon	40
Warscythe	9

OFFICIO ASSASSINORUM UNITS

UNIT	MODELS PER UNIT	POINTS PER MODEL (Including wargear)
Callidus Assassin	1	70
Vindicare Assassin	1	80

SISTERS OF SILENCE UNITS

UNIT	MODELS PER UNIT	POINTS PER MODEL (Does not include wargear)
Prosecutors	5-10	10
Vigilators	5-10	10
Witchseekers	5-10	10

SISTERS OF SILENCE WARGEAR

WARGEAR	POINTS PER ITEM
Executioner greatblade	5
Flamer	6

SPACE MARINES UNITS

UNIT	MODELS PER UNIT	POINTS PER MODEL (Does not include wargear)
Aggressor Squad	3-6	21
Assault Squad with Jump Packs	5-10	15
Attack Bike Squad	1-3	25
Bike Squad	3-9	21 (Attack Bike is 25)
Captain in Cataphractii Armour	1	95
Captain in Gravis Armour	1	90
Captain in Terminator Armour	1	95
Captain on Bike	1	88

SPACE MARINES UNITS

UNIT	MODELS PER UNIT	POINTS PER MODEL (Does not include wargear)
Cataphractii Terminator Squad	5-10	26
Centurion Devastator Squad	3-6	40
Chaplain in Terminator Armour	1	90
Company Veterans	2-5	14
Contemptor Dreadnought	1	88
Dreadnought	1	60
Drop Pod	1	63
Hunter	1	80
Inceptor Squad	3-6	25
Intercessor Squad	5-10	17
Ironclad Dreadnought	1	70
Land Raider	1	200
Land Raider Crusader	1	200
Land Raider Redeemer	1	180
Land Speeders	1-3	50
Librarian	1	88
Librarian in Terminator Armour	1	102
Librarian with Jump Pack	1	112
Primaris Captain	1	78
Primaris Chaplain	1	77
Razorback	1	70
Redemptor Dreadnought	1	105
Repulsor	1	185
Scout Bike Squad	3-9	21
Servitors	4	5
Stalker	1	75
Sternguard Veteran Squad	5-10	14
Stormraven Gunship	1	192
Tartaros Terminator Squad	5-10	23
Terminator Assault Squad	5-10	23
Terminator Squad	5-10	23
Terminus Ultra	1	250
Vanguard Veteran Squad	5-10	14
Vanguard Veteran Squad with Jump Packs	5-10	17
Venerable Dreadnought	1	80
Vindicator	1	125
Whirlwind	1	70

UNIT	MODELS PER UNIT	POINTS PER MODEL (Including wargear)
Captain Lysander	1	130
Captain Sicarius	1	110
Chaplain Cassius	1	85
Chaplain Grimaldus	1	90
Chief Librarian Tigurius	1	115
High Marshal Helbrecht	1	150
Kor'sarro Khan	1	90
Pedro Kantor	1	150
Roboute Guilliman	1	400
Sergeant Chronus	1	30
Sergeant Telion	1	65
Vulkan He'stan	1	135

SPACE MARINES WARGEAR

WARGEAR	POINTS PER ITEM
Assault bolter	10
Assault cannon	22
Assault plasma incinerator	17
Astartes grenade launcher	6
Auto bolt rifle	1
Auto boltstorm gauntlets	12
Auxiliary grenade launcher	0
Bolt pistol	0
Bolt rifle	0
Boltstorm gauntlet	22
Centurion assault launchers	0
Cerberus launcher	0
Chainfist	11
Chainsword	0
Combi-flamer	8
Combi-grav	13
Combi-melta	15
Combi-plasma	11
Cyclone missile launcher	38
Dreadnought chainfist	38
Dreadnought combat weapon (other models)	30
Eviscerator	11
Flamer	6
Flamestorm gauntlets	15
Force axe	10
Force stave	8
Force sword	8
Frag grenades	0
Grav-gun	12
Grenade harness	0
Heavy flamer	14
Heavy onslaught gatling cannon	30
Heavy plasma cannon	16
Hurricane bolter	10
Icarus stormcannon	10
Ironclad assault launchers	5
Krak grenades	0
Master-crafted power sword	6
Meltagun	14
Missile launcher	20
Multi-melta	22
Plasma cannon	16
Plasma cutter	5
Plasma exterminator	17
Plasma gun	11
Plasma pistol	5
Power fist	9
Power sword	4
Predator autocannon	40
Reaper autocannon	10
Relic blade	9
Seismic hammer	40
Servo-arm	0
Sniper rifle	2
Stalker bolt rifle	0
Storm shield (CHARACTERS)	10

SPACE MARINES WARGEAR

WARGEAR	POINTS PER ITEM
Storm shield (other models)	2
Twin assault cannon	44
Twin heavy plasma cannon	24
Twin lascannon	40
Twin multi-melta	40
Typhoon missile launcher	38
Volkite charger	3
Whirlwind castellan launcher	15
Whirlwind vengeance launcher	20
Wrist-mounted grenade launcher	0

SPACE WOLVES UNITS

UNIT	MODELS PER UNIT	POINTS PER MODEL (Does not include wargear)
Contemptor Dreadnought	1	88
Dreadnought	1	60
Drop Pod	1	63
Hunter	1	80
Intercessors	5-10	17
Land Raider	1	200
Land Raider Crusader	1	200
Land Raider Redeemer	1	180
Land Speeders	1-3	50
Primaris Wolf Lord	1	78
Primaris Wolf Priest	1	80
Redemptor Dreadnought	1	105
Repulsor	1	185
Rune Priest in Terminator Armour	1	102
Servitors	4	5
Skyclaws	5-10	15
Swiftclaw Attack Bikes	1-3	25
Swiftclaws	3-9	21 (Swiftclaw Attack Bike is 25)
Venerable Dreadnought	1	80
Wolf Guard	5-10	14
Wolf Guard Cataphractii Terminators	5-10	26
Wolf Guard Tartaros Terminators	5-10	23
Wolf Guard Terminators	5-10	23
Wolf Lord in Cataphractii Armour	1	95
Wolf Lord in Gravis Armour	1	90
Wolf Lord in Terminator Armour	1	95
Wolf Priest in Terminator Armour	1	95

SPACE WOLVES WARGEAR

WARGEAR	POINTS PER ITEM
Astartes grenade launcher	6
Auto bolt rifle	1
Auxiliary grenade launcher	0
Bolt pistol	0
Bolt rifle	0
Cerberus launcher	0
Chainfist	11

SPACE WOLVES WARGEAR

WARGEAR	POINTS PER ITEM
Chainsword	0
Combi-flamer	8
Combi-melta	15
Combi-plasma	11
Cyclone missile launcher	38
Dreadnought combat weapon	30
Flamer	6
Flamestorm gauntlets	15
Frag grenades	0
Grenade harness	0
Heavy flamer	14
Heavy onslaught gatling cannon	30
Heavy plasma cannon	16
Icarus stormcannon	10
Krak grenades	0
Master-crafted power sword	6
Meltagun	14
Missile launcher	20
Multi-melta	22
Plasma cannon	16
Plasma gun	11
Plasma pistol	5
Power fist	9
Power sword	4
Reaper autocannon	10
Servo-arm	0
Sniper rifle	2
Stalker bolt rifle	0
Storm shield (CHARACTERS)	10
Storm shield (other models)	2
Twin lascannon	40
Twin multi-melta	40
Typhoon missile launcher	38
Volkite charger	3
Whirlwind castellan launcher	15
Whirlwind vengeance launcher	20
Wrist-mounted grenade launcher	0

T'AU EMPIRE UNITS

UNIT	MODELS PER UNIT	POINTS PER MODEL (Does not include wargear)
XV88 Broadside Battlesuit	1-3	35
XV8 Crisis Battlesuits	3-9	27
XV8 Crisis Bodyguards	3-9	30
TY7 Devilfish	1	70
XV95 Ghostkeel Battlesuit	1	70
TX4 Piranhas	1-5	30
TX78 Sky Ray Gunship	1	80

UNIT	MODELS PER UNIT	POINTS PER MODEL (Including wargear)
Commander Farsight	1	125
Commander Shadowsun	1	110
MV1 Gun Drone	N/A	10

UNIT	MODELS PER UNIT	POINTS PER UNIT (Including wargear)
The Eight	22	1120

T'AU EMPIRE WARGEAR

WARGEAR	POINTS PER ITEM
Advanced targeting system (all other models)	6
XV8-02 Crisis Iridium battlesuit	10
Cyclic ion raker	32
Flamer	6
Fusion blaster	18
Fusion collider	30
High-output burst cannon	16
Ion accelerator	50
Missile pod	15
Plasma rifle	8
Pulse driver cannon	50
Quad ion turret	30
Rail rifle	12
Railgun	30

THOUSAND SONS UNITS

UNIT	MODELS PER UNIT	POINTS PER MODEL (Does not include wargear)
Chaos Cultists	10-40	5
Chaos Land Raider	1	200
Chaos Spawn	1-5	25
Defiler	1	120
Forgefiend	1	100
Helbrute	1	60
Heldrake	1	120
Maulerfiend	1	120
Mutalith Vortex Beast	1	125
Rubric Marines	5-20	16
Scarab Occult Terminators	5-10	30
Sorcerer	1	90
Sorcerer in Terminator Armour	1	102

UNIT	MODELS PER UNIT	POINTS PER MODEL (Including weapons)
Flamers	3-9	25
Horrors	10-30	
- Blue Horrors		5
- Pairs of Brimstone Horrors		3
- Pink Horrors		7
Screamers	3-9	28

THOUSAND SONS WARGEAR

WARGEAR	POINTS PER ITEM
Combi-flamer	8
Combi-melta	15
Daemonic Icon	15
Ectoplasma cannon	20
Flamer	6
Hades autocannon	20
Havoc launcher	6
Heavy flamer	14
Heavy stubber	2
Heavy warpflamer	17
Helbrute fist (single/pair)	30/40
Helbrute hammer	30
Helbrute plasma cannon	16
Hellfyre missile rack	15

THOUSAND SONS WARGEAR

WARGEAR	POINTS PER ITEM
Inferno bolt pistol	0
Instrument of Chaos	10
Missile launcher	20
Multi-melta	22
Plasma pistol	5
Power scourge	35
Reaper autocannon	10
Soulreaper cannon	10
Twin heavy flamer	28
Twin lascannon	40
Warpflame pistol	3
Warpflamer	10

TYRANIDS UNITS

UNIT	MODELS PER UNIT	POINTS PER MODEL (Does not include wargear)
Biovores	1-3	50
Broodlord	1	115
Exocrine	1	170
Harpy	1	105
Haruspex	1	170
Hive Crone	1	135
Hive Tyrant with Wings	1	190
Lictor	1	30
Maleceptor	1	150
Neurothrope	1	90
Pyrovores	1-3	25
Tervigon	1	180
Toxicrene	1	140
Tyranid Prime	1	70
Tyrannocyte	1	75
Tyrannofex	1	151

UNIT	MODELS PER UNIT	POINTS PER MODEL (Including wargear)
Deathleaper	1	60
The Red Terror	1	50
The Swarmlord	1	250

TYRANIDS WARGEAR

WARGEAR	POINTS PER ITEM
Heavy venom cannon	18
Massive scything talons (two or more pairs) (Trygon and Trygon Prime)	40
Stranglethorn cannon	15
Venom cannon	12

UPDATED POINTS VALUES: FORGE WORLD

As part of our update of point values, we have also reviewed Forge World's range of units. The points values for the units and items of wargear that appear in one of the tables below replace those that appear in books with an earlier publication date, and also take precedence over points-value lists that have no publication date at all. If a unit or item of wargear does not appear in any of the tables below, continue to use the points values for it that are listed within the most recently published datasheet for that Faction.

ADEPTUS ASTARTES UNITS

UNIT	MODELS PER UNIT	POINTS PER MODEL (Does not include wargear)
Caestus Assault Ram	1	250
Contemptor Mortis Dreadnought	1	88
Deimos Relic Predator	1	90
Fire Raptor Gunship	1	280
Infernum Pattern Razorback	1	70
Land Raider Achilles	1	230
Land Raider Helios	1	215
Land Raider Prometheus	1	250
Land Speeder Tempest	1-3	95
Lucius Dreadnought Drop Pod	1	80
Relic Cerberus Heavy Tank Destroyer	1	680
Relic Contemptor Dreadnought	1	110
Relic Deredeo Dreadnought	1	120
Relic Falchion Super-heavy Tank	1	840
Relic Fellblade Super-heavy Tank	1	740
Relic Javelin Attack Speeder	1	110
Relic Land Raider Proteus	1	225
Relic Mastodon Super-heavy Transport	1	934
Relic Sicaran Punisher	1	155
Relic Sicaran Venator	1	170
Relic Typhon Heavy Siege Tank	1	720
Siege Dreadnought	1	80
Sokar Pattern Stormbird	1	2000
Tarantula Air Defence Battery	1-3	70
Tarantula Sentry Gun	1-3	20
Thunderhawk Gunship	1	1330
Thunderhawk Transporter	1	1000
Xiphon Interceptor	1	110

ADEPTUS ASTARTES WARGEAR

WARGEAR	POINTS PER ITEM
Assault cannon	22
Castellum battle cannon	55
Combi-flamer	8
Combi-melta	15
Cyclone missile launcher	38
Dreadnought chainfist (single/pair)	38/48
Dreadnought combat weapon (single/pair)	30/40
Flamer	6

ADEPTUS ASTARTES WARGEAR

WARGEAR	POINTS PER ITEM
Grav-flux bombard	65
Heavy flamer	14
Heavy plasma cannon	16
Leviathan siege claw (single/pair)	30/40
Leviathan siege drill (single/pair)	40/50
Magna-melta cannon	50
Meltagun	14
Missile launcher	20
Multi-melta	22
Plasma destroyer	40
Power fist	9
Predator autocannon	40
Punisher rotary cannon	0
Seismic hammer	40
Servo-arm	0
Twin accelerator autocannon	0
Twin assault cannon	44
Twin autocannon	30
Twin heavy flamer	28
Twin lascannon	40
Twin multi-melta	40
Typhoon missile launcher	38
Whirlwind castellan launcher	15

ASTRA MILITARUM UNITS

UNIT	MODELS PER UNIT	POINTS PER MODEL (Does not include wargear)
Armageddon Pattern Medusa	1-3	115
Artemia Pattern Hellhound	1-3	73
Avenger Strike Fighter	1	150
Cyclops Demolition Vehicle	1-3	60
Dominus Armoured Siege Bombard	1	600
Earthshaker Battery	1-3	115
Earthshaker Carriage Battery		
- Earthshaker Carriage	1-3	105
- Guardsmen Crew	4-12	4
Gorgon Heavy Transporter	1	300
Griffon Mortar Carrier	1-3	77
Heavy Quad Launcher Battery		
- Heavy Quad Launcher	1-3	85
- Guardsmen Crew	3-9	4
Hydra Battery	1-3	75
Imperial Fortress Walls	1	800
Leman Russ Annihilator	1-3	122
Leman Russ Conqueror	1-3	122

ASTRA MILITARUM UNITS

UNIT	MODELS PER UNIT	POINTS PER MODEL (Does not include wargear)
Leman Russ Stygies Vanquisher	1-3	160
Lightning Strike Fighter	1	125
Manticore Battery	1-3	110
Medusa Carriage Battery		
- Medusa Carriage	1-3	100
- Guardsmen Crew	4-12	4
Primaris Redoubt	1	700
Rapier Laser Destroyer		
- Rapier Laser Destroyer	1	80
- Guardsmen Crew	2	4
Salamander Command Vehicle	1	110
Stygies Destroyer Tank Hunter	1-3	160
Stygies Thunderer Siege Tank	1-3	160
Tarantula Battery	1-3	20
Thunderbolt Heavy Fighter	1	125

ASTRA MILITARUM WARGEAR

WARGEAR	POINTS PER ITEM
Artemia inferno cannon	20
Autocannon	10
Defence searchlight	20
Demolisher cannon	20
Flamer	6
Grenade launcher	3
Heavy flamer	14
Heavy stubber	2
Hellstrike missile	30
Meltagun (model with a Ballistic Skill of 4+)	10
Meltagun (other models)	14
Missile launcher	15
Multi-laser	5
Multi-melta	15
Multiple rocket pod	8
Plasma cannon	10
Plasma gun (model with a Ballistic Skill of 4+)	7
Plasma gun (other models)	11
Power fist	8
Twin assault cannon	44
Twin heavy flamer	28

ASURYANI UNITS

UNIT	MODELS PER UNIT	POINTS PER MODEL (Does not include wargear)
Corsair Cloud Dancer Band	3-9	20
- Corsair Cloud Dancer Felarch	0-1	25
Corsair Reaver Band	5-15	7
- Corsair Reaver Felarch	0-1	12
Corsair Skyreaver Band	5-10	10
- Corsair Skyreaver Felarch	0-1	15
Hornet	1-3	60

ASURYANI UNITS

UNIT	MODELS PER UNIT	POINTS PER MODEL (Does not include wargear)
Phoenix	1	183
Revenant Titan	1	2000
Scorpion	1	700
Skathach Wraithknight	1	420
Vampire Hunter	1	1500
Warp Hunter	1	175
Wasp Assault Walker	1-3	55
Wraithseer	1	100

ASURYANI WARGEAR

WARGEAR	POINTS PER ITEM
Aeldari missile launcher	20
D-cannon	45
Deathshroud cannon	45
Flamer	6
Fusion gun	14
Hornet pulse laser	25
Prism blaster	25
Prism rifle	20
Scatter laser	7
Shuriken cannon	10
Sonic lance	60
Starcannon	13
Twin shuriken cannon	17
Twin shuriken catapult	2
Twin starcannon	24
Wraithcannon	15

CHILDREN OF THE WARP UNITS

UNIT	MODELS PER UNIT	POINTS PER MODEL (Including weapons)
Aetaos'rau'keres*	1	1500
An'ggrath the Unbound*	1	888
Giant Chaos Spawn	1	150
Mamon Transfigured*	1	200
Plague Toads of Nurgle	3-9	58
Pox Riders of Nurgle	3-9	63
Samus*	1	155
Scabeiathrax the Bloated*	1	777
Spined Chaos Beast	1	150
Uraka the Warfiend*	1	150
Zarakynel*	1	666

There may only be a single unit of this type in any given army.

CHILDREN OF THE WARP WARGEAR

WARGEAR	POINTS PER ITEM
Daemonic Icon	15

DAEMON BOUND UNITS

UNIT	MODELS PER UNIT	POINTS PER MODEL (Does not include wargear)
Blood Slaughterer of Khorne	1	165
Greater Blight Drone	1	170
Greater Brass Scorpion of Khorne	1	650

DAEMON BOUND WARGEAR

WARGEAR	POINTS PER ITEM
Butcher cannon	25
Kytan gatling cannon	80
Soulburner petard	60

DEATH KORPS OF KRIEG UNITS

UNIT	MODELS PER UNIT	POINTS PER MODEL (Does not include wargear)
Death Korps of Krieg Command Squad*	4	7
Death Korps Combat Engineer Squad*	5-10	7
Death Korps Commissar	1	15
Death Korps Death Rider Commissar	1	35
Death Korps Grenadier Storm Squad*	5-10	8
Death Korps Leman Russ Mars Alpha Battle Tanks	1-3	122

* If models in these units form Heavy Weapons Teams, there is no change in the unit's points cost.

DEATH KORPS OF KRIEG WARGEAR

WARGEAR	POINTS PER ITEM
Ablative storm armour and mine plough	10
Autocannon	10
Demolisher cannon	20
Eradicator nova cannon	15
Executioner plasma cannon	15
Exterminator autocannon	17
Flamer	6
Grenade launcher	3
Heavy flamer	14
Heavy stubber	2
Hot-shot lasgun	0
Hot-shot laspistol	0
Medi-pack	5
Meltagun (model with a Ballistic Skill of 4+)	10
Meltagun (other models)	14
Missile launcher	15
Multi-laser	5
Multi-melta	15
Multiple rocket pod	8
Plasma cannon	10
Plasma gun (model with a Ballistic Skill of 4+)	7
Plasma gun (other models)	11
Power fist	8
Twin heavy stubber	8
Vanquisher battle cannon	15

DRUKHARI UNITS

UNIT	MODELS PER UNIT	POINTS PER MODEL (Including wargear)
Tantalus	1	400

ELYSIAN DROP TROOPS UNITS

UNIT	MODELS PER UNIT	POINTS PER MODEL (Does not include wargear)
Elysian Command Squad*	4	7
Elysian Veteran Squad*	10	7

* If models in these units form Heavy Weapons Teams, there is no change in the unit's points cost.

ELYSIAN DROP TROOPS WARGEAR

WARGEAR	POINTS PER ITEM
Auxiliary grenade launcher	0
Flamer	6
Grenade launcher	3
Heavy flamer	14
Medi-pack	5
Meltagun (model with a Ballistic Skill of 4+)	10
Meltagun (other models)	14
Missile launcher	15
Multi-melta	15
Multiple rocket pod	8
Plasma gun (model with a Ballistic Skill of 4+)	7
Plasma gun (other models)	11
Power fist	8

EYRINE CULTS UNITS

UNIT	MODELS PER UNIT	POINTS PER MODEL (Does not include wargear)
Chaos Fire Raptor Assault Gunship	1	280
Chaos Hell Blade	1	90
Chaos Hell Talon	1	180
Chaos Sokar Pattern Stormbird Gunship	1	2000
Chaos Thunderhawk Assault Gunship	1	1330
Chaos Xiphon Interceptor	1	110

EYRINE CULTS WARGEAR

WARGEAR	POINTS PER ITEM
Balefire missiles	30
Havoc launcher	6
Reaper battery	30
Twin lascannon	40
Twin multi-melta	40

GREY KNIGHTS, INQUISITION & SISTERS OF BATTLE UNITS

UNIT	MODELS PER UNIT	POINTS PER MODEL (Does not include wargear)
Inquisition Land Raider Prometheus	1	250
Sororitas Repressor	1	91
Thunderhawk Assault Gunship	1	1130
Vortimer Pattern Land Raider Redeemer	1	215
Vortimer Pattern Razorback	1	70

GREY KNIGHTS, INQUISITION & SISTERS OF BATTLE WARGEAR

WARGEAR	POINTS PER ITEM
Heavy psycannon	24
Incinerator	13
Multi-melta	22
Twin psycannon	50

HELLFORGED UNITS

UNIT	MODELS PER UNIT	POINTS PER MODEL (Does not include wargear)
Chaos Space Marine Crew	N/A	10
Hellforged Cerberus Heavy Destroyer	1	650
Hellforged Contemptor Dreadnought	1	88
Hellforged Deredeo Dreadnought	1	120
Hellforged Dreadclaw Drop Pod	1	115
Hellforged Falchion	1	840
Hellforged Fellblade	1	740
Hellforged Kharybdis Assault Claw	1	325
Hellforged Land Raider Achilles	1	230
Hellforged Land Raider Proteus	1	225
Hellforged Mastodon	1	934
Hellforged Predator	1	95
Hellforged Sicaran	1	150
Hellforged Sicaran Venator	1	150
Hellforged Typhon Heavy Siege Tank	1	700

HELLFORGED WARGEAR

WARGEAR	POINTS PER ITEM
Butcher cannon	25
Butcher cannon array	40
Combi-flamer	8
Combi-melta	15
Combi-plasma	11
Dual malignatas saker	40
Ectoplasma blaster	11
Ectoplasma cannon	20
Havoc launcher	6
Heavy flamer	14
Hellforged chainclaw (single/pair)	38/48
Hellforged deathclaw (single/pair)	30/40
Hellforged siege claw (single/pair)	30/40
Hellforged siege drill (single/pair)	40/50
Infernal flamestorm cannon	30
Magna-melta cannon	50
Malignatas beam laser	0
Meltagun	14
Multi-melta	22
Plasma destroyer	40
Predator autocannon	40
Soulburner	30

HELLFORGED WARGEAR

WARGEAR	POINTS PER ITEM
Soulburner bombard	90
Twin accelerator autocannon	0
Twin autocannon	30
Twin heavy flamer	28
Twin lascannon	40
Twin multi-melta	40

HERETIC TITAN LEGIONS UNITS

UNIT	MODELS PER UNIT	POINTS PER MODEL (Including wargear)
Chaos Reaver Battle Titan	1	4000
Chaos Warhound Scout Titan	1	2000
Chaos Warlord Battle Titan	1	6000

LORDS OF RUIN UNITS

UNIT	MODELS PER UNIT	POINTS PER MODEL (Including wargear)
Necrosius the Undying*	1	135
Zhufor the Impaler*	1	120

There may only be a single unit of this type in any given army.

LORDS OF RUIN WARGEAR

WARGEAR	POINTS PER ITEM
Combi-melta	15
Flamer	6
Infernal axe	0
Soulburner pistol	0
Voidcutter	0
Warpfire lance	30

NECRONS UNITS

UNIT	MODELS PER UNIT	POINTS PER MODEL (Does not include wargear)
Canoptek Tomb Sentinel	1	145
Canoptek Tomb Stalker	1	130
Gauss Pylon	1	475
Night Shroud	1	185
Sentry Pylon	1	70
Tesseract Ark	1	160

UNIT	MODELS PER UNIT	POINTS PER MODEL (Including wargear)
Toholk the Blinded	1	125

NECRONS WARGEAR

WARGEAR	POINTS PER ITEM
Staff of light	10

ORKS UNITS

UNIT	MODELS PER UNIT	POINTS PER MODEL (Does not include wargear)
'Chinork' Warkopta	1	74
Kill Tank	1	365
Squiggoth	1	160

ORKS WARGEAR

WARGEAR	POINTS PER ITEM
Big choppa	5
Killkannon	15
Lifta-droppa	0
Rack of rokkits	24
Supa-kannon	30
Twin big shoota	10

QUESTOR IMPERIALIS UNITS

UNIT	MODELS PER UNIT	POINTS PER MODEL (Does not include wargear)
Acastus Knight Porphyrion	1	600
Cerastus Knight-Lancer	1	360
Questoris Knight Magaera	1	380

QUESTOR IMPERIALIS WARGEAR

WARGEAR	POINTS PER ITEM
Autocannon	10
Castigator bolt cannon	50

RENEGADES AND HERETICS UNITS

UNIT	MODELS PER UNIT	POINTS PER MODEL (Does not include wargear)
Malefic Lord	1	80
Renegade Command Squad*	4-14	6
Renegade Disciple Squad*	5-15	6
Renegade Militia Squad*	10-20	4
Renegade Cultists	10-30	5

* If models in these units form Heavy Weapons Teams, there is no change in the unit's points cost.

RENEGADES AND HERETICS WARGEAR

WARGEAR	POINTS PER ITEM
Autocannon	10
Flamer	6
Grenade launcher	3
Heavy stubber	2
Meltagun (model with a Ballistic Skill of 4+)	10
Meltagun (other models)	14
Missile launcher	15
Plasma gun (model with a Ballistic Skill of 4+)	7
Plasma gun (other models)	11
Power fist	8

T'AU EMPIRE UNITS

UNIT	MODELS PER UNIT	POINTS PER MODEL (Does not include wargear)
Blacklight Marker Drones	N/A	7
TX7 Fire Support Hammerhead Gunship	1	100
XV9 Hazard Support Team	1-3	40
TX7 Heavy Bombardment Hammerhead Gunship	1	100
Manta Super-heavy Dropship	1	2000
DX-6 Remora Stealth Drone Squadron	1-6	30
KX139 Ta'unar Supremacy Armour	1	750

T'AU EMPIRE WARGEAR

WARGEAR	POINTS PER ITEM
Burst cannon	8
Fusion blaster	18
Missile pod	15
Plasma rifle	8
Rail rifle	12

TITAN LEGIONS UNITS

UNIT	MODELS PER UNIT	POINTS PER MODEL (Including wargear)
Reaver Battle Titan	1	4000
Warhound Scout Titan	1	2000
Warlord Battle Titan	1	6000

TRAITOR QUESTORIS UNITS

UNIT	MODELS PER UNIT	POINTS PER MODEL (Does not include wargear)
Renegade Knight Lancer	1	360
Renegade Knight Magaera	1	380
Renegade Knight Porphyrion	1	600

TRAITOR QUESTORIS WARGEAR

WARGEAR	POINTS PER ITEM
Autocannon	10
Castigator bolt cannon	50

TYRANIDS UNITS

UNIT	MODELS PER UNIT	POINTS PER MODEL (Does not include wargear)
Barbed Hierodule	1	420
Hierophant Bio-titan	1	2000
Malanthrope	1-3	140

TYRANIDS WARGEAR

WARGEAR	POINTS PER ITEM
Massive scything talons (one pair)	22
Massive scything talons (two or more pairs)	60

UPDATED DATASHEETS

This section of *Chapter Approved* contains updated datasheets for several different units. The datasheets presented here replace those published in earlier publications and reflect the very latest rules and wargear options for the units they describe.

This section contains five updated datasheets. If you are playing a matched play game (or another game that is using points values), where points for the units and wargear described in this section have been revised, they can be found in the updated point values section of this book (pg 124-139).

Intercessors

Since *Codex: Space Marines* was released, new upgrade packs have been released for Intercessors, alongside *Codex: Blood Angels*, *Codex: Dark Angels* and *Codex: Space Wolves*. The relevant options for these upgrade packs can be found within the datasheets for each respective codex, and all are represented in *Codex: Deathwatch*. However, since then we have released a further upgrade pack. The updated datasheet for Intercessors allows Intercessor Sergeants to be equipped not only with the options released in this new upgrade pack, but also from all previously released upgrade packs, irrespective of their Chapter. It therefore replaces the Intercessor Squad datasheet in *Codex: Space Marines*, *Codex: Blood Angels* (replace the <CHAPTER> keyword with BLOOD ANGELS) and *Codex: Dark Angels* (replace the <CHAPTER> keyword with DARK ANGELS). It also replaces the Intercessors datasheet in *Codex: Space Wolves* (change the datasheet title to Intercessors, replace Intercessor Sergeant with Intercessor Pack Leader throughout, remove the Combat Squads ability, replace the <CHAPTER> keyword with SPACE WOLVES and replace the INTERCESSOR SQUAD keyword with INTERCESSORS). The datasheet for Intercessors in *Codex: Deathwatch* already includes all previous upgrade packs, so instead of reprinting the entire datasheet here we will instead add the following errata.

Page 73 – Intercessors, Wargear Options
Change the third bullet point to read:
'• The Intercessor Sergeant may either replace their bolt rifle with a chainsword, power sword or power fist (pg 91) or take a chainsword, power sword or power fist in addition to their other weapons.'

Fiends and Flesh Hounds

Since *Codex: Chaos Daemons* was released, new models have become available for Fiends and Flesh Hounds. The datasheets included here reflect these models and take into account the new options both gain for unit champions. These datasheets replace the Fiends of Slaanesh and Flesh Hounds datasheets respectively from *Codex: Chaos Daemons*.

Horrors

Horrors have appeared in three different codexes, and their datasheet has changed each time following feedback from the community, leading to some confusion about which is the correct datasheet. The Horrors datasheet published here replaces those found in *Codex: Chaos Space Marines* and *Codex: Thousand Sons*.

Bloodcrushers

Since *Codex: Chaos Daemons* was released, we have received lots of feedback about Bloodcrushers and have decided to improve their profile. The datasheet included here reflects this and replaces the one in *Codex: Chaos Daemons*.

INTERCESSOR SQUAD

NAME	M	WS	BS	S	T	W	A	Ld	Sv
Intercessor	6"	3+	3+	4	4	2	2	7	3+
Intercessor Sergeant	6"	3+	3+	4	4	2	3	8	3+

This unit contains 1 Intercessor Sergeant and 4 Intercessors. It can include up to 5 additional Intercessors (**Power Rating +5**). Each model is armed with a bolt rifle, bolt pistol, frag grenades and krak grenades.

WEAPON	RANGE	TYPE	S	AP	D	ABILITIES
Auto bolt rifle	24"	Assault 2	4	0	1	-
Bolt pistol	12"	Pistol 1	4	0	1	-
Bolt rifle	30"	Rapid Fire 1	4	-1	1	-
Stalker bolt rifle	36"	Heavy 1	4	-2	1	-
Chainsword	Melee	Melee	User	0	1	Each time the bearer fights, it can make 1 additional attack with this weapon.
Power fist	Melee	Melee	x2	-3	D3	When attacking with this weapon, you must subtract 1 from the hit roll.
Power sword	Melee	Melee	User	-3	1	-
Frag grenade	6"	Grenade D6	3	0	1	-
Krak grenade	6"	Grenade 1	6	-1	D3	-

WARGEAR OPTIONS	
	• All models in the unit may replace their bolt rifle with an auto bolt rifle or stalker bolt rifle.
	• For every five models in the unit, one may take an auxiliary grenade launcher.
	• The Intercessor Sergeant may either replace their bolt rifle with a chainsword, a power sword or a power fist, or take a chainsword, a power sword or a power fist in addition to their other weapons.

ABILITIES	
	And They Shall Know No Fear: You can re-roll failed Morale tests for this unit. **Combat Squads:** Before any models are deployed at the start of the game, an Intercessor Squad containing 10 models may be split into two units, each containing 5 models. **Auxiliary Grenade Launcher:** If a model is armed with an auxiliary grenade launcher, increase the range of any Grenade weapons they have to 30".

FACTION KEYWORDS	IMPERIUM, ADEPTUS ASTARTES, <CHAPTER>
KEYWORDS	INFANTRY, PRIMARIS, INTERCESSOR SQUAD

FIENDS

NAME	M	WS	BS	S	T	W	A	Ld	Sv
Fiend	14"	3+	-	4	4	4	4	7	6+
Blissbringer	14"	3+	-	4	4	4	5	7	6+

This unit contains 1 Fiend. It can include up to 8 additional Fiends (**Power Rating +2 per model**). If this unit contains at least three models, one Fiend can be upgraded to a Blissbringer. Each model attacks with dissecting claws and a vicious barbed tail.

WEAPON	RANGE	TYPE	S	AP	D	ABILITIES
Dissecting claws	Melee	Melee	User	-1	2	Each time you make a wound roll of 6+ for this weapon, that hit is resolved with an AP of -4 instead of -1.
Vicious barbed tail	Melee	Melee	User	-3	D3	A model can only make a single attack with this weapon each time it fights.

ABILITIES	
	Daemonic, Quicksilver Swiftness, Daemonic Ritual (see *Codex: Chaos Daemons*) **Disruptive Song:** PSYKERS within 12" of any enemy models with this ability must subtract 1 from the result of Psychic tests they take. **Soporific Musk:** Units within 1" of any enemy models with this ability cannot Fall Back unless they can FLY.

FACTION KEYWORDS	CHAOS, SLAANESH, DAEMON
KEYWORDS	BEAST, FIENDS

HORRORS

NAME	M	WS	BS	S	T	W	A	Ld	Sv
Pink Horror	6"	4+	4+	3	3	1	1	7	6+
Blue Horror	6"	5+	-	2	3	1	1	7	6+
Pair of Brimstone Horrors	6"	5+	-	1	3	1	2	7	6+

This unit contains 10 Pink, Blue or pairs of Brimstone Horrors, in any combination. It can include up to 10 additional Horrors (**Power Rating +4**) or up to 20 additional Horrors (**Power Rating +8**). Pink Horrors attack with coruscating flames, while Blue Horrors and Brimstone Horrors simply scrabble at anyone who comes too close.

WEAPON	RANGE	TYPE	S	AP	D	ABILITIES
Coruscating flames	18"	Assault 2	User	0	1	-

WARGEAR OPTIONS	• For every ten models in the unit, one Pink Horror may take an Instrument of Chaos. • For every ten models in the unit, one Pink Horror may take a Daemonic Icon.

ABILITIES

Daemonic Ritual (see *Codex: Chaos Space Marines* or *Codex: Thousand Sons*)

Daemonic Icon: If you roll a 1 when taking a Morale test for a unit with any Daemonic Icons, reality blinks and the daemonic horde is bolstered. No models flee and D6 slain Pink Horrors are instead added to the unit.

Split: Each time a Pink Horror is slain, you can add up to two Blue Horrors to its unit before you remove the slain model. Each time a Blue Horror is slain, you can add one pair of Brimstone Horrors to its unit before you remove the slain model. The replacement models cannot be placed within 1" of an enemy model. Note that Horrors that flee do not generate any extra models for their unit.

Matched Play: In matched play you must pay reinforcement points for each and every Blue and Brimstone Horror model that you add to a unit of Horrors, but the additional models can take the unit above its starting strength.

Instrument of Chaos: A unit that includes any Instruments of Chaos adds 1 to their Advance and charge rolls.

Iridescent Horror: When you set up this unit for the first time, you may select a single Pink Horror in the unit – that model has an Attacks characteristic of 2, instead of 1.

Magic Made Manifest: A unit of Horrors can attempt to manifest one psychic power in each friendly Psychic phase, and attempt to deny one psychic power in each enemy Psychic phase. However, when you do so, only roll a single D6 for the Psychic test or Deny the Witch test, and use the result to determine the outcome. Note that this means the Horrors cannot roll a double 1 or 6 to suffer Perils of the Warp. In addition, if the unit manifests the *Smite* psychic power whilst it contains less than 10 Pink Horror models, it only inflicts 1 mortal wound rather than D3.

Ephemeral Daemons: Pink Horrors have an invulnerable save of 4+. Blue Horrors have an invulnerable save of 5+. Pairs of Brimstone Horrors have an invulnerable save of 6+.

Magical Horde: Change the Type of this unit's coruscating flames to Assault 3 whilst the unit contains 20 or more Pink Horrors.

PSYKER

This unit can attempt to manifest one psychic power in each friendly Psychic phase, and attempt to deny one psychic power in each enemy Psychic phase. It knows the *Smite* power. When manifesting or denying a psychic power, first select a model in the unit – measure range, visibility, etc. from this model. If a Brimstone Horror is selected, it is slain after the psychic power has been attempted and, if successful, resolved.

FACTION KEYWORDS CHAOS, TZEENTCH, DAEMON

KEYWORDS INFANTRY, PSYKER, HORRORS

BLOODCRUSHERS

NAME	M	WS	BS	S	T	W	A	Ld	Sv
Bloodcrusher	8"	3+	3+	5	4	4	3	7	4+
Bloodhunter	8"	3+	3+	5	4	4	4	7	4+

This unit contains 1 Bloodhunter and 2 Bloodcrushers. It can include up to 3 additional Bloodcrushers (**Power Rating +7**), up to 6 additional Bloodcrushers (**Power Rating +14**) or up to 9 additional Bloodcrushers (**Power Rating +21**). Each model is armed with a hellblade and rides a snorting Juggernaut that attacks with its bladed horn.

WEAPON	RANGE	TYPE	S	AP	D	ABILITIES
Rider						
Hellblade	Melee	Melee	User	-3	1	Any attacks with a wound roll of 6+ for this weapon have a Damage characteristic of 2 instead of 1.
Juggernaut						
Juggernaut's bladed horn	Melee	Melee	5	-1	1	After a model riding a Juggernaut makes its close combat attacks, you can attack with its mount. Make 3 additional attacks, using this weapon profile.

WARGEAR OPTIONS	• One Bloodcrusher may take an Instrument of Chaos. • One Bloodcrusher may take a Daemonic Icon.	
ABILITIES	**Daemonic, Unstoppable Ferocity, Daemonic Ritual** (see *Codex: Chaos Daemons*) **Daemonic Icon:** If you roll a 1 when taking a Morale test for a unit with any Daemonic Icons, reality blinks and the daemonic horde is bolstered. No models flee and 1 slain Bloodcrusher is instead added to the unit.	**Devastating Charge:** Add 2 to the Strength of a Juggernaut's bladed horn attack if its unit charged in the same turn. **Instrument of Chaos:** A unit that includes any Instruments of Chaos adds 1 to their Advance and charge rolls.
FACTION KEYWORDS	**CHAOS, KHORNE, DAEMON**	
KEYWORDS	**CAVALRY, BLOODLETTER, BLOODCRUSHERS**	

FLESH HOUNDS

NAME	M	WS	BS	S	T	W	A	Ld	Sv
Flesh Hound	10"	3+	-	4	4	2	2	7	6+
Gore Hound	10"	3+	6+	4	4	2	2	7	6+

This unit contains 5 Flesh Hounds. It can include up to 5 additional Flesh Hounds (**Power Rating +4**), up to 10 additional Flesh Hounds (**Power Rating +8**) or up to 15 additional Flesh Hounds (**Power Rating +12**). Each model attacks with gore-drenched fangs.

WEAPON	RANGE	TYPE	S	AP	D	ABILITIES
Burning roar	8"	Assault 1	4	0	1	This weapon automatically hits its target.
Gore-drenched fangs	Melee	Melee	User	-1	1	-

WARGEAR OPTIONS	• For every 5 models in this unit, one Flesh Hound can be upgraded to a Gore Hound. Each Gore Hound attacks with a burning roar in addition to its gore-drenched fangs.
ABILITIES	**Daemonic, Unstoppable Ferocity, Daemonic Ritual** (see *Codex: Chaos Daemons*) **Collar of Khorne:** This unit can attempt to deny one psychic power in each enemy Psychic phase.
FACTION KEYWORDS	**CHAOS, KHORNE, DAEMON**
KEYWORDS	**BEAST, FLESH HOUNDS**